REPORT FROM FORMOSA

REPORT *from* FORMOSA

by

H. MACLEAR BATE

EYRE & SPOTTISWOODE
London

This book, first published in 1952, is printed in Great Britain for Eyre & Spottiswoode (Publishers) Ltd., 15 Bedford Street, London, W.C.2, by Chiswick Press, Brunswick Park Road, New Southgate, London, N.11

Contents

Acknowledgments

I AM indebted to so many people for assistance in collecting data in a very short time, that I am reluctant to particularise. However, Mr. "Johnny" Shen, a P.R.O., burned much midnight oil with me in Formosa and travelled hundreds of miles on my behalf as the proverbial guide, philosopher and friend, while in London Mr. A. V. Sellwood gave me the greatest possible assistance; I am most grateful to them. Others in London who made my trip possible were Dr. F. T. Cheng, Mr. Y. M. Lee, former First Secretary at the Chinese Embassy, Mr. John Ralph and Mr. Barry Horniblow, former Editor of the *Sunday Graphic*. Of course, the personnel of the Philippine Air Lines could not have been more courteous and helpful during trips that aggregated 25,000 miles.

Introduction

In the course of my work as a newspaperman I have travelled the length and breadth of the African continent, traversed two great deserts, the Kalahari and the Sahara, and have crossed the Atlantic several times. However, not until this year did I have the good fortune to find a way of returning to the Far East.

During the war I begged the army to send me to China where I was born and where I spent the first fourteen years of my life so that I learned to speak the Mandarin dialect simultaneously with my mother tongue. The army, in its unfathomable wisdom decided otherwise, although they could not have known that I had long since forgotten my Mandarin. I suppose, in view of the dreadful fate that awaited the British Forces in the Far East, I should thank Providence that my many applications were pigeon-holed.

In the last stages of the war, when Germany had been beaten, I became associated with Chinese naval officers undergoing training at the Royal Naval College at Greenwich. Duty took me there for a short time which meant a great deal to me because my father had also passed through Greenwich before being commissioned. Those days were among the happiest of my life mainly because of the pleasure I derived from the friendship of the Chinese officers.

At the beginning of this year the urge to go back to China became almost irrepressible. There were so many things I wanted to find out for myself, so many people I wanted to see again, boyhood friends, men who knew my father so much better than I did—and in particular I wanted to know the fate of my Greenwich friends.

Earlier this year the situation in Korea was deteriorating, China was taking an increasing part in the war and our chargé d'affaires was making no headway in Peking. There seemed no doubt, in retrospect, that the Government had been over-hasty in recognising the communists. I realised, of course, that there is no such act known to international law as "de-recognition" but it did seem to me that a case was certainly building up to withdraw our consular and other official representatives from the country in which they were being so studiously insulted.

What was even more worrying was that on this matter of recognition of communist China we were not marching in step either with the Dominions of Australia, New Zealand, South Africa, and Canada, or with the United States. Yet the Government of China, the Kuomintang headed by Generalissimo Chiang Kai-shek, still retained its seat at the United Nations with the overwhelming support of the other members. Surely this was a most unhappy situation and merited examination from a newspaperman's point of view.

The questions to which I wanted to find the answers were varied, but I especially wanted to know whether Generalissimo Chiang Kai-shek has any hope of returning to the mainland of China. I think I found the answer to that. I also wanted to know what sort of an army was left to him and to try and assess its value and the support it might expect from the Army Air Force and the remnants of the Chinese Navy.

Late in December, 1949, the State Department issued the confidential directive to its officials abroad to take any opportunity to decry the importance of Formosa to the United States from a strategic point of view. In the course of my work as a diplomatic correspondent I knew of this confidential directive, as did most of my colleagues. It was obviously a fatuous piece of work. When, therefore, six months later the State Department did its complete policy somersault and dramatically ordered Formosa to be protected at all costs, I had that smug "I thought so" feeling which, with all the goodwill in the world, is sometimes so difficult to smother.

I was delighted that Formosa had come into its own politically because it justified certain theories regarding the island's importance which I had tried to propagate.

The thing to do now was to find out whether these theories still held water, because if they did, then there are certain pointers to the future which must be published.

I remember my father telling me how in 1908 (the year in which I was born in Newchwang, Manchuria), a United States fleet had visited Australia. It had been welcomed in Australian waters with a warmth akin to hysteria because of the meteoric rise of Japan on the political horizon. It foreshadowed to Australia the dreadful challenge which she did in fact have to meet within a lifetime. Far seeing Australians realised that in Japan, their country and the United States had a common potential enemy. They shared with other nations misgivings about the Anglo-Japanese Treaty. Australians were also on common ground with the United States in that the integrity of the incalculably rich Philippine archipelago, with its 7,000 islands, was vital to both of them; to America on economic grounds in addition to her political obligations; to Australia because an enemy in the Philippines was much too close to be comfortable.

There was no doubt in the minds of the realists that Japan would strike west into China and South-east – if she could. In China she might be contained by the rivalry of every country in Europe and only allowed such spheres of influence as might be agreed upon by the other "concessionaires". South-east Asia, however, was very different.

Formosa was then the southernmost part of the Japanese Empire and no one was under any illusion as to its strategic importance. The Marshall Islands were only mandated to Japan after the 1914-18 war. It was also appreciated that Japan would utilise Formosa and the neighbouring Pescadores, with all the military cunning of which she has proved herself possessed in high degree.

I wanted to know whether Chiang Kai-shek was in a position to make use of Formosa's natural advantages as had the Japanese, and if so, to what extent.

Then, in July 1950, came the news of General MacArthur's dramatic meeting with Generalissimo Chiang Kai-shek and I really felt the time had come to sort out the rumours that American troops were to go to Formosa and, moreover, that Formosa had actually been offered to the United States.

There were delays which could not be avoided so for eight months I spent as much time as I could at the Public Records Office and other reference libraries doing a little research on Formosa, some of the results of which are included in this book. At this critical stage of Formosa's history and the island's relationship to world affairs, these historical references may seem of academic rather than of practical interest. However, I found some of the information so interesting and sometimes so amusing, that I included it in the hope that it would make towards a fuller understanding of the Formosan background.

Unfortunately I was unable to stay in Formosa for as long as I wanted, but this did not militate against my being able to find the answers to my questions for two reasons. Firstly, I was fortunate in that I was immediately given facilities such had never before been accorded to a visiting British journalist, and one can do a great deal in forty days and nights, specially in a small place not much larger than Vancouver Island. Moreover, I had every form of modern transport at my disposal and in any case, the activities in which I was interested and the people whom I wished to see, were in concentrated areas.

Secondly, I found many old friends, including Dr. George Yeh, the Foreign Minister and my naval friends, three of whom had attained high rank. One, Rear-Admiral Liu Kwang-kai, is in command of the squadron based on Kaohsiung in southern Formosa and mainly responsible for the arrest and detention of ships carrying strategic materials to Communist China. Another, Captain "Chris" Soong, is officer commanding the naval ratings' depot and second-in-command is Commander "Bing" Shih, all "late of the R.N. College".

I was with them on VJ Day, in Glasgow. They had been visiting Scottish shipyards as the guests of Viscount Kemsley and had become well-known in Glasgow. That night on leaving Kemsley House we literally had to seek police "protection", so enthusiastic were the crowds outside. I doubt if there has ever been a greater public demonstration of Anglo-Chinese goodwill. I am convinced that the warm hospitality of the British people during those days has had a lasting influence and in no small measure accounts for the fact that there is still a tremendous reservoir of goodwill for Britain among the naval officers in Formosa. In some countries the Services guide Government policy—from my observations this applies in the Kuomintang. It was undoubtedly due to the presence of these old friends in Formosa that the way was made smooth and the official coolness towards Great Britain never evinced towards me.

It was not a little embarrassing to be told by my own countrymen time and again that I seemed to be "privileged" although I think that they must have learned through one way and another that it was not a case of "privilege" but rather of fortuitous goodwill accumulated during a lifetime of interest in China, moreover, friendships forged in the heat of war stand great strain. Indeed, my interest in China is hereditary in that my father and mother spent the best days of their lives there and only the death of my father in Tientsin broke the continuity of nearly a century of family association with China, as an obelisk in the grounds of St. John's Cathedral, Hong Kong, bears witness.

It was not difficult for me to pick up the threads.

There were other practical reasons why I could not remain longer in Formosa. To be seen in its proper perspective, Formosa must be looked at from a global point of view—not just as an interesting and beautiful island, now the last bastion of a régime which may be either terminating or preparing for a re-entry. This was what I wanted to ascertain. It is so placed geographically that Australia, no less than the United States, has a vital interest in its future, so have the British in Hong Kong and Malaya. That is a premise that needs justification which I have sought to provide.

The obvious way to do this was to visit those places where Formosa is looked upon, not just as an island whose ownership is being disputed, but as a country whose fate is a matter of deep concern. There I would find people who could express considered opinions.

The quest for this took me to Hong Kong and to the Philippines where once again I was fortunate in that I met with nothing but co-operation, and specially through the kind offices of Colonel Andries Soriano, president of the Philippine Air Lines and of the San Miguel Brewery. Through the Colonel and his friend, Mr. Edward Bolton, I was introduced to General Carlos Romulo, the Foreign Minister, and through the personal efforts of Mr. Peter Richards, Reuter's Correspondent, and Mr. James Woodruff, D.F.C., I obtained in a week more background than an ordinary visitor could hope to obtain in months and an insight into life in Manila which has made me determined to go there again.

In spite of the pleasures which were a serious distraction to the more serious business, I was able to learn something of the problem of communism in the Philippines and the fear with which responsible Filipinos regard its extension in South-east Asia. I have tried to sum up to what extent those fears are based on reason and to what extent on historical animosity between landowners and peasantry. The people also have an important legacy of Spanish influence as well as the Roman Catholic religion which was not grafted on to any form of paganism because the people have "always" been Catholics.

Hong Kong is a problem in itself, full of political, social and economic dynamite, one of the few places in the Commonwealth where the pound sterling can be changed for U.S. dollars openly and where men, as well as currency, are quickly sorted out at their real worth in terms of Hong Kong values. From Hong Kong it was obviously necessary to find out what I could about Macao, the last remaining foothold of Portugal in the Far East, never more thriving than at present, due to the war in Korea and the embargo on trade between Hong Kong and China. It is a case of Hong Kong's poison being delicious meat for Macao. This Tangier of the East is a dangerous, immoral place and all the more interesting for that. Through Macao scrap iron from India and Indonesia, drugs from Germany and electrical goods from other countries, in fact all the scientific sinews of war, find their way into Communist China without infringing any local laws, but at Macao's price. It is a port which weathers wars and storms because it is willing to serve all masters at once, and where agents of every kind gather to keep some track of each other's villainies.

All this and much more is part of a swaying edifice in which Formosa is the fulcrum.

H. MACLEAR BATE

Ruckinge,
Kent.

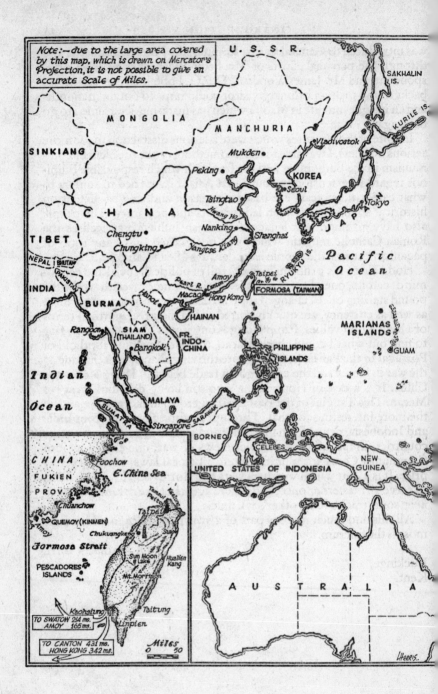

Note:— due to the large area covered by this map, which is drawn on Mercator's Projection, it is not possible to give an accurate Scale of Miles.

U.S.S.R.

SAKHALIN IS.

KURILE IS.

MONGOLIA

MANCHURIA

SINKIANG

Vladivostok

Mukden

Peking

KOREA

Tsingtao

Seoul

C H I N A

Hwang Ho

Nanking

Tokyo

TIBET

Chengtu

Chungking

Yangtse Kiang

Shanghai

J A P A N

NEPAL BHUTAN

PAKISTAN

Pacific Ocean

INDIA

BURMA

Pearl R.

Amoy canton

Taipei

RYUKYU IS.

Macao

Hong Kong

FORMOSA (TAIWAN)

Hanoi

HAINAN

MARIANAS ISLANDS

Rangoon

SIAM (THAILAND)

FR. INDO-CHINA

Bangkok

PHILIPPINE ISLANDS

GUAM

Indian

Ocean

MALAYA

SARAWAK

Singapore

BORNEO

SUMATRA

CELEBES

UNITED STATES OF INDONESIA

NEW GUINEA

CHINA

Foochow

E. China Sea

FUKIEN PROV.

Chuanchow

QUEMOY (KINMEN)

Amoy

Tamsui Keelung

Pettou

TAIPEI

Chukuangken

Sun

Formosa Strait

Sun Moon Lake

Hualien Kang

PESCADORES ISLANDS

Mt. Morrison

A U S T R A L I A

Keohsiung

Taitung

TO SWATOW 214 ms.
AMOY 165 ms.

Linpien

TO CANTON 431 ms.
HONG KONG 342 ms.

Miles

0   50

L.HARRIS.

1. *Arrival in Formosa*

OVER a green blue sea the DC4 throbbed towards the Problem Isle – a huddle of mountains on the distant sky line, of peaks partly veiled by the white mists of the morning.

Then, quite unexpectedly, almost sternly, the dark-eyed, dark-haired Filipino air hostess called, "Draw the curtain, please".

She passed along the aisle. Semi-comatose passengers nodded and dozed in the cushioned seats on either side. Her voice, slightly sing-song and American accented, cut into my half-awareness through the dull rhythmic beat of the engines.

"Close your curtains, *please*. You are now approaching Formosa. Close your curtains. You are *forbidden* to look out. . . ."

Thus, in as little as forty-one hours from London Airport, does one reach a war – a strange and silent war relegated to three or four inches in *The Times* or *The Daily Telegraph*, ousted from prominence by the headlines of Korea.

To Europeans the centre of this conflict – this bitter struggle between Chiang Kai-shek and Mao Tse-tung is known as Formosa, or the Beautiful Island. To the Chinese it is Taiwan, or the "Terraced Bay", the island where mountain range above range marches with steady progress to the sky, where the rice crop springs in torrential rain, and the sugar cane flourishes on stream-laced, sea-fringed plains.

Below, its surface seems fair and smiling but beneath the perennial blossom, sleek gun barrels jab towards the Straits. From out at sea one can sometimes discern with the aid of binoculars, camouflaged pill boxes, converted from natural and man-made caves, so that the embrasures look like evil, elongated eyes.

"Close your curtains, *please*". The order was repeated, this time directed to me alone and I obeyed with guilty haste. My sudden zeal was so thorough, the curtain nearest me came off its runners, and the window was unscreened. I tried to hide my surprise, satisfaction, and slight apprehension – and continued to look down.

I caught no glimpse of military installations, tank barriers or trenches, only a wide expanse of sand, a sprawl of white and red buildings, of palm trees blossoming like green smoke across broad boulevards, and in the far distance foaming breakers over a reef of coral.

It was all so peaceful until two specks of silver shot past from out of the sun, and twin Mustang Fighters rolled their wing tips and climbed again beyond my view for a destination unknown, as if to say;

"Formosa is at war. Look; her winged guardians are alert and vigilant!" I felt my victory had its sourer fruits and I noted that the hostess was faintly perturbed behind her smile and I wondered what the penalty might be. "Adjust your safety belts, please." Ten minutes later we were on the last remaining territory of Generalissimo Chiang Kai-shek.

We touched down on the tarmac of Taipeh* airfield–one of those from which the Japanese bombed Hong Kong and Manila. The buildings of Flying Control slid in a blur of brick and concrete past my guilty eye and the engines slowed to silence. The young Chinese student who had travelled from an American university to volunteer for Chiang in the war against the communists, smiled and said, "I congratulate you on having obtained a view–you English are so er– persistent". The door opened and smartly uniformed officials–armed with Colt pistols–stood by the gangway to usher us towards the customs and immigration buildings.

My fellow passengers and I parted at the barrier, a very mixed group, representative of the daily influx to the island from the world outside. One was a Texan complete with high-heeled boots, stetson, and the commendable assurance of the Lone Star State–the badge of which he wore in his lapel. He came to Taipeh to join an American engineering firm whose activities necessitated every man employed by it to be politically reliable. Another was the bickering wife of an American officer attached to the United States Military Mission. Yet another, a rather scared looking Chinese child–just who she was, who would be waiting for her, what part of the island she was visiting, or why she should be on this trip at all, I was left to wonder.

With an attaché who had been sent to meet me, I stepped into the dust, sunshine and the noise of a Formosan street where a battered jeep stood by to run us into the city.

So much for the general picture. What are the hard, cold facts? Just what are the factors political, moral and military, that are now being weighed so meticulously by the statesmen and so variously interpreted, so emphatically disagreed upon. Were the good things here– if there were any–sufficiently good to overshadow the things that were most obviously bad? Strategically the island of Formosa may well be vital for the west's security against a hostile China. The question is–can an alliance with General Chiang Kai-shek be considered as desirable to a democratic world on moral grounds, or even as a simple matter of political expediency?

*The official spelling in Formosa is Taipei.

The questions came crowding in and here, as in all Asiatic affairs it is necessary to go back to origins, to consider the backcloth before applauding or condemning, the actors.

It was on December 1, 1943, that the United States, Great Britain and China solemnly declared at Cairo that all territories "stolen" by Japan from China–among them Manchuria, "Taiwan" and the Pescadores Islands–would be returned at the war's ending.

This agreement between agents who had not consulted their principals was reaffirmed in the Potsdam Declaration of May 1945, where it obtained the additional, if dubious, blessings of the Soviet Union.

On September 2, a few days after the atom bombs had collapsed the walls of the Mikado's Empire, the cheering, flagwagging students of Canton and Chungking celebrated with fireworks and march-pasts the island's formal retrocession. The deed was done, but was it wisely done?

Six weeks later a strong force of Chinese troops set foot at last on the soil that for fifty years had formed an important part of Japan's Empire and over the wide, tree-lined streets the Japanese had built, rumbled the trucks and tanks of the forces of "Liberation". The national flag waved high above the great dome of the Provincial buildings and days of joy and festival were duly proclaimed, and dutifully fulfilled.

Despite the junketings, the welcome was by no means unqualified to many of the "natives", the 7,000,000 Formosans who are of pure Chinese descent. Although Formosans had been barred from every worthwhile position in commerce and politics (or maybe, because of it?) the Japanese administration had earned a considerable degree of respect. Japanese policy–while brutally repressive to all who dared offend–at least left unharmed and in peace the majority of the Islanders.

The Japanese had made a prosperous colony from virtually nothing and had suppressed, most painfully, the pirate and the bandit. They had, as part of their Asiatic version of "self sufficiency", heavily subsidised the island's sugar and rice industries and developed its mineral resources. Finally, with the subtlety of their race, they had taken great pains to inculcate among Formosans a certain contempt for their struggling compatriots on the mainland.

The storms of the Boxer rising in 1900, the rise of the Republic; the collapse of Yuan Shi-kai, the conflicts with the War Lords, all these might convulse the mainland but they passed the Formosan by.

It was small wonder that, despite the iron fist and long claws beneath the Japanese glove, the average peasant came to consider himself as fortunate in being part of the "booty" collected at the end of the Sino-Japanese war in 1895.

Small wonder too that as a result of comparisons embellished by Japanese propaganda—the majority of the disaffected tended to press for independence of both Japan and China rather than for a return to the island's ancient allegiance!

The Cairo Declaration, the Potsdam Agreement, changed the *status quo* but they did not change the ultimate aims of the "patriots".

Chiang's men received cheers and tributes from many of the population, the others, suspicious from the start, turned hostile within a year or so for the claims of the independence movement suddenly found queer champions—the Chinese communists who now decided the time was ripe to unleash their war on the Kuomintang.

All along the 240 mile length of the Island the embers of discontent were fanned by the winds of Marxist rhetoric, and China, ravaged after eight years of war against the Japanese, distracted again by the onslaught of the communists, could do little to help the once prosperous Formosans regain the balance that had been so rudely upset by World War Two.

The glib spokesman of Mao Tse-tung—although their creed was distrusted by the wealthy leaders of the independence movement—promised those leaders at least an opportunity of unseating the existing Chinese overlordship.

On the mainland the forces of Chiang passed from defeat to catastrophe, even the peace-loving politically unconscious masses of Formosa—by far the vast majority of its people—began to feel the wisdom of the well tried Asiatic custom of making friends with the winning side!

Furthermore, to quote one of them, they "groaned" beneath the extortions of a government that Chiang, in his bigger abstractions, could do little to control. Then came the crisis, and the massacre.

As the armies of the Kuomintang struggled in their death agonies, over a million refugees began to pour into the sanctuary of the island. The place was put on a war footing and thousands of Chinese soldiers, sailors and airmen followed in the wake of the refugees to prepare for what promised to be a last desperate and possibly unavailing stand, and Formosans in Taipeh and other places began to evince uneasiness.

The full story of those terrible days of February, 1947, is still unknown. Some supporters of Chiang say that the rioting was the prelude to a widespread communist engineered revolt, others that it was the spontaneous expression of a people bewildered at seeing their homes "invaded".

We do know, however, that the rioting came to an end in a cascade of machine-gun fire and that when the guns fell silent the Governor of Taiwan, General Chen Yi, sent parties of picked troops to every part of his territory.

They killed, they tortured, they raped and in less than a week the leaders of the independence movement had been formally shot on Taipeh's disused racecourse, or informally butchered in their beds.

Europeans, resident there at the time, told me that some victims of Chen Yi's firing squad were so brutally treated on first being arrested that they had to be carried to the place of execution, their limbs having been broken by beatings.

Houses of families related to offenders were reduced to ashes, and after all the demonstrations in the capital had been quelled Nationalist troops indulged in an orgy of looting.

Within a very short time the radio station at Taipeh was all too truthfully announcing that the "revolt" had been crushed, and that order had been restored. For the majority of Asiatics it is nothing new for a story to begin with a chant of slogans and to terminate in a blast of gunfire. General Chiang Kai-shek, however, did not consider the story closed and that impressed Formosans as the most surprising phenomenon in their history.

By all the rules of the game he should either have been content with the action of General Chen Yi, or else have taken advantage of the islanders' crushed and demoralised condition to consolidate his position by even more drastic "reprisals", but he did neither.

After sending one of his most trusted lieutenants to investigate, he ordered the arrest of the General and other instigators of the massacre. They were tried, found guilty of murder and conspiracy and sentenced to death. Certain of Chiang's followers pleaded for leniency for the men who had shown such a commendably strong hand at a time when his entire empire was rapidly collapsing to his enemies, but he refused.

Like ultra cautious rabbits from their burrows the Formosans blinked warily at this astonishingly Roman solution and asked themselves if this was the bait of some colossal trap, some masterly scheme to lure into the open the remaining disaffected?

They sought for reassurance, and then when they realised that their new master really meant to keep his word they released their pent up hatred for the former Governor in a particularly macabre manner.

His execution was scheduled to take place on the racecourse that lies only a few miles from the centre of Taipeh.

The Formosan women carefully wrote curses on rice paper and then with their prayers for vengeance tucked into the hollow ends of bamboo sticks, they paraded through the streets and marched to the racecourse there to invoke the damnation of the General's soul for ever.

At the racecourse the mob—thousands strong, assembled to watch the unfortunate man end his life on earth, and so hardly did the throng press upon the police and guards that Chiang, afraid of further disorders that would involve the soldier supporters of the General with the people, ordered his condemned erstwhile "follower" to be executed in private. His orders were obeyed at dawn on June 18, 1950.

Today, if you can spare the time for a chat in one of the innumerable cafés in the hustling streets of Taipeh you will be told of this rough justice, and that Chiang, by effecting it, gained ten times more than if he had displayed weakness.

Was Chiang's decision activated by an honest desire to see justice done or was it a gesture of political expediency designed to gain native support? His opponents are not slow to insinuate that he could afford to be "generous". Maybe after General Chen Yi had liquidated the island's opposition it might not have been so convenient to have left him in a position to talk.

I am inclined to rule out the sinister innuendo of this last argument. By his action Chiang risked a breach with some of his oldest supporters, supporters who urged that all men strong enough to stand by the Kuomintang in its hour of stress should have their hands completely free to deal with those who would not. Nor has the Generalissimo always been so lenient to offenders against his régime, on the contrary he has been remorseless at times. He is not in the position to be completely impartial in his justice, even supposing he had the desire to be so.

A Secret Police of "Iron Curtain" efficiency gives to Communist plots—both real and fictitious—a termination that is as speedy as it is unpleasant. Throughout my stay I was haunted by the shadow of a Police State malevolent in its objectives and far reaching in its methods. "Keep your mouth shut and you'll be all right", was the advice given to me when I first joined the British Army. To the average Formosan this advice would appear to hold good today—although "private" grumbling over details, as distinct from open disaffection regarding principles, is frequent and unhampered.

Chiang's administration must be debited with the curtailment of political liberty; the ruthless liquidation of all who oppose the régime. To its credit is the fact that the Formosan despite the presence of 500,000 exiled troops and all the military and civil precautions inevitable in an island on the defensive against a merciless enemy, need have no fear for his life, his property, or even his daily food provided he keeps within the law.

Chiang, as I was to see for myself, has done much to remedy the abuses originally so prevalent among the corrupt and extravagant administrators of the Kuomintang. He has replaced an administration similar to that which caused his downfall in China by an efficient and practical régime. Beggars and starving children, so conspicuous a feature of Eastern cities, are not to be seen and there is very little non-political crime. For the better things in Formosa much of the credit must go to the island's governor, Dr. K. C. Wu—formerly mayor of

Chungking and Shanghai, where he did more than any man before him to combat vice and maladministration. Much too, is due to the other men who are now with Chiang, men of proven virtue like Premier General Chen Cheng and Foreign Minister Dr. George Yeh.

Formosans now hold high positions in industry and administration, and if Formosan elections cannot be regarded as free by the standards of the west, they have nevertheless been considerably more democratic in character than anything yet known in the Far East outside Hong Kong. The secret ballot prevails but no candidate fundamentally opposed to the régime would have the temerity to stand for election. The railway operates safely—and right on schedule! The streets are as clean as anywhere in Asia—with the exception of Japan and Hong Kong. The currency is backed by gold. The first steps have been taken towards the realisation of the "Principles of the People's Livelihood", those principles of democracy so dear, in theory, to the early revolutionaries but which were later to be ignored so thoroughly by their successors.

Since Chiang's final retreat from the mainland, Formosa has been variously described as "The Last Bastion of the Nationalist Cause", and "The Unsinkable Aircraft Carrier" for an attack on the forces of Mao Tse-tung.

At first there seemed small hope that it could long survive a Red assault. Mutiny was rife—even in that *élite* force of the Nationalists represented by the Chinese navy. The cruiser *Chungking* (formerly H.M.S. *Aurora*) deserted the Nationalists and was subsequently bombed and sunk by the airmen of Chiang.

The army was demoralised, and, as the events of 1947 so clearly showed, brutalised as well by its long succession of ignominious defeats.

The air force remained loyal throughout, but most of its aircraft were obsolescent in pattern.

Today, owing to the advent of the Korean war, the position has changed. The army is well disciplined and reflects justifiable self-respect. It is smartly uniformed, reasonably well equipped, and instead of living locust-like on the native population, has actually adopted measures to make itself partly self-supporting in food.

The navy has been restored to its loyalties by many successes in intercepting "blockade" runners encouraged by a liberal provision of prize money and a weeding out of malcontents.

The air force has a reserve of twelve hundred pilots and, although still unprovided with jets, is well drilled, efficient, and full of fighting fervour.

Shaped like a tobacco leaf, split from north to south by a mountain chain, this island fortress—approximately the size of Holland or the combined areas of the States of Massachusetts and Connecticut – is indeed the home of contrast and paradox. Two-thirds of its area is covered by forest clad mountains, the remainder is the coastal plain where rice, more than sufficient to feed its population, and sugar cane – necessary to obtain foreign currency–flourish. In the more inaccessible forest regions–and many have never been explored–the aborigines lead their primitive lives, and it is hinted that they still enjoy the occasional relaxation of head-hunting. They are the forgotten 150,000 of the island. In the cities the average Formosan plumps for less sanguinary pleasures–a visit to the pictures to see the latest Wild West thriller or gangster film or a quiet evening at the traditional Chinese games of chequers or even Mah Jong, or the opera which is particularly popular.

It is a land where until quite recently the mining of coal was forbidden. Neither mountain nor green hill might be disturbed as it was said that such western practices would disturb the dragons that slept beneath, the self-same dragons that were the "founders" of Formosa and terrible indeed would be the consequences of their annoyance!

Yet they man one of the most powerful radio stations in all Asia, and anti-aircraft guns stab at the sky from the roofs of tall buildings.

Tank traps and temples–the latter named after former national heroes–keep a crazy comradeship beside swift flowing streams and willow pattern bridges.

In Taipeh the jeep–my constant form of transport–is infinitely more ubiquitous than ever was the rickshaw in days gone by, while buses and bullock carts vie with American limousines and army lorries to form the world's noisiest and most chaotic traffic.

Everywhere, or so it seems, you will find American soldiers, not one of them under the rank of Top Sergeant, attached to the formidable Military Mission soon to number 700.

America has certainly realised the strategic importance of the island, and from her capacious pockets has produced the weapons of war, despite the fact that the Kuomintang is in power.

At the time of its collapse on the mainland, the Kuomintang had become the label for every variety of shabby administration, political jobbery and graft. Chiang, yesterday's hero of the west, was suddenly portrayed, in the exaggeration of American disappointment, and in the adulation of British left-wingers for Mao Tse-tung, as a dyed-in-the-wool thick-headed mandarin without the faintest glimmerings of political sense or military strategy.

Madame Chiang, formerly the lady lion of democratic tea parties, became to the disgruntled, after a violent radio attack on Britain for acknowledging the Red Government, a spendthrift, an ungrateful woman with a taste for sheer stockings and high heeled shoes, the most avaricious of a rapacious family, with an unhealthy flair for high finance. The confusion in Asia that followed the fall of the Right was easily matched at home by a confusion not only regarding the character of Chiang Kai-shek but also that of his opponent.

To some Mao Tse-tung was a communist of the orthodox type but to most he was just a man of humble origin, ambitious, who had "made good" in the face of obstacles; moderate in sentiment, benevolent of purpose, who simply used the term communist to describe his movement because he did not know a better one.

This latter view was then curiously prevalent among those with financial interests in China—even among many British and American business men. "Sic transit gloria mundi" they murmured knowingly of Chiang.

When they had their doubts about the New Man they remembered a book called *From Log Cabin to White House* and drew due relief. No doubt they also remembered Chiang Kai-shek's two books—*China's Destiny*—the first edition of which was discreetly edited so that the second and expurgated edition read rather less anti-foreign.

The attack on Korea—the persistent refusal of Red China to reciprocate or even avail herself of the benefits of diplomatic recognition offered by Britain, changed many opinions regarding the reasonableness of Mao Tse-tung and continues to do so.

Whether the Korean war has done anything to restore the damaged prestige of Chiang Kai-shek in western eyes is quite another matter. My experience has been that whenever one raises the question of the recognition of Mao Tse-tung with British Foreign Office officials they seem to lose something of their traditional *savoir-faire* and become almost irritable—like normal men react when their consciences are touched, or their good sense impinged.

Meanwhile, in hard pressed Formosa the arguments are as varied and infinitely more bitter than any yet uttered in the clubs of London and Washington or in the western legislatures.

Point to the difference between the Nationalist régime on the island and its career on the mainland and the cynical will readily affirm that it is Chiang's desire to "work his passage" back rather than any intrinsic change of heart that has led him to ensure that Formosa is a "show piece" of efficiency and resolution.

Point to the brutalities practised by his subordinates against communist "infiltrators" and you will be told that the island is fighting an enemy of infinite ruthlessness whose tyranny is much worse than anything that Chiang has yet attempted.

To an observer who endeavoured, as I endeavoured, to obtain an honest and unprejudiced viewpoint, it was all more than a little trying. It was also extremely fascinating.

2. *The romantic past*

FROM the fun of the dragons arose Formosa, back in the days when Jason pursued the Golden Fleece, and Aphrodite was born in the spray of a wave that broke on the rocky shores of Cyprus.

At this time, says local legend, some dragons who lived at "Five Dragon Gate" near Foochow on the south China coast slipped out to sea. Under the ocean bed they travelled due east for a hundred miles, and then, in a holiday mood, they stopped to frolic. So violent were their submarine contortions, so ecstatic the swishing of their scaly tails, that a chain of mountains was created where hitherto there had only been a vast expanse of the Pacific. From these mountains, proof positive of their origin, belched the fire that had sprung from the nostrils of the monsters. The highest and most majestic of their creations – 12,000 feet high (it now bears the undragonlike name of Morrison) – was hurled directly astride the Tropic of Cancer, a fortuitous phenomenon to successive generations of navigators plotting their courses.

Where the seas receded from the western slopes, volcanic plains of astounding fertility were left, while to the east the cliffs dropped 6,000 feet sheer to the water's edge, the highest in the world.

After their astonishing high jinks, the dragons curled up and went to sleep in the slopes of the hills, emitting upon occasion, a warning snore or two to disturb the head hunting proclivities of a most unpleasant set of natives and to act as deterrent to sea-roving Chinese to claim the island other than nominally.*

Formosa, the pirate's lair; the place where one, quite literally, just could not keep one's head, had few charms to offer the merchant adventurers of the mainland. The grotesque eyes on the bows of their laden junks saw evil in the silhouetted peaks, and warned their masters to safer anchorages. Even when the Europeans arrived with trade demands – plus pikes and guns to back them – the island, apart from scattered coastal forts which changed possession from Spaniard to Dutchman, remained with its steaming streams of sulphurated water, its lush green forests where violent death by decapitation awaited the unwary, the Forbidden Territory of the Far East, to say nothing of a reputation built up over many decades of the terrible fate that invariably awaited shipwrecked mariners.

Only when the storms of civil war raged on the Chinese mainland; only when the Manchus wrested the Dragon Throne from the effete occupation of the Mings; then only did the "Terraced Bay" begin to

---

*There is an average of one earth tremor a day somewhere in Formosa and major earthquakes every few years. There are no active volcanoes now.

yield its secrets. It is to this epoch that the supporters of Generalissimo Chiang Kai-shek – now more confident than at any time since 1945 – will refer you for a historic parallel with the events of today.

The parallel is a peculiar one, involving as it does a comparison between the activities of the sober uniformed "Methodist General", and Koxinga, the offspring of a bloodthirsty pirate; the sailor who later made himself a soldier and a king.

The name Koxinga means little to the average westerner. But in Formosa it is a name which is revered, and, as the deeds of this seventeenth century hero are being studied by the officers of Chiang with a view to modern adaptation, no report from the island would be complete without his story.

This story assumes particular significance, now that the United States, dramatically reversing the policy that it adopted in the days of the mainland defeats, has allocated to the Nationalists $200,000,000 (US) representing forty per cent of the entire Military Aid Programme for the Far East for guns and aircraft.

Many fears have been expressed that as a result Chiang will be encouraged to attack China. To these the Administration has replied that such aid is for defensive purposes – a precaution against fresh communist aggression. Major General Chase reiterated this view on September 10, 1951. It is in the nature of a guarantee of the preservation of the *status quo* and to prevent the island from becoming a hostile territory, couched menacingly between the Philippines and Japan. It is denied that assistance will be given to Chiang's forces to stage a return to the mainland.

The diplomatic delicacies involved in the U.S. policy need small comment, and Chiang is not the only "realist" in the Orient or elsewhere who draws from it the analogy of a soldier issued with a tommy gun, and then, with one hand tied behind his back, told not to shoot unless the enemy has a chance of shooting first!

Meanwhile the reverent manner in which the new and efficient officers of the Nationalists are taught to regard the memory of Koxinga may provide a useful indication as to the ultimate effectiveness of any such well meaning restrictive clauses.

The story of this hero they are now pledged to emulate began in the seventeenth century when – like the Kuomintang – the cowardly, corrupt but cultured dynasty of the Mings was discourteously upset by the bloody onslaught of the determined Manchus.

Koxinga was the son of tailor from Macao; a tailor who, thanks to the Jesuits, was known to many by the baptismal name of Nicholas Gaspard and who, thanks to his subsequent exertions was known by many more varied *noms de guerre*.

A man of enterprise, he migrated to Japan, married a Japanese girl, and then, as times were bad in the Koxinga household, forsook his shears and yard-stick and tried his hand at piracy–a grossly over-crowded profession in which, nevertheless, he graduated so notably that he became the most successful buccaneer of them all.

In the meantime–beneath the fierce onslaught of the Manchus–a barbaric Northern people, bred in the vast regions of Manchuria, and toughened by centuries of campaigning in countries where even the climate ensured that only the strong survived–the splendid façade of the Ming Empire began to crack. In circumstances not dissimilar to the campaign of 1947, the miserable armies defected *en masse*. In droves the pig-tailed Mandarins went to kotow to the Conqueror and pay him tribute. The bonds of the Empire appeared to be as fragile as the parchment on which its extravagant decrees were so elaborately inscribed.

It was at this time that the Emperor, wilting beneath the disasters of the North, heard of the fresh depredations caused by Nicholas' private enterprises along his seaboard, and despairing of humbling him, resorted to the typical Chinese method of making an enemy a friend by offering him high office.

This time-honoured stratagem was an unexampled success. The astonishing Nicholas kept to his new allegiance and fought bravely until, trapped by the Tartars, he died a martyr's death.

He could have gained his freedom at any time had he cared to desert his master. But this he would not do, and so, weighed down with shackles, he died, very slowly and painfully even for those days, in a small bamboo cage.

When Koxinga heard of his father's death and the nature of it, he went to the temple of Confucius in Nanking and there, burning in-cense to the departed's spirit, he vowed to continue to fight for so long as he lived. He kept his word and in doing so he changed the face of China's history.

Terror stricken civilians, fleeing from the hordes of the north just as their descendants were later to flee from the armies of the com-munists, seized junks and sampans to carry them by sea away from the menaced province of Fukien. Dreading blowpipe and head hunter, dragon and the devils unknown far less than the Manchus and the devils they knew, they chose Formosa as the nearest convenient land in which to hide.

Back in the fighting line meanwhile Koxinga, an outstanding general fought–like several unpraised Nationalist commanders in the latter stages of the Civil War–a brave and desperate battle, but, as those commanders were to discover in the bitterness of their own conflict, the issue had already been decided by previous corruptions, treacheries, defections and defeats. To Koxinga, staggering with his army back to the coast, came word from the refugees of the wonders of Formosa, its timber resources, its soil so suitable for rice, and of the "black fire nourishing rock" that the westerners were later to tersely name "coal."

No doubt Koxinga had heard more than enough already from the embellished yarns of his father's enterprising captains about this island of coves and anchorages, of natural fortresses and mountain caverns.

The conclusions which induced Koxinga to remove his main forces from the continent were fundamentally the same as those that were later to be adopted by Chiang.

Like the Nationalists of today the Mings were superior to their enemies at sea and Formosa provided a convenient rallying point to regroup and rest their battered armies before switching to attack; an ideal sally port for periodic raids on the Chinese mainland.

Koxinga sailed for the island in 1651 with the main body of his forces. Like Chiang, in later years, he left a garrison on the mainland to fight a rearguard action at Amoy. Unlike Chiang he had the good fortune to possess a garrison that was actually willing to fight the rearguard action! Chiang's guerillas are as yet of unknown quality or quantity, although reports come through of frequent acts of sabotage.

Koxinga's son Cheng-ching commanded the army on the mainland and later, in succession to his father extended Formosan resistance by twenty years. Chiang's younger (adopted) son has the task of spearheading with his armoured forces any future nationalist return to the mainland. Formosa was delivered to Chiang by the statesmen of the west. Koxinga was opposed by a European power.

The Dutch, taking over the territories of the Spaniards whom they had attacked and defeated thirty-five years before, had introduced to the island eighty-one missionaries, many cannon, and a list of reprisals against native treachery that included crucifixion and boiling in oil.

They were as thorough and as brutal in their time as the Japanese and like the Japanese were equally ready to try conciliation and sweet reason whenever they thought that force might fail.

On this occasion they thought it might and when Koxinga's preparations for invasion reached the vigilant ears of their innumerable agents, the envoys of rightly alarmed Dutch Governor–Frederick Coyett—proceeded to Koxinga's headquarters as quickly as they could.

With valuable presents and conciliatory intent, they inquired if His Excellency's plans were aimed at the Dutch settlement. Playing for time, Koxinga told them that they were not, but Coyett was unsatisfied by these glib assurances and sent to Batavia for reinforcements.

The reinforcements arrived, but after a period of inactivity, departed before Koxinga's host of junks, containing 25,000 soldiers, appeared off Keelung. The Ming armada arrived in April, 1662, while the commander of the "relief expedition" was hastening home to report that Coyett was a fool and an alarmist! His call to surrender rejected, Koxinga attacked Zeelandia Castle in the south, the Dutch having evacuated Providentia Castle which was within gunshot of Zeelandia. He was repulsed, and a red flag of defiance flew over the fort until the following January, when the valiant Dutchmen surrendered through lack of food and ammunition.

Like Chiang, Koxinga brought a new and not altogether welcome broom to the islanders. Koxinga had the task of rooting out the influence of the Dutch–a task entailing such diverse precautions as recalling the hunting permits they had issued to the natives and renaming Zeelandia, Anping Ching, or the City of Peace.

Chiang had the job of stamping out all trace of the Japanese occupation, all efforts aimed at creating an independent Formosa.

Like Chiang also, Koxinga was constantly in touch with guerilla movements, and with those fragments of the regular army that still continued to harass China's new masters.

Will history repeat itself still further? In Koxinga's day the Ming force on the mainland was able finally by skilful manoeuvre to compel the Manchus to evacuate the Fukien coast for a depth of ten miles, and so formidable did it become at one stage, that it managed to reach the outskirts of Nanking.

In Formosa the Nationalist intelligence services report that the communists are clearing civilians from a large belt of the coastline opposite the island and concentrating upon the preparation of coastal defences.

Crowned king in Formosa, but still a zealous adherent to the Mings to the end, Koxinga was unable to put into effect the plans he had always nourished for a return to the mainland. He failed to reach his final objective because he lost his fleet, and then death suddenly struck him down.

A few weeks before he died Koxinga was also planning a punitive raid on Manila where the Chinese population had suffered a massacre by the Spanish. It is interesting to conjecture what may have happened had this punitive expedition ever been launched and attended with success and to recall that the Japanese did invade the Philippines from Formosa. Koxinga's last words, much impressed upon the Nationalist cadets, were "How can I face my Emperor in Heaven now that my mission is unfulfilled?" Beneath the great dome of the Municipal building in Taipeh the officers of the fighting forces of Chiang Kai-shek are now studying the logistics of an offensive. Everywhere I heard among them the talk of the "Great Return", a significant change indeed from the days when the only slogan of the few who remained loyal was the despairing negative defiance of "Death rather than Mao Tse-tung".

Whether we, or the Americans, like or dislike it, the fact remains that the declared aim of the Generalissimo, as expressed publicly upon many occasions, is and must by necessity always be "The re-establishment of the Government of the Republic of China on the mainland of China".

Whatever the reservations of the men they command, whatever the diplomatic restrictions urged by Washington, the officers of Chiang have every intention of supporting this aim, and in so doing to succeed where Koxinga failed.

It is strange that this attitude does not appear to have been generally appreciated in the west as yet. It is equally strange that the west should imagine that the future of Formosa can be solved by putting the island into "quarantine" until its future is decided – presumably by the Big Powers – in the cool and antiseptic atmosphere of some hypothetical conference of settlement.

To a world motivated by sweet logic and bereft of the human passions, such a situation might no doubt be practicable.

To the world of the present, Mao Tse-tung, still faced with resistance on the mainland – as the lists of executions that were regularly broadcast by Peking Radio all too faithfully demonstrate – cannot tolerate a position where the people who are instigating that resistance are kept out of his reach by foreign warships.

Similarly, Chiang Kai-shek – puzzling and sometimes infuriating to a west which has persistently regarded itself as the generous giver and him as the poor acquaintance of doubtful antecedents – obviously cannot tolerate for ever the equivocal position in which he is armed to defend one part of "his" territory, and forbidden to help his friends who are still fighting in the rest.

How long can Formosa continue to maintain a status that is so artificial as the present? And if the conferring statesmen decide that the island goes to Mao how are they going to enforce their writ? If they decide that it legally belongs to Chiang, how are they going to prevent him eventually from extending this legal right to the logical conclusion of an invasion of China?

A granary for the mainland, the world's seventh exporter of cane sugar, formerly the partial rice bowl of Japan, how could an "independent Formosa" (another suggestion of the west) possibly exist without forces to defend it? Chiang's men, with some apparent reason, argue that America, having approved their cause as preferable to that of the communists, and having decided to supply them with war equipment, must accept the implications of its approval and not confine them to the prolongation of an artificial status. Originally relieved by President Truman's decision to "neutralise" the island, they are now afraid that this very "neutralisation" may commit their régime to an indefinite exile, and, perhaps, a premature death.

They are pleased by the decision to re-equip their war torn forces, but they are worried lest the very "vested interest" of the Americans in Chiang which this decision implies may not cause opportune moments for a counter attack to go by default. And, if not noticeably Churchillian in their previous practices, their appeal at the moment at any rate is well expressed by "Give us the tools and we will finish the job".

Whether or not this boast could be made good is another story, but while the world outside asks if America is throwing good money after bad, the Nationalists plan on, always maintaining a wary eye upon the activities of the people whose home they now so uncomfortably occupy in a role mid-way between visiting landlord and sitting tenant.

The Chinese, whether of Chiang or Mao, claim Formosa as theirs, historically and racially as recognised at Cairo and Potsdam.

The Japanese—although to employ a ju-jitsu term they have been temporarily forced to "yield"—must still look at Formosa longingly, and who knows, maybe aspire to exercise sovereignty over it again.

The aborigines—the 150,000 who survived the successive Japanese "Subjugation or Death" campaigns—can still make the fringes of their forests a fatal place for strangers. The Japanese kept them in their forest fastnesses by electrifying barbed wire fences and by other vicious measures, and so they never became an economic or social asset. The "true" Formosans—the seven million descendants of the mainlanders—would like very much to believe that Formosa might be theirs. From the fun of the dragons arose Formosa. From the ill humours of men all pious Formosans are praying for protection. They have had more than their fair share of strife and bloodshed—at one time Chinese historians officially described them as staging "every five years a rising and every three years a rebellion!"

They have also had more than their fair share of western intervention, for after Koxinga came two hundred years of fantastic misrule, a misrule into which intruded occasionally the enquiring gun muzzles of exploiting "Foreign Devils", and, while the island's associations with the mainland were ruinous, its associations with the west were to say the least, unprofitable.

The ties with the mainland are of race and language—Formosans speak the Fukien dialect of the seventeenth century. But the passing of time has weakened those ties which have been strained under the extortion of successive Chinese Viceroys who were more interested in filling their capacious sleeves than in the welfare of their people.

True these Manchu viceroys were under the onerous obligation of visiting the island once a year, but as they invariably defaulted in this duty, the corruption of the unsupervised officials became a scandal to even the case hardened.

In such circumstances rebellion followed upon rebellion. Seldom was the island occupied by less than 10,000 soldiers. And never did the unfortunate islanders, despite initial successes, succeed in their objectives.

Typical of these insurrections which were invariably led by men of the people, was the rising organised by a duck minder, Choo Ynkee who gambled for the support of a powerful band of outlaws by feasting them on his entire flock. By this generous entertainment he gained the goodwill of his guests and then, at the head of an insurgent host marched on to the capital, where he was proclaimed ruler.

Alas for poor Choo Ynkee. His victory cost the Viceroy the death of two senior officers who distinguished themselves by committing suicide when fleeing to the mainland. Subsequent defeats resulted in Choo Ynkee's capture and his transportation in the proverbial bamboo cage along nearly one thousand miles of rough roads to Peking. There he was sentenced to be crucified as an example to other potential rebels. An even more serious rebellion occurred in 1786, in which the Government lost 100,000 men before the order was restored. As late as 1930 two hundred Japanese are said to have forfeited their heads to the Chin-Hwan (Green Savages) and, as mentioned in the last chapter, thousands of Formosans were subsequently killed in the rising of 1947.

Superficially this history of intransigence lends weight to the arguments of those who claim that the Formosans, as distinct from the aborigines, are a single minded people who insist that they have never owed allegiance to whatever government happened to be ruling China at any time.

They also point out, with considerable emphasis, that in fifty years the Japanese were unable completely to restrain the insurrectionary tendencies of the islanders, a fact attested by the records of the Japanese themselves. On the other hand it should be appreciated that in their insurrections and rebellions the Formosans were actuated by many motives that it would be unwise to catalogue as organised nationalistic feeling. They can hardly be regarded as signs and symptoms of a people living in a state of duress.

In some cases a "rising" was purely the revolt of dissatisfied soldiery and banditry out for loot: in others it was born from fear–to quote one instance, the fear of villagers that they would be conscripted by the Japanese to fight the dreaded aborigines.

The Communist can truthfully boast that certain of the "plots" unmasked by the Japanese were Marxist in origin and intent. The

C

Nationalists, equally truthfully, can point to the Japanese records to show that many Formosans gave their lives to assist Chiang when the Japanese attacked China.

A typical example of the way in which history can be interpreted— (and not only in the Far East)—to suit the motives of the political zealots of the day is exemplified by the different conclusions drawn from the history of the First Formosan Republic.

In 1895 a defeated China ceded Formosa and the Pescadores to Japan as part of the price of peace.

Indignantly the "patriotics" declared a republic, and then, with solemn gravity, celebrated their announcement by despatching messages to all the Great Powers, and a special telegram to the Emperor at Peking, in which they described themselves as the "Literati and People of Formosa" and declared somewhat obscurely for "an independent island republic, at the same time recognising the sovereignty of the sacred Tsing dynasty".

For this new order a great enthusiasm was shown by a handful of officials and others in a position to profit by the large monetary "transactions" that took place! But "The People of Formosa" seemed, in the main, unmoved.

The Republic had a splendid flag—a great golden tiger with an abnormally long tail portrayed on a blue background with a yellow border. It had a Great Seal. It had postage stamps. It had a comic opera army. And, in southern Formosa, it lasted ten days. Then the great tiger curled up its long tail and died.

Cost to the Japanese? One hundred and sixty-four killed, five hundred and fourteen wounded. The remainder of their casualties were due to disease and climate rather than the warlike qualities of their opponents.

While the hasty flight of the Republic's "Second President"—"Black Flag" pirate chief Liu Yung-fu, commander of Chinese forces in the earlier war against France, who came to power after the first President's flight—was preceded by the firing of the republic's main buildings by the republic's own soldiers! It is unnecessary to add that the subsequent mopping up was conducted in the usual Japanese tradition of ruthless thoroughness. But let us study the way the story is developed today. According to the (Formosan) Nationalists the inception of the Republic—the first in Asia—is proof positive that the island's (organised) will to be free is of mature growth. The defeats of the Republic they blame on the base spirit of the "regular" troops on the Island—"rude mercenaries" from Canton. All tales of loot they lay at the same door.

Chiang's men, from their viewpoint will argue gravely that the rise of the Republic, and the subsequent clashes between Formosans and

Japanese, demonstrated the basic loyalty of Formosa to the Motherland. Surely, they argue, that to couple the announcement of a republic with an acknowledgment of the Emperor's sovereignty could
only have been a device to ensure that "one part of China" still fought
on without prejudicing the negotiations of the Central Government.

The mouthpiece of Mao urges that the whole thing is an example of
Chinese Fascists cashing in on people's righteous hatred of "Japanese
Fascism". That's why the Republic couldn't succeed, they declare. It
was organised for gain, and, when adversity came, it was betrayed.
The people who fought were "martyrs" for a freedom in which their
bosses did not believe. The Japanese have yet a different version.

They claim, glibly quoting contemporary records, that only 150
prominent people decided to stay behind when offered the alternative
of "fight or get out" by the Republic's Government. The Government, say the Japanese, was so heartily abhorred by its "subjects" that
they welcomed the arrival of the Imperial Guard as an army of liberation.

From the appearance of the cities of ferro-concrete, on the wide and
tree lined streets of Taipeh, Keelung and Kaohsiung, it is difficult to
realise that this apparently happy-go-lucky eastern people has behind
it, and perhaps before it, a terrible history of pillage, and murder, war
and muddle.

Wreckers, pirates, and aborigines, all found profit from the constant shipwrecks which occurred on the eastern shores, and through
their profit the unfortunate Formosan majority suffered the perpetual
attention of enquiring European gunboats and avenging expeditionary forces.

Even the "black fire nourishing rocks" that had been noted by
Koxinga and his men were to bring pain instead of profit to the
islanders. As steamships replaced the ships of sail it became of primary
importance for the "new fangled" steamers—now laden with
increasingly valuable cargoes of tea, silk, and other oriental produce,
to possess adequate facilities for coaling.

America, significantly, was the first of the western lands to become
inquisitive about the mineral wealth of the island, and in 1842 the ships
of Commodore Perry—Perry who had opened by force the markets of
Japan to the world outside—swept into Keelung to examine and report
on the coal resources of the island.

Eagerly the islanders discussed with joy the prospects of fortune introduced by these emissaries of heaven to whom they offered an immediate supply at the price of four shillings ($1) a ton. Alas for their
expectations. On the subject of mining coal the minds of the
mandarins were fully made up. In Koxinga's day the realistic peasant
had been by no means averse from using the providential rock, but

the mandarins who followed him, educated men possessed of all the geomantic and theological law of the day, had opposed the mining with vigour.

They recalled the legendary origin of Formosa, and after conducting various experiments and tests, were satisfied that their original opposition was justified and that the caverns from which the coal was won were, in fact, the abode of the genii.

To a dragon worshipping intelligentsia this was the most exciting discovery, and on their representations tablets were erected declaring that the mining of coal, under severe penalty was, "absolutely and for all eternity prohibited". Thus, with a sense of timing and tact that was in the best mandarin tradition, the official edicts were issued just in time to spoil the islanders' little deal with the west!

In 1850 Britain emerged as a suitor for Formosa's sudden wealth, and the reply of the Peking Government, after a prologue of stately officialese, "thanked the British Minister for his kind offer" to which it said it "had given careful consideration".

It continued:

"Upon examining records it is necessary state that as the surrounding hills contain the dragons pulse for all Formosa, the gentry and people had repeatedly prohibited interference therewith, and it is obviously right to comply with the wishes of the people. It would, moreover, be inexpedient forcibly to insist upon the opening of the mines. It might lead to trouble and furnish occasion for disasters".

The British filed the letter for future reference and left it at that, although more than one Admiral grumbled, including my great uncle, John Fiot Lee Pearse Maclear, R.N.

The French were not so polite. After the Chinese Governor of the island had thought fit to place the mandarins' superstitions second to the necessity of obtaining fuel for his arsenal, the cruiser *Volta* under the command of a Captain Tournier, sailed into Keelung to demand coal. He got it. His simple method involved turning the guns of his ship upon the town and threatening to open fire unless his requirements were immediately met.

"Such an officer as the *Volta's* commander would seem marked for a career", sarcastically noted an American in his diary. As it happened, such a career was forthcoming and Tournier became a "mediator" in armistice discussions following the Franco-Sino War of 1884-5.

In the interim three French warships pounded Keelung's forts to rubble with the loss of a few French sailors from a landing party, two of whom were killed by Formosans in revenge for a raping. The French reprisals were heavy.

In their time the islanders have seen landing parties of British, American, German and Japanese march through their streets to protect the lives and properties of their nationals from disorganised soldiery. They have experienced in less than seventy years the successive occupations of the French (for a very short time), and Japanese and now the armies of Chiang Kai-shek.

One of the most important questions is just how do the Nationalists stand in the eyes of the Formosans? On the answer depends rather more than just the matter of internal security.

The iniquitous system whereby tenant farmers were compelled to pay up to 70 per cent of their produce by way of tribute has been abolished by the reforming zeal of the Provincial Government, and for this the islanders are duly grateful, a matter which is discussed more fully later. The army is restrained in its indiscipline, and much effort has been devoted to ensuring that justice is done to those who would unduly oppress the islanders. It would, however, be idle to pretend that the troops are popular as a whole with the Formosans. Nor is there any gainsaying the fact that a good 70 per cent of the total Formosan budget is being spent on the armed forces and this is naturally much resented.

Yet at least these soldiers are not parasites. They are now growing much of their own food. They build their own barracks, make their own shoes and, like western soldiers, "moan" instead of loot.

Certainly the Formosans who said when the Nationalists took over from the Japanese: "the dogs have gone but the pigs have come", would be at a loss for epithets to describe the communists if they were to land! Although they have little love for Chiang's supporters, they have even less for those of Mao Tse-tung, and, up to a point, they undoubtedly regard it as only reasonable that the cost of the army should be borne – in part – by the islanders.

This agreement, however, carries the important proviso that the army behaves itself as an army should – especially if called upon to defend the people who are paying for it.

On this score – let alone the possibility of the soldiers making their much publicised, much opposed, victorious return to the mainland – the Formosans seem more than a little sceptical.

I had an opportunity of carrying on a miniature poll among friends who were in contact with Formosans and the majority thought that first and foremost they would like sovereign independence – as an alternative they would welcome status as a trusteeship territory under the United Nations or American tutelage. They were divided in their views as to whose rule was preferable – Chiang's comparative freedom or Japanese repression which had at least meant order. None professed preference for the communists.

3. *The Nationalist garrison*

WHO are the men who man the castle? How trustworthy are they? How well equipped? And what guarantee is there that should the opportunity occur they would not follow the example of the armies of Chiang that surrendered so easily upon the mainland? And what of their commanders? Will they prove as amenable to bludgeon and bribe as so many of the Generalissimo's former "right-hand men"?

When the armies of the Kuomintang reeled in panic from the Yangtze, western observers prophesied that the life of the Nationalist régime could be numbered in weeks.

The prophets were confounded, but not, let it be said, by any intrinsic military virtue displayed upon the field of battle; they lost rather by default. Chiang Kai-shek withdrew to Formosa and it seemed for a while that even this island refuge would not long avail against the efficiently regimented forces of Mao Tse-tung. On the mainland – a hundred miles away – picked communist formations began to assemble in the ports and harbours, while motorised junks and a few other craft crowded the inlets and anchorages ready, or so it was believed at the time, for the attack.

That attack did not come. And within two days of the outbreak of the Korean war President Truman had declared that the island would be "neutralised" and that the war would not be permitted to reach it.

Immediately units of the U.S. Seventh Fleet took up position in the Straits. American army and navy aircraft commenced widespread patrols from their bases in Okinawa and Clark Field near Manila. Into the hands of Chiang's weapon hungry forces arrived the bazookas and tommy guns of America. And then, in July 1950, came the much criticised, but from Chiang's view, most providential, arrival of General MacArthur.

The MacArthur visit was followed by a thawing in American opinion – for some time past almost glacier-like in its temperature towards General Chiang Kai-shek – while the interim dollar aid that followed to the estimated value of fifty million was the fore-runner of the existing aid proposals. But what of the Nationalists themselves? Are they worth the money? And, despite the outspoken determination of their leaders to some day launch an attack, are the rank and file even capable of maintaining a defence?

In a Dakota of uncertain vintage, piloted by a Chinese Air Force officer, I flew to the tiny island of Quemoy (or Kinmen as it is also known). And there, within only a few hundred yards of its single war-scarred runway, I thought I had found an answer.

Quemoy is one of Chiang's "other islands". It is the island that nobody ever hears about. It is the island that, militarily untenable according to all the laws of strategy, has been held by his express command, and despite the views of some of his military advisers. It is the island that has held out against odds that, even to better equipped defenders might be classed as overwhelming.

I had often heard of this brave defiance, but not until I saw the spot did I realise just what this defiance entailed. Quemoy is bare of all trees, and has no foliage. It is a place of coral, sand, and withered grass, a place lacking all natural obstacles to a determined attacker. Swept by gales and baked by sun, it is only two miles off the Chinese coast–approximately one quarter of the distance between Southend and the southern side of the Thames!

It is unique in that its "crack" garrison outnumbers the civilian population of 35,000 by almost two to one. It is unique also by reason of its weird civilian background–where singularly unperturbed peasants, among them, in their loose jeans and gay slacks, the women who are reputed to be among the most beautiful in the Orient, scratch a living from a soil that has trenches for its boundary fences, and pill boxes instead of barns; where fishermen ply their trade only beneath the guns of protecting warships and batteries of American 105's.

A frequent exchange of "gun fire", I was told, has been going on since October 1949, a date that may prove of considerable significance to students assessing the efficiency or otherwise of the Nationalist forces.

For it was in this month that the communists–flushed with their great land victories–launched an invasion attempt in which it is claimed nearly 30,000 men took part. This attempt, although supported by shore batteries and directed from the fort of Amoy, less than ten miles distant, was most bloodily repulsed.

Without necessarily accepting the Nationalists' subsequent estimates of Red casualties–their figure of 2,000 killed and captured would indeed seem exaggeration–it is obvious that the incident provided a severe setback for Mao Tse-tung.

Although local in its immediate military effect, the Quemoy repulse was in fact the first symptom that not all of the armies of Chiang Kai-shek were demoralised by defeat.

Similarly the communists' incredible failure either to repeat the experiment successfully, or to break by blockade and bombardment the will of the defenders to resist, was a symptom that not every Red Division was prepared to wade over its dead to victory, and that at least one Nationalist army is apparently endowed with staying power as well as initial ardour.

I saw, beside a field of scruffy undersized bananas, with a covering of white dust across their "XGI" marching boots, a handful of machine-gunners jump to action stations and train their Browning at a pack of seagulls riding peacefully on the wave-tops of the Straits. The emphasis throughout the practice lay in speed. The "home" of these men (typical of the "homes" of many of the garrison) is a pit dug in the sand, supported by wood and covered by camouflaged tarpaulins. Their food is the basic bowl of rice. Fresh vegetables are singularly few, grown on miserable little "allotments" or flown in by air or brought from Formosa in gunboats. Occasionally units of the garrison are allowed a little leave on Formosa. For bleak, unfriendly and by all standards unbeautiful, the island is only fifty square miles and the extent of its civilisation is numbered in the occasional clusters of baked mud dwellings that form the Quemoy "villages", which are periodically used by the communist guns as markers for practice shoots!

I am not revealing any profound military secret when I say that the army on the island relies very little upon motorised transport. With communist field glasses inquisitively inspecting the landscape from less than 4,000 yards away, the expectation of life for any jeep or truck that stirs along its coastal tracks, is limited. And, only a day or so before my arrival, a move to pass a convoy of six vehicles to the north was detected and immediately smashed by howitzer fire.

Yet despite these obvious inconveniences morale is high. Chiang's men in their foxholes and block-houses have actually developed a degree of "shell happiness". Several told me that artillery marksmanship was one of the weakest qualities of the Red army, while there is no doubt that the Nationalist guns have made things extremely unpleasant for the besiegers.

Discipline is strict. As in that other Chinese army, political indoctrination is an integral part of military training, and one company I visited had written, in its own blood, a manifesto of allegiance to General Chiang Kai-shek, and its resolution to fight on to victory.

Long, long ago Quemoy was the hide-out of the pirates who infested the sea-ways between Hong Kong and the north. Today units of Chiang's fleet sail from it to harass the blockade runners. For like Formosa, this tiny island is an excellently placed base from which to intercept traffic between the mainland ports. It is only 300 miles from Hong Kong and its warships frequently make a successful "catch".

The Pescadores, Quemoy and Formosa—these are the territories that remain loyal to Chiang Kai-shek.

It is problematical how long they would remain should the link between them break: the link that is provided by the seldom publicised Nationalist navy which since the mutinies of 1949, has remained loyal. It has the advantage of having as complete a numerical superiority afloat as the Communists have ashore. And furthermore, many of its officers and petty officers are trained in the British tradition.

Some measure of its growing prestige and importance may be gathered when one realises that a representative from Lloyd's of London was in Formosa while I was there trying to negotiate with the Nationalists for some portion of the money derived from the sale of seized cargoes.

Before leaving England, I had sought out the addresses of Chinese naval officers with whom I had been associated during the war. They had spent a year or more at the Royal Naval College at Greenwich and several of them had served with the Royal Navy before returning to China. I was naturally most anxious to renew their acquaintance and travelled to Kaohsiung, the commercial port and naval base that lies in the south of the island. Beside the ensigns of the Kuomintang – everywhere evident – flew the Stars and Stripes of an American destroyer, a unit of the Seventh Fleet using the harbour at the end of a patrol.

But most impressive were the grey ships of Chiang. On the still, hardly ruffled waters of the harbour they lay grimly quiet. But on their turrets, radar detectors steadily searched the skies for hostile aircraft, the seas for "blockade busters".

Once upon a time, I recalled, as I looked at these surprisingly vigilant craft, the navy of Chiang had been dismissed as "The Flat Iron Fleet". What sign was there that this appellation was no longer justified?

I could only make invidious comparisons between them and the huddle of untidy sloops and gunboats (normally with the washing of their crews giving an illusion of being "dressed overall") that I remembered seeing as a small boy at Chefoo and other places along the China coast. Remembering such naval curiosities, how could my first impressions of Chiang's fleet be anything but favourable?

In fact, however, Chiang's navy, although formidable to a civilian looking from the shore, probably comprises the most heterogeneous collection of warships afloat.

Its destroyers – estimated to number between sixteen and twenty – are either of the small American "escort" type or else none too new Japanese craft that were surrendered after the ending of the Pacific War.

Some of its sloops saw service with the Royal Navy, others were built in China, the landing craft are American and for good measure one of its gunboats came from Italy. It was a coincidence, but I remembered her well as a trim little gunboat, the *Sebastian Cabot*. I had had lunch on board with her Commander and my father in 1923 at Tientsin. Its largest ship probably has a displacement of about 2,000 tons.

By Western standards therefore, it is most certainly neither of impressive dimensions nor of formidable fighting quality. But Western standards do not govern the Chinese war, and Chiang's fleet is undoubtedly efficient and well disciplined enough to do the jobs now required of it.

It has no submarines. It does not need them. It has no aircraft carriers, although many young naval officers are urging that it should be permitted to bring itself up to date in this latter respect. They argue that two or three of the small aircraft carriers now "mothballed" in America would be of the utmost service:

(a) in tightening still further the blockade,

(b) to effect a further dissipation of communist strength by strengthening points on the mainland, and

(c) in enabling, by the support of their fighters, the Nationalist navy to proceed much further afield than it has done to date.

Opposed to these arguments are those of one or two of the senior naval officers who state that, even were America willing to part with a carrier, the navy could ill afford to part with precious officers for the time necessary to train them in a new technique. Those who hold this view are far more perturbed by the state of the machinery in certain of the older craft and are anxious to obtain new frigates, corvettes and L.S.T.'s.

Kaohsiung is the headquarters of the Chinese First Squadron, and at the time of my visit, there was another squadron based on the former Japanese secret harbour in the Pescadores.

It is to Keelung, the northern base however, that most of "the ships that make headlines", namely the ships detained under suspicion of carrying contraband, are escorted. Here one can usually see at least one Panamanian ship. For several weeks while I was there, the German ship *Mai Rickmers* lay in the harbour high out of the water, having been relieved of a million pound (sterling) cargo. And it is at Keelung, also, that one hears the most bitter arguments about "British misrepresentation".

Nationalists complain that ships flying the British flag are, next to the craft which fly the flag of Panama are the worst offenders.

They argue also, that newspapers often claim that "British" ships have been detained when, in fact, they are not British owned, but only wearing the Red Ensign because of their legal obligation to fly the flag of the port of registration (Hong Kong). The same argument of course, is equally sound of ships flying the Panamanian flag.

They also point to their "forbearance" in not using their batteries at Quemoy Island to stop British ships passing near the island and ask, not without some pertinency, what the communists would do in similar circumstances!

But despite these differences and a certain degree of hurt pride at the manner in which the Admiralty recalled two warships lent to the Nationalists following the *Chungking* affair, I encountered a very real affection for the Royal Navy among the officers. At the naval officers' club at Tso Ying, six-and-a-half miles north west of Kaohsiung, their splendid reading room boasts most of the service and technical magazines produced by the Americans. But there are no similar British publications available to the members and they would like to know why not, for their "British Tradition" is dying very hard.

The night after my arrival at the Kaohsiung base I attended a banquet at which fourteen of the naval officers present had received their training in Britain. But my host had not.

He was Admiral Kwei Yung-ching, one of the most colourful figures in Formosa.

Admiral Kwei graduated to his present position after nearly forty years of service in the Chinese Army in which he is a five star General. Trained at Whampoa Military Academy, so dear to General Chiang Kai-shek, he later went to a German Staff College, fought the communists in the two civil wars, and the Japanese in World War Two. He came to Britain in 1946 as head of the Chinese Military Mission.

Although probably only the topsyturvydom of the Nationalists could ever result in a General becoming Commander-in-Chief of a navy overnight, the experiment, as so many other odd experiments in the Far East, appears to work!

In Kwei, originally called upon to root out "disaffected" elements and investigate widespread rumours of factions within the navy, Chiang possesses a tough disciplinarian; a man devoted to the régime, and possessed of a rare ability for getting things done. He has purged and he has built. He has doubled the pay of naval officers, he has sent traitors to the firing squad.

The navy, after some initial suspicious grumbling, appears to have accepted him with enthusiasm. Americans in Formosa told me that the speed with which the naval officers' training depot was built from the ruins of the former Japanese headquarters was largely due to the inspiration of Admiral Kwei, and I saw for myself, in the radar training section of the depot, just how his young men are enthusiastically attempting to master the equipment of modern sea-war.

As a host, the Commander-in-Chief possesses great qualities of charm, and an almost frightening thoroughness. At the feast to which I was invited and at which I was the guest of honour, twenty-three courses were served, and they were followed by a series of Gambai's* (ceremonial toasts) that lasted for two hours! It was from Admiral

*"Gambai" is a salute with full glasses and the person toasting and the recipient both empty their glasses.

Kwei's staff that I learned what is apparently common knowledge in the island, that at a farewell party to the *Amethyst* he had urged a postponement of its departure down the Yangtse River. The Admiral told me himself that he warned his British friends that the communists would probably open fire from their shore batteries. The British ignored Kwei's advice and the sequel became front page news so long as officers and ratings were being killed. It was through Admiral Kwei's efforts and good offices that the British wounded were evacuated and in performing this brave and friendly service, Admiral Kwei told me he lost one of his best officers.

In affairs military and political his reputation as a fire eater is proverbial, and the course of political indoctrination to which he submits the men he commands would, for its happy disregard of all claim to objectivity, be a credit to the Kremlin. A few impressions, taken from my diary, of a typical evening's "education" for the ratings of the First Squadron.

In a vast hall in the naval depot 1,800 sailors came to their feet. Down the centre aisle I walked beside the admiral, followed by his aides. At the end of the hall was a stage. On it, bowing low, were a group of actors whose job it is to boost the fighting men's morale.

The admiral signified permission to sit down. The audience sat, and the show began. The theme of the entertainment was the "two-facedness" of the Red deceivers over the Straits. One of the sketches depicted a peasant who is sufficiently excited by communist promises to redistribute the land to kill an unpopular landlord. We then, of course, witnessed his subsequent revulsion and disillusionment. For what happened to the hero and the people of the village beneath the Red yoke?

A row of prostrate actors covered the stage. A figure unmistakably resembling the hated Stalin—immense nose and long moustache emerged from the wings to slash madly at them with a long whip. The bodies moaned and heaved. From backstage came the screams of a woman, punctuated by the raucous laughter of communist soldiers and the "Ay Yah; Ay Yah"; the cry of despair.

Was all lost? Of course not! A thousand times no! Suddenly the audience was deafened by exploding fire crackers. The screen at the back of the stage was lit by the red glow of "incendiary bombs". The heroes had come to the rescue.

I was amazed at the roar of voices behind me. The 1,800 jumped to their feet, bellowing approval and then as the lights faded. Representatives of the army, navy, air force and civilian resistance movement marched, with arms swinging, across the stage. The refrain of the Nationalist war songs were taken up by the voices of the audience and, in between times, an attractive girl with a good microphone technique

hurled rhetorical questions to the sailors, questions which drew fren-
zied cheers, cries of agreement, and repeated vows that Chiang Kai-
shek's banner will be carried by the fighting men back to the mainland
and reconquest.

I have mentioned this episode, for two reasons. Firstly it demon-
strates the insistence of "The Return". Secondly, however primitive
in plot to western eyes, the sketches are undoubtedly effective in
counteracting the type of propaganda that has for so long been provided by the communists.

Certainly they would appear to produce an enthusiasm infinitely
more fervent than would be the result of a Nationalist equivalent to
the ABCA or the British Council or even the Voice of America! But
just how would this vociferous resolution stand up to the hard test of
repeated reverses?

I recalled the case of the *Chungking*. What guarantee, I asked, was
there that if Chiang's fortunes change for the worst, other warships
would not follow her example of defection. At any reference to this
5,000 ton cruiser—former pride of the Chinese navy—faces grow
glum. It is not good form to talk about the *Chungking*. The shame is
still so bitterly felt.

They tell you probably with a considerable degree of truth, that the
desertion occurred only after the officers had been overpowered at
the pistol point. And with, perhaps, less accuracy, they assure you
that the mutineers were a "minority" who seized the ship by surprise.

I do not know the force of this argument. But one thing is certain.
If it *was* a minority that took possession, then ships' majorities will be
considerably more watchful in future, for the *Chungking*, as mentioned
earlier, was bombed out of the water by the men of the Nationalist air
force as soon as the news reached Formosa.

Probably the most concrete evidence of the navy's abiding loyalty
lies in the fact that, by nature of their calling, Chiang's ships are often
in positions where desertion would be a relatively simple matter. And
they show no desire to avail themselves of the opportunity!

I left Kaohsiung with impressions of the Nationalist navy that still
remained favourable—despite a few reservations caused by the sight of
the disrepair of certain of the smaller craft!

And before I left I watched, from an ex-American gunboat, the new
and much boosted Chinese marine corps perform a routine day's
training.

This force was formed only two years ago. But it is now said to comprise some 10,000 men. The training closely resembles that of the
British and American marine and commando formations and the
men are "hand picked" front line fighters and from the tasks which I

saw them perform on the 600-feet high precipitous cliffs in the neighbourhood, I daresay the training is superb.

The marines, designated optimistically as the spearhead of a Nationalist return, are well equipped with automatic weapons, are smartly uniformed, and have a high morale.

Furthermore, they would probably – should there be a little relaxation of the American "neutralisation" policy – be used almost immediately for commando and sabotage roles along the mainland.

But, even here, there is a considerable shortage of war material such as DUKWS and waterproofed vehicles. And, at the moment, the Nationalists possess less than twenty landing craft, of varying types, age groups and working efficiency.

The state of the army is the most imponderable of the many factors that have to be considered when assessing the military situation of Formosa.

By far the largest of the three services, its personnel, with the exception of the undaunted garrison of Quemoy, has had small chance of recovering the prestige lost during the battle for China proper.

Officially, its strength totals 500,000 officers and men. Its discipline is higher than that of any other army of the Kuomintang. And it has the benefit of considerable American advice.

But not withstanding these factors, foreign military observers believe that only about two-fifths of the force is in a fit state to fight anything but a defensive delaying action.

The "two-fifths" comprise those show pieces of Chiang – the few picked divisions. The remainder of the garrison is seldom seen. It is scattered in holding positions along the island or else in remote training camps.

There are certain problems peculiar to the army that confuse attempts to estimate with any degree of accuracy its fighting qualities.

To commence with, unlike the navy and the air force with its reserve of 1,200 trained pilots, it has not seen action since the withdrawal of the last troops from Hainan Island and the Chusan Archipelago.

Despite the rigidity of Chiang's censorship it has naturally heard of the Red successes of last year in Korea and, it is probable that many of its troops condemned to inaction feel a certain tinge of admiring envy for the prestige that the men of Mao have acquired.

And whatever the enthusiasm of its leaders, the equipment of the army still leaves much to be desired but, even more important than the shortcomings in this direction, is the tussle that is going on between the army leaders and the Administration regarding the soldiers' food.

I first heard of this sorry business from General Sun Li–jen.

General Sun Li-jen is fifty-two years old and trained at the Virginia Military Academy. He fought with distinction in the China-Burma war area in 1942 and 1945. He has the C.B. and the C.B.E. and is a personal friend of Field-Marshal Sir William Slim–to whom, upon my return to England–I conveyed a message of goodwill. He speaks English fluently, is a great admirer of things English and is most highly thought of by the men he commands.

It came as a considerable shock, therefore, to hear this able, loyal supporter of Chiang, tell me that his men are the victims of malnutrition through dependence on the governmental buying system.

There was a look of anguish in his eyes when he said: "The position is crazy. The army is forbidden to buy its food direct, all provisions must be purchased by the Government and later allocated to the forces.

"The Government dealers do not seem to realise that by employing surplus middle men, agents and other people, they are paying twice the price the army would pay. They have, by their action, grossly increased the price of the rations which means that the army is getting far less food than it should. How can men's morale be maintained indefinitely on handfuls of rice?"

Since then, however, the recommendations of the Chase Military Mission have probably been implemented or are well on their way to being so. To one who remembers the incredible stupidities of Chiang's former administrations, these criticisms sound unpleasantly familiar but, in all fairness, it should be added that Sun Li-jen also emphasised that it was only upon this particular issue that he had found cause for discontent.

In other directions, he said, the administration was doing extraordinarily brilliant work. And he, as well as other officers I spoke with, emphasised that leadership today is no longer the perquisite of a deep purse and an influential relative!

Prominent, of course, among the officers of Nationalist China is Chiang's younger son Chiang Wei-kuo–but even here it would seem that personal ability rather than "influence" has governed the appointment.

Popular with the men he leads, and dissimilar in this respect and others from his elder brother, young Chiang is head of the mechanised warfare department of the army.

He has had the opportunity of learning his trade from good mentors. He graduated in the armoured schools of Germany and after further training with the armoured formations of America and personal front line experience against the communists in China, Chiang Wei-kuo is described by foreign military observers as a "first class armoured officer". I was told that on the sand table and the map his methods displayed an originality based on sound premises but that practical training was handicapped by a serious shortage of tanks and other vehicles. Self-propelled guns are few, while there are, as yet, no really efficient field workshops.

American aid may soon create a world of difference but should his men fail to make the best use of the equipment that is available in the meanwhile, it will be through no fault of their commander.

Chiang Wei-kuo and his junior officers are displaying considerable ingenuity in providing "mock ups" of the weapons that would have to be handled in combat. All sorts of tank attacks are "simulated" in the absence of practical equipment.

Like Sun Li-jen, he believes morale still has at least a favourable ratio to material. Good morale he says, does not arise from idleness or ease, or even from the adoption of roles that however politically desirable are defensive and therefore, in the military sense, uninspiring. Morale is indeed the imponderable factor in the Formosan situation today.

Apart from the desire of the – perhaps too optimistic – leaders much has been made by the the official propagandists of the "individual will" to return to the mainland, and it is true that the average soldier is as anxious as his officers to shake the volcanic dust of Formosa off his sandals and get back to his family.

But, although this desire might induce him to set out for the Mainland without complaint is there any guarantee that he might not then find smoother and faster ways of reaching "home" than by fighting?

The elder son of the Generalissimo, Lieut. General Chiang Chengkuo, would seem to have had his doubts in this direction, and the Secret Police system that he has established is well worth study and consideration.

4. Is Formosa a "democracy"?

THE stars were hard and bright in the skies above the mountains. Below, in the gardens of the Air Force Officers' Club, ornamental lanterns swayed from bending palm trees and multi-coloured electric lights bobbed and shimmered like beads on a necklace as the wind blew cool across a host of flowers and magnificent lawns. A dance orchestra, as accomplished as any I have ever listened to, played on a gaily decorated rostrum while in the background flowered exotic shrubs and bushes. A hundred dancing couples – men in white dinner jackets or spotless khaki uniform, women wearing "Shanghai frocks" which accentuate the slim figures of the Chinese women, slit up the side as far as the knee. I could not help wishing that a magic carpet would transport just one couple to the Occident for its edification.

The only European invited to this function at Formosa's most exclusive club, I was the guest of Dr. Shen Chang-huan, one of the Presidential advisers and the Government Spokesman.

For a moment, I stood outside to appreciate the scene that, in all its elegant extravagance, was so typical of a softer grace and age. Then I saw the "other men" outside.

Quietly, unobtrusively, they stood back in the shadows. There was no conversation between them. And as I became aware of their regard I realised, yet once again, the grim realities that lie beneath the island's gay appearances. For this was a special occasion – the most powerful, and some say, the most feared man in Formosa was visiting the club with a party of intimate friends.

His name: Lieutenant General Chiang Cheng-kuo, the elder son of General Chiang Kai-shek and – with the title of Chief of the Ministry of National Defence – boss of the island's complicated, efficient and thoroughly ruthless secret police and security network.

He is the man who, more than any other, has earned for Formosa the unpleasant but correct appellation of "Police State". But he is also, let it not be forgotten, the man whose job it is to ensure that an even worse form of suppression is not imposed upon the island.

Not even his most ardent admirer could claim that Chiang Cheng-kuo is popular with his compatriots, while his hatred of communism is said to be accompanied by an instinctive distrust and dislike of all foreigners.

Stocky, stout and slightly scowling, he is reported to be as reticent in conversation as he is ready in action. He shows little mercy to others, and to his credit would probably not ask for mercy for himself should his fortunes ever meet a serious reverse.

As I saw him on that evening, his behaviour seemed to belie the reports of his arrogance, moodiness and general unsociability. If anything he was almost boyishly exuberant, and it was difficult indeed to realise that this paunchy, beaming, black haired fellow had approved probably more death sentences than any one else outside the Iron Curtain.

The blare of a saxophone, the clash of cymbals, a ripple of hand clapping and a rank of gay smiles – from my contemplation of Chiang Cheng-kuo I turned to see the Generalissimo's son bow to the audience and, to my surprise but apparently nobody else's, take the drummer's seat in the orchestra. Many were the reports I had heard of the "difference" in character of the sons of the General.

Chiang Wei-kuo, mentioned in the previous chapter as the head

D

of the Nationalists' armour, is studious only in his military profession. He is gay and debonair and as popular with all classes of the army and the people as his brother is disliked. Between the two, it is whispered that there is a singularly pronounced lack of brotherly affection, although I noticed little of their alleged jealousies.

The band struck up again. Two or three minutes later Chiang Cheng-kuo was, incongruously, heading a laughing jiving throng, while Chiang the younger increased the general frenzy with the drum beats at which he is expert.

With Chiang Cheng-kuo was his Russian born wife, a tall, attractive brunette. She is now a naturalised Chinese and is said by some, with what truth I do not know, to have suffered at the hands of the communists before leaving "Mother Russia".

Chiang Cheng-kuo–significantly when one considers the ramifications of the organisation of which he has now control–is Russian trained. He was a guest of the Soviets for years and has had first hand experience of Soviet methods. In addition, he was at one time a great admirer of Russia–so much so that he fell out of favour with his father, and his bitter disillusionment has now been accompanied by the usual violent reactions.

All in all, his experiences may account for his ruthlessness, they may also explain why the weapon with which he now tackles the communists is so carefully modelled upon the communists' own pattern!

For the Nationalist Government it is said, by reputable United States experts, employs 25,000 political "commissars" in the army alone!

These "commissars", or Political Officers as they are more euphemistically labelled, are permanently attached from company level, and each battalion has a political section as an administrative unit.

Like their communist counterparts, one of their jobs is to "politically educate" the soldier, to convince him of the righteousness of his own cause and the evil of its rival. Like the communists also they have a more sinister occupation, to detect and root out "defeatism", to smash all opposition to the régime within the armed forces!

The "P.O.s" are responsible only to the Ministry, to whom they report direct, and one very quick result of their activities has been the denunciation of many malcontents, most of whom, it is said, are summarily executed.

These political officers, however, form only one group of the many men who are working to support Chiang Cheng-kuo's exacting task.

For to the Ministry of National Defence come not only the reports of the Political Officers but also information from the Municipal Police, the Military Police, and the Peace Preservation Corps (an organisation of picked members of the Party).

The reports are sifted by a special counter-espionage section that is part of the much dreaded Secret Police of which, of course, Chiang Cheng-kuo is also the head. And the Secret Police, within the limit imposed by numbers and resources, has powers approximating to that of the Russian N.V.D.

It has its own agents, answerable only to their Chief, established in all of the "junior" police forces. It has absolute powers to arrest, detain and "interrogate" suspects. It has its own "private" army. And it provides the execution squads that have disposed of so many political offenders.

Among its branches can be numbered the Foreign Affairs Police, some of them fluent linguists and the amiable "guides" of foreigners; and the department which controls the men who guarded Chiang Cheng-kuo so effectively on that very pleasant night.

For, despite the gold bars promised by the communists for his premature, unaccidental death, Chiang Cheng-kuo left the club as intact as usual in the small hours of the morning. And I, like many others, was left guessing about the extraordinary good humour he had shown until, a little later, I heard about "a wholesale communist plot" – its discovery, its breaking up, and the arrests of its members.

The Government announcement, with an economical choice of phrasing said:

"The Ministry of National Defence announces the cracking up of a big communist plot involving 107 men and women. All but one, Yu Fei, have been arrested, and eighteen have been convicted and executed." The plotters, the communiqué continued, included schoolteachers and journalists", while one man had succeeded in becoming an employee of the American Consulate! The activity of the Secret Police is not confined to the work of counter-espionage; nor is its field of operations limited to the boundaries of Formosa. It has agents on the mainland to report on the problems of Mao Tse-tung, and keep in touch with the guerilla groups that, almost unnoticed by the West, are becoming daily more harassing to the communist régime. It has agents, also, in practically every quarter of the Far East and operates even in London and New York.

This claim to possess an international network of intelligence may seem, at first sight, to be a little overdrawn. One tends to think of the influence of Chiang only in relation to the territory that he actually controls, and to compare its minute population and scant resources with the millions of Mao Tse-tung. The tendency to overlook the influence that the Nationalists have upon the discontented in China, as the only organised and coherent body of "official" resistance to the communists, is perhaps inevitable.

Yet, in fact, there are continual clashes on the mainland between the supporters of the "New China" and those who, for a variety of reasons, would like to see its end. I discovered when visiting Hong Kong that the Secret Police of Chiang *have* made good the boast of functioning with some efficiency in this area which, together with the Portuguese possession of Macao, has now become the clearing house of Far Eastern intelligence.

Also, in assessing the efficiency of Nationalist intelligence the influence of the "patriotic societies" overseas cannot be ignored. These function wherever there is a Chinese population; they dispose of considerable financial resources, and receive innumerable secrets. In their ranks are some of Chiang's wealthiest supporters. The alleged ramifications of the Chiang Cheng-kuo network are not uninteresting.

The Nationalists claim to have rendered invaluable service to the British in "tip offs" from time to time regarding the activities of Chinese communists in Malaya—a claim that, as far as I know, has not been denied.

While in the Philippines, I was advised that Manila received frequent, and accurate, reports from Formosa regarding the designs of the Huks (the near communists who are fighting the régime of President Quirino).

In Indo-China Nationalist agents have been assisting deserters from the armies of Mao Tse-tung to reach French territory.

But what effect has the Secret Police upon the lives and everyday affairs of that large majority of Formosans that is neither "communist" nor "Nationalist" but merely wants to go about its own business in its own unspectacular way?

According to the "leftist" publicists outside Formosa, a "reign of terror" rules the island of Chiang Kai-shek. While according to the Nationalists their Government is a "democracy" without blemish!

What are the real facts?

Through a variety of circumstances I arrived in Taipeh without a visa and, instead of being detained, as would most certainly have happened in the western democracies, I was allowed to go where I chose while the courteous authorities made inquiries that resulted in my passport being returned to me the very same day. I think this incident provides something of an answer.

My desire to keep up with the news led me to a bookstall on which, for all who chose to buy, were American and British newspapers and magazines, some of them containing the most savage attacks on the Nationalist administration. I later heard considerable and apparently uninhibited grumbling regarding various aspects of the régime. It was intriguing to learn from government circles that Formosa possessed no such thing as a press censorship, nor was there a censorship of mail, nor was there a curfew, excepting in Kaohsiung the naval port. The street scene was most reassuring.

In the world's most chaotic traffic – the Taipeh streets were never designed to support the traffic of today – a bewildered looking traffic control policeman, with his automatic pistol, perched on a strange raised platform, strove to control a people that seemed remarkably obedient to the signals but when out of sight seemed to abandon all road sense. In what appeared to be the Formosan equivalent of Hyde Park, orators held forth loudly from improvised platforms. And three of Chiang's putteed, steel-helmeted military police walked along the pavements without pushing everyone else off them, in Asia a noteworthy phenomenon indeed!

The tinkling of the bells of the ice-cream vendors; the trade calls of the sellers of sweetmeats; even the metallic pings of the air guns that, mounted on tripods and aimed at targets attached to trees are the favourite toys of the amiable islanders, convey an atmosphere of tranquillity to the traveller that is far removed from his preconceived opinions regarding the appearance of a Police State.

Initial impressions of Formosa, especially if one has had experience of the Far East, are smooth and fair indeed.

The children are plump and clean. There is no unemployment. And disease, so often part of the Oriental street scene, seems here to be in decent hiding behind the walls of modern hospitals, although the incidence of tuberculosis is high.

Crime is at a discount. The cells in the Police Stations are clean. Justice, though very severe, appears to be impartially administered. And so that illiterate offenders are not unduly exploited by the police, their statements are recorded and played back to them.

You can leave your wallet on the table of your unlocked bedroom. You have no need to pay cash should you wish to ask a policeman the time. While the ostentation of the rich – that eternal insult to the Asiatic poor – is here officially discouraged.

For while the housewife grumbles at the price she has to pay for fresh vegetables, the business man has more reason to curse the Government's car tax which, under this "Right Wing" régime, approximates annually to the cost of the car when new!

Fair and lofty indeed is the façade of the Formosan castle until, of course, the visitor recovers from his delighted intellectual stupor and begins to look a little more carefully at the quality of the mortar that binds the bricks.

There is no curfew – but all people out of doors after dark are liable to be detained at the nearest Police headquarters until they can provide a satisfactory explanation for their wanderings. And they may also be required to explain why they are not in their own dwelling houses should the police choose to call as they sometimes do. And freedom of one's mail from official scrutiny might depend, I was informed, on employing "test" letters, on a variety of factors–the type of paper of which the envelope was made, the type of gum used, and to where the letters were addressed. In actual fact, the only astonishing thing about such elementary precautions as these is the infinite trouble the Nationalists take in inferring that they do not exist. But in other directions the picture is more disturbing.

Despite the Nationalist boast of a free press, an editor is by no means a free agent in the western sense of the word. He can print what he likes. There is no "committee" to consult before publishing. But once the paper is on the streets he is responsible for any "defeatism" that its articles might engender and as "defeatism" is a crime against the State he can be tried, in secret and by a military court.

My Chinese friends would indeed privately criticise "methods", but they would never dare publicly criticise the principle of the régime; while the variety of speeches offered by the soap box orators had a theme as carefully underwritten by "The Party" as would any peroration bellowed through the amplifiers in Red Square. At times indeed the security complex of the Nationalists had an atmosphere that savours of the comic opera.

I soon received information from two separate European sources that the handsome, polite and remarkably cultured young man who had volunteered to be my driver was an agent of the government. Whether he was or not I don't know. But he was certainly an excellent driver and always cheerful even when rain and gale made driving in a jeep most uncomfortable–nor did he ever remonstrate when my business kept me out until the early hours of the morning. But he is the only chauffeur I have ever had who had his own telephone extension in a Foreign Office. Anyway, whatever his other calling, he was kind, friendly and efficient.

At the Friends of China Club–club-cum-hotel–the managerial staff was famed for its Civil War association with the intelligence service.

The keeper of the well known curio shop (a charming fellow) turned out to be a naval intelligence officer, and that courteous member of the Foreign Affairs Police who had met me at the airport proved almost embarrassing at times in his efforts to ensure that I "saw the island at its best". His devotion to my welfare was most touching, the more so since it was genuine. Life is by no means difficult for the foreigners, whom Chiang Cheng-kuo reputedly dislikes so much.

At times, in fact, the opportunists find that great benefits may be obtained from exploiting the zeal of the island's guardians. There is, for example, the true story of a western journalist who complained bitterly to a Chinese "friend"–whom he knew to be a member of the Foreign Affairs Police–that the rough unpaved road outside his bungalow ruined his tyres. A road in such a miserable condition, said the journalist, was a shocking reflection upon the vaunted efficiency of the régime—a régime then anxious to create a good impression in the west. The road-menders arrived next morning.

In my own case I was advised by foreign friends to leave my luggage unlocked in my rooms. This would, it was hinted, enable any "check-up" on their contents by the hard working secret agents to be effected without undue embarrassment or inconvenience to either them or me.

I complied with this thoughtful suggestion but never troubled to find out whether or not my papers were scrutinised because their contents were not confidential. Gold sovereigns and currency were certainly never disturbed, which is pleasant in these days of "spivvery" and violence elsewhere.

I wanted to get some rough approximation of the number of foreigners on the island. Within a day of asking if this could be arranged, I received a detailed and up-to-date "breakdown" of every foreigner in terms of nationality, profession and address. Life on Formosa is full of Gilbertian situations.

But, after all the stories about the policemen of Chiang have run their round throughout the bar, after the lights have faded and the European sleeps, grim things are likely to occur.

Typical of the continuous and brutal war that is being waged on the island is the story of the Amoy Street Plot; where good looking Li-Peng, one time staff member of the U.S. Information Services and, subsequently, a reporter for the "*Time and Life*" group, met his death at the hands of the "SP".

Li-Peng, say those who knew him as a colleague, was a "nice guy". To the Nationalist Police, however, he was identified as "The Chief Agent of the Cominform in Taiwan".

Li had a mistress—the Chief Nurse, or Matron, of a Taiwan hospital. Through her brother, who worked with the navy, she obtained vital information and passed it on.

The group had two other leading members. One of them, Cheng-ho, had formerly served with the Nationalist intelligence service, while Pei-chun, his wife, was well known in amateur dramatics!

According to the Nationalists, Cheng-ho was instructed by the Cominform to leave the mainland for Formosa in the autumn of 1949. He arrived there on October 29 of the same year, having been "tailed" by the "SP" all the way. The conspirators took a small shack—Number 103 Amoy Street—as their H.Q. The Secret Police watched the plot take shape. For five months they held their hand. And then they struck. Leng-ho and Pei-chun were asleep when the jeeps of the "SP" tore into Amoy Street on that March night. They were awakened by the prodding barrels of tommy guns, and a sentry was placed in their bedroom while the rest of the squad started to ransack the house. After a while he said he heard Pei-chun whisper to her husband. According to the sentry she said that the time had come to kill themselves. "By prompt action" they were prevented.

From them were taken three small bottles and a packet of drugs of the silver nitrate group (stock equipment with communist agents). Further search revealed a radio transmitting set.

All four received the death sentence. They seemed singularly unmoved by it. They were shot shortly afterwards and the Secret Police supplied the firing squad.

Every method is employed by the communists to obtain recruits for the "war within the island". They have the weapon of blackmail–the threat to make a man's relatives on the mainland suffer if he does not comply with their requests. They have unlimited financial resources. And it is obvious that, among one and a half million refugees, the opportunities for planting agents are numerous and they are not neglected.

The coastline is ceaselessly patrolled by large forces of soldiers and special police. But the places favourable for landing are many, and for every junk, launch or sampan that is captured there must be many more that have succeeded in their mission.

Communists so far trapped by the security forces have, significantly, often belonged to the "educated" classes: the students who benefited from the colleges of Chiang and then, disappointed at not being able to obtain the too scarce careers to which they thought their learning entitled them, fanatically espoused the teachings of the Marxists.

Several of them have been equipped with transmitters of Russian make–fascinating sets that, especially constructed for the purpose of espionage, are of less than handbag size.

Several others have been armed and have "shot it out" with their would be captors. Others have succeeded in committing suicide.

The details of "Treason Trials" are rarely published until after the accused's conviction, and normally the announcement is reserved until after sentence–death by shooting, or a spell in one of the "rehabilitation centres" that are tucked away in the hinterland.

The accused–there are usually several of them–stand behind a "dock" of polished wood, surrounded by armed police. The judges are military officers. There is no jury. The actual proceedings are "in camera". Sometimes, as has been noted, the condemned arrive at the execution ground physical wrecks.

Some substance to these reports is provided by the Government's attitude to press correspondents requesting permission to witness the shootings.

Apply to do so, and you will receive full permission. They cannot do enough for you. Papers are issued and duly approved. There is nothing to stop you attending – nothing at all. And then, somehow there *is*.

You either get to the racecourse an hour or two too late ("such a pity, some fool must have given you the wrong time", they say). Or else (if you accept their pressing invitation and allow *them* to provide the transport) your jeep does not arrive.

To those who believe in Democracy the short execution posts on Taipeh racecourse, those grim posts to which the condemned are roped before being shot in the back of their heads provide a terrifying commentary on the state of political relationships in the world today. If allies employ such methods is it wise to employ such allies? The question is a natural one.

But it is necessary, before too self-righteously deploring the brutality of the Nationalists towards "political offenders" to remember the circumstances in which that brutality operates.

Left wing circles in Britain have succeeded in representing its victims as single minded, homely, honest, decent people; the martyrs to a Fascism that will brook no opposition. But to many Chinese the picture looks a little different.

However "single minded", however "decent", the men and women who end their lives at the racecourse have been convicted of aiding an enemy whose own brutality makes that of Chiang Cheng-kuo seem, by comparison, mild indeed.

For however soft and "liberal" the impression of the Chinese communists that is conveyed by their publicists in Britain and America, the tone of Mao Tse-tung, when addressing the people he has so successfully "liberated", betrays the mainland's methods with *its* opposition.

"Fascists", "Bandits", "Brigands", "Warmongers" – surely never before has the mainland been infested with such a multitude of villains! and how fortunate for the people that these villains, according to the communist boasts, are so often liquidated, eliminated, and disposed of.

It is only by studying the blandishments, threats and boasts of the mainland radio stations and newspapers, that a westerner can even begin to appreciate the basis of the hatred and fear that actuates the Secret Police of the Nationalists. "The horse that is not yet caught should listen to the voice of the man in the saddle of the horse that is", quoted a Chinese acquaintance of mine.

To the refugee merchant in Formosa – the man who left his wealth to be pillaged by the Reds; to the peasant who reached the island after he'd seen his friends and neighbours murdered as part of the communist "land reform" programme: to the small shop-keeper I met whose son had been killed by a communist purge in 1950, the idea of showing "mercy" to those communists who are stupid enough to fall into Nationalist hands is grotesque in the extreme.

Formosa—or "Free China" as the Nationalists frequently call it—cannot afford to entertain scruples.

That is why the Secret Police are so important, and why Chiang Cheng-kuo is now so powerful!

When I was in a small town in the south of the island, one incident was told to me by the local postmaster, a man highly respected as a good citizen. Close to this town is the island's main air force training centre and a few months previously a cadet who had just been awarded his "wings" imprudently wrote to his parents in Shanghai telling them of his success. He had taken the precaution of sending the letter by a regular underground route. Not unnaturally, the young pilot asked his father and mother for a recent photograph.

It was months before the reply came. Excitedly the boy opened the envelope containing the photograph of his beloved father and mother.

The photograph showed their freshly decapitated heads lying on a table.

5.   "*It is not like home*"

IN the steaming white tiled bath at Pei-tou, where the water of the bubbling sulphur streams comes directly from the hills above, sat the American Forces "brass hat", his moon like face and huge corporation pink as much with blushing as with scrubbing.

My naval acquaintance of a few days was by no means the only westerner whose sense of decorum had been flouted by Formosa's enthusiastic observance of the Japanese hospitality of the Geisha technique, the tradition whereby, when you take a bath at a smart hotel, a posse of attractive young women swoops upon you to make sure that, by their ministrations, you emerge the cleaner for your visit!

Bewildered, shamefaced, but with the stubborn resolution of one who refuses to beat a retreat, or else finds retreat too late, he confessed to me: "It's the first time this has happened to me since Maw shoved me in the tub back home . . . And that", he said, with a rambling, nostalgic quaver, "was a good few years ago!"

So between us, in these odd circumstances, developed that essential solidarity of the two branches of the Anglo-Saxon family; that queer, half grudging friendship that only manifests itself when, in accordance with our peculiar temperaments, we forget our mutual suspicions and inhibitions to express to each other our disapproval of the queer goings on of someone else!

"Yank"— the *nom de plume* is to save him from embarrassment—steeled himself to his ordeal by sucking a cigar, a huge cigar, which, alas, no longer burnt after the first preliminary puff, but drenched in water, lost its utility in every respect except that of building morale.

I, having had the advantage of preceding him in entering the water by about ten minutes, assumed with the return of dignity some measure of lofty detachment, as is the way with the English.

The behaviour of my American, when reluctantly involved in practices that would be deemed at least unorthodox in Main Street Home, epitomised, I thought, the western attitude to the affairs of Chiang Kai-shek.

The "democracy" of Chiang Cheng-kuo is as eastern as the baths of Pei-tou, and, whereas in the latter the blatantly aggressive cigar may provide a link with the homely and the familiar and yet still appear misplaced, so in the former do repetitions of "the rights of life and liberty" serve to give moral support for one's presence and yet appear asininely out of place when compared with local harsh political realities!

Any western assessment of the morality, venality, or just plain cussedness of the Kuomintang administration must take into account the habits and character of the people among whom that administration has been introduced.

The problem Isle is Topsyturvy Land; the place that is unlike any other place; the place which possesses a people who do not behave like any other people; the place where, because it's so enchantingly different, it is difficult to take oneself so seriously as the very serious situation would appear to warrant.

To others, such as my American friend, the place is quite disgusting.

Our dignity restored, our digestion perhaps imperilled, we discussed it over local beer which we sipped sitting on the floor, Japanese style, in front of low tables.

"Mighty fine fighting men", he conceded reluctantly, "mighty fine material—if properly led. But democratic—my foot, nobody here knows what the word means!"

This sort of sweeping summary is habitual, and perhaps understandable among the islands' (foreign) defenders. To those who go there with illusions—favourable and unfavourable alike—the surprise is great indeed, for Formosa plays havoc with preconceived ideas.

Next to the Japanese the Formosans have the highest standard of literacy in Asia—thanks to the Japanese provision of universal elementary education during their reign.

The Formosans have a system of government that is, with all its faults, yet more merciful than any tucked behind the Bamboo Curtain. They have, upon occasion, a strong, though warped, sense of humour.

And they have some of the oddest customs ever. Their treatment of animals is cruel; in this the Chinese characteristic is adamant and revolting.

It is not surprising that Democracy there is not like Democracy back home. Main Street Formosa never even bore a shadow of resemblance to Main Street Home, not even in the pets it keeps or the food it eats!

Warren White, Reuter's correspondent in Formosa, was my constant companion whilst I was in Taipeh.

A tall, lean, young Australian, with the happy-go-lucky attitude towards life which seems to characterise most Australians abroad, he said to me one day, "Come along for a walk and I'll show you where I bought my pet".

We went to a little shop in the market place; a shop that was lined with baskets and cages in which there reposed, to my surprise, a collection of snakes of all types and varieties.

They were for sale by the catty (one and one-third of a pound) at a price depending on the species, and with a python fetching rather more than a cobra!

I then discovered that this popularity of the python was due to its excellence as a rat catcher and, later on, I met Europeans as well as natives who kept these unpleasing companions in the space above the ceiling of their Japanese style bungalows.

Warren said the average python was more effective than a household cat and, he inferred, a lot more affectionate. His own "pet" was kept in a round basket in the corner of his bedroom-cum-office. A young and unpleasant looking character—about five foot eleven inches long—it lay coiled at the bottom, its eyes wide open. Warren replaced the lid rather quickly. "Of course it can't bite, you know," he hastened to add. He said it only cost him one egg a fortnight and a little milk to keep it happy and contented. "Not even a licence", he added!

The snake, however, has other uses than the purely domestic!

Many restaurants produce, as special delicacies, cooked cobra and python to titillate the palates of their wealthier Cantonese customers.

Boiled, stewed or jellied, they are as acceptable as any underdone sirloin to the westerner. "And after all", say the cooks, "if you don't like snakes why do you eat eels?"

In other cafés they claim, although I did not put their boast to the test, that nothing can be so pleasant to the careful gourmand than a carefully cooked repast of monkey's brains—a food that, according to the old fashioned, imparts certain mystic virtues as well as physical nourishment.

The more spectacular dishes only achieved popularity in the island—

and then not amongst the majority of the "natives"–following the arrival of the refugees from the mainland, people from all parts of China, with very divergent habits of eating, speech and even thought!

The forebearing Formosan, so used to catering for unexpected guests and modifying local ideas and methods at the instructions of others, began to cater for their needs.

One of the results of this catering may today be seen in the diversity of menu presented by the innumerable small cafés–some catering for the Cantonese, the people who are fond of snakes, and others suitable for visitors from the north. Northerners have a penchant for duck, but even this innocent and harmless sounding dish gives some offence to unacclimatised Europeans.

For the duck is presented to one in a state that, although perhaps of absorbing interest to students of the art of surgery, is guaranteed to turn the average stranger's stomach upside down. Slit from crown to tail, it is "folded open" (I am at a loss to describe the operation more succinctly) upon one's plate, and the choicest piece of that duck, you are told, is the head, from which a glazed, malevolent eye confronts your upraised fork; or chopsticks.

Formosa is a land where the serum of snakes is purchased as a cure for stomach ailments. It is also a land where, thanks to a Scandinavian anti-tuberculosis team financed by the World Health Organisation, the school children are inoculated with B.C.G., the so-called "wonder vaccine" that is not yet properly available in Britain.

In Formosa all trains run meticulously to schedule. In Formosa also four-fifths of the population relies on sweating bullocks, hauling carts as primitive as those of pre-Roman Britain, for locomotion and transport. It is a place where they hold discussion groups in the cities and, among the aborigines, surreptitious head hunts in the wilderness.

Even apart from the "well to do" elements–the men in their smart American style suits, and the women in well cut flowered frocks and expensive nylons–your Formosan is probably numbered among the world's most trim dressers.

In straw hats, of shape somewhat similar to pointed lampshades; in "raincoats" made of reeds and heavier than anything short of armour; in plaited sandals and exotic scarves, they will pause in their business at any time to purchase highly scented gardenias from the urchins of the street, to beflower themselves or purchase at a stall the highly scented oils and perfumes with which they love to adorn their sleek and shining hair! In the streets of the native quarter one seems far away indeed from the files and calculating machines of the municipal buildings.

The tinkling of ice cream bells, the blare of jazz and Chinese classical music from an infuriating number of juke boxes provides a musical accompaniment to the street cries of the banana sellers, the appeals of children selling lottery tickets, the purveyors of sweetmeats.

In these shadowy arcades – alleys with roofs that contain the living quarters of the shops beneath – life is as colourful, though less odoriferous than in the Baghdad of the fairy tales.

In one dark doorway a native woman suckles her child. In the other there is an improvised stationers – for notepaper, at fabulous prices is, inexplicably, one of the best selling commodities in Formosa.

From the elderly street artist, his easel jammed among the passing throng, his charcoal sketches selling for a few cents apiece, to the man who plays traditional – and inharmonious – music upon a cracked flute, this happy-go-lucky crowd, with apparent indifference towards the polemics of either Chiang or communist, pursues its none too rapid, quite unorganised way.

Here and there a bland trader will, for many dollars, pass on the packets that contain the crushed powder of the much valued rhinoceros horn, first used in the East when, twelve hundred years ago, the gay painted junks of the early Chinese explorers brought it from east Africa, and made fortunes that the spice trade could never have provided.

For, said superstition, the rhinoceros horn, when ground to powder, was noted for its aphrodisiacal qualities. There were many buyers. There still are, and the superstition dies hard. No, it's not like High Street Home one little bit!

Splendid Swiss wrist watches – how they came to Formosa I did not have time to fathom; mats and baskets, locally plaited; bilious looking mineral waters, sold by the glass; images of Buddha in ivory, jade and agate; the tenets of Confucius and the latest American "shocker"; pornographic photographs and vicious looking cutlery – in rich profusion, in untidy heaps, the wares of the vendors clutter up the side streets, while great banners of crimson, gold and green, draped from the "better class" establishments, plead with the traveller to visit "Honest Wu – the friendly pharmacists" or "Noble Yeng the seller of sweetmeats".

Strange indeed are some of the things that the salesmen of Taipeh press upon the passer-by – strange also the sense of values in a changing world which pays for such rich and wonderful productions with bundles of paper, "guaranteed" to be worth in all yet so many bigger bits of paper!

For it is among these surroundings so ridiculous, so picturesque, so unwestern that one is forced to take a new and pride-debunking look at the standards we accept so easily back home.

It is impossible to do otherwise if you visit one of the city's innumerable jewellery shops where, depending on the size of the wad of greasy dollar bills or pounds sterling in your pocket, you can receive lessons in history, geography and finance that may be turned to extensive profit on one's return (the Customs willing!).

For there they lie, in a cluster of gold, the mighty tokens of the West of an era long gone by–the sovereigns which cannot fail to evoke nostalgic reminiscences even in the mind of the most case-hardened anti-Imperialist; the golden roubles–those even more tragically, if slightly less recently, deceased messengers of the Tsar.

The fifty peso piece of Mexico, the occasional odd Napoleon of France, the currency of Abdul the Damned–appropriately they say, more than somewhat debased–lie among bullion less illustriously renowned on little counters where bowing, insignificant dealers spread deprecating arms as they assure you that your offer is much appreciated *but* "*perhaps* another three dollars fifty?"

The insignia upon most of these coins–the once proud emblems of the Hohenzollern and the Hapsburg–have no longer any political value save that of the moral imparted by the study of their history. Yet, in the money markets of the world the coins are more important than in the most glorious noon of the men who issued them.

The gold is placed on the counter scales. It is sold by the weight of the piece and no consideration of nationality, or of the ornamental detail so dear to a collector's heart, the date of issue, influences the transaction. Behind the seller, chalked on a blackboard, is the prevailing free market price allowed per ounce. And so, weight for weight, the weight of gold against paper proffered do they jingle on their way.

I purchased an 1847 sovereign for less than the price of a George V sovereign in this way, and I wondered as I did so if some day some future merchants of Taipeh will offer for different notes the variegated coloured currencies of today!

In the shops it cost me five shillings for a bottle of locally brewed beer, ten shillings for an indifferent Chinese meal. A ham sandwich and a glass of mineral water meant the expenditure of eight shillings and sixpence, while an American Air Force pilot who had dined in the States only four days earlier, posted beside the menu of the Friends of China Club the bill of fare of one of the smartest New York restaurants. The U.S. price was by far the less expensive.

For the visitor, or the well to do, about the only thing that is cheaper in Taipeh than in the west are the ministrations of the hairdresser. And even here–where a haircut, shave, shampoo and facial massage totals about three shillings–the prices, I was told, are about a third more than they used to be. How do the "locals" contrive then to look so prosperous?

The pay of the average peasant is very low. It might surprise those who accuse Chiang of establishing a "military caste" to know that the average miner who is a Formosan, earns more than a junior commissioned officer of the Nationalist army. The latter receives a salary that would not suffice to buy a good meal in a Taipeh restaurant, forty Formosan dollars a month, or twenty shillings! Yet here again the Formosans have confused the prophets.

Their living standards demand a goodly quota of rice, a modest amount of vegetables and fish—all of which being locally produced are plentiful; all are cheap.

The local, low wage group toper relies not on the western type liquors but on the potent home-brewed rice beer. In the cities the cinema seats cost only a few Formosan dollars and, as far as I could discover, the major entertainment item on the average house-keeping budget was the purchase of medicine, and from the type of medicine he possessed a man's social standing could be estimated with a considerable degree of accuracy!

For the peasant there are more cheap "cure-alls" available than in any other corner of the globe. "Brewed" by whiskered gentlemen squatting behind stalls where flies make perpetual pancake landings—normally unopposed—they include such ingredients as snake venom and a mysterious compound that I was told—truthfully or not—is extracted from bull frogs.

In the modern Japanese style stores that line the smart and almost western city centre, a more prosperous class of client is catered for, and the shelves here are full of the most marvellously comprehensive array of western drugs—including penicillin and the sulphanimide groups to say nothing of benzedrine and even streptomycin.

For a certain laxity, delightfully democratic, though possessed of lethal possibilities, appears to govern the health regulations laid down by the Provincial government regarding both its chemists, its chemists shops and their profuse and indiscriminate use by laymen. This recklessness with the techniques of modern medical science would drive British practitioners to exchange in advance their occupation and simply become undertakers.

Yet, they say, the island has never been healthier, while, as against this indulgence of the haphazard whims of the ignorant can be set the fact that the Administration's hospital and medical services proper are of the most advanced western type. The pay of the army presents, however, an increasingly serious problem to both the national and municipal treasuries.

So far the army officer—who, after all, lives rent free and eats free—has managed to supplement his income by entering into private trade during his spare time.

There are few important businesses in the island which do not possess serving officers as part of their sales and intelligence network. Such distractions from the calling to which they are ostensibly devoted have results that are easy to imagine and I was told in Taipeh that the whole pay system is shortly to be revised with a view to eliminating this undesirable but at present necessary practice.

A story, by no means apocryphal, of what happened recently to the defaulting creditor of an army captain, illustrates the uneasiness of these bewildering marriages between military science and commerce. Faced by the obduracy of his erstwhile partner the infuriated officer brought to the realms of finance a technique successfully employed by eastern soldiers in other theatres since time began. He promptly despatched a platoon of his men to his creditor's business premises. To the stupefaction of the neighbouring shopkeepers, he loaded all the furniture and merchandise on to a waiting army truck.

I was told later that the legal problems inherent in obtaining the return of the booty and judging between the respective claims of the defaulter's other creditors promise to emulate the most involved complications of Dickens' circumlocution office!

"Justice is not always so slow in reaching a decision", a Formosan friend assured me. "But in cases such as this we have to consider so many differing factors. On the one hand we have to avoid giving the civilians a feeling that law is on the side of the army. But on the other we have to ensure that the army does not become discontented because it feels it is at the mercy of evilly disposed civilians." In tackling less complicated affairs, Chiang's justice cannot be said to favour the armed forces unduly. If an army driver negligently runs over a civilian and kills him, he can receive the death penalty. Rape and several other offences against the person are punishable by death, and time after time again the Nationalists have proved that these penalties do not just exist on paper, but receive the final confirmation of the firing squad!

This emphasis upon the protection of the virtues is especially interesting when compared with the uninhibited sexual careers of previous Chinese armies, for Chiang Kai-shek has spared few efforts to establish a feeling of security among a people shaken in the past by its bitter experiences of the brutal and exacting demands of "outside" armies.

It must be admitted, however, that the more puritanically minded of Chiang's admirers in the west would frown on one of the methods by which the Nationalists maintain their exiled army in a state likely to be inoffensive to the innocent. Although sexual assaults are harshly punished, legalised prostitution flourishes to a degree which although faintly shocking to the Anglo-Saxon is probably necessary with armed

forces of 500,000 plus about 400,000 exiled civilian males, suddenl
uprooted and placed in an island of seven million people.

Throughout the Far East the Formosan women are famed for thei
beauty and their vanity. I have seen them ploughing the fields, guidin
their oxen, working in the mines, mending the roads, and in militar
cantonments. In these manifold activities, these labours which seen
unnatural to women, they contrived to maintain something that wa
mysteriously reminiscent of the verve and appeal of the Wester
girl. From the cinemas, abundant in the cities, they have learnt an
as usual exaggerated, ideas of glamour. But, before the cinemas came
their mothers had acquired most of the tricks in make-up!

And now, despite the necessity for war materials to take priority i
the precious shipping available to Chiang, there is no apparent em
bargo on the import to the island of the latest and most alluring
American and Japanese cosmetics, an import that must be consider
able.

A favourite jeer of the sophisticated male is that it's a pity peopl
who spend so much on cosmetics cannot afford the time to make them
selves new sandals. For although the working class Formosan beauty
when engaged in rough outdoor work, shrouds her face in a scarf to
preserve her complexion from the sun she invariably has the peasants'
preference for bare feet.

As can readily be imagined, despite the efforts of the government to
maintain a cordial relationship between the mainlanders and the
natives, the Formosan woman is often unpopular with her mainland
sister, and for a reason by no means unconnected, the mainland soldier
is often unpopular with the younger elements of the peasant class of
the island's males. Out on the roads of the country behind the cities
the dust rises from the sandalled feet of the marching columns of
Chiang's ever parading army. In steel helmet, peaked cap, or the
traditional straw of the Formosan native, they march and patrol
through a landscape that quite surely must be one of the world's most
beautiful, most outwardly serene.

I shall not easily forget my first impressions of it.

The day before I had been walking among the European style Vic-
torian buildings erected along the banks of the river by the merchant
adventurers of England. I had been talking with the representatives
of Jardine, Matheson—the firm whose magnitude in the China trade
has obtained for them the respectful title of "The Princely Hong".
Now this homely European atmosphere had disappeared.

It was night. I was travelling on the express to Kaohsiung from
Taipeh. My sleeping compartment was beautifully clean—a surprise
indeed to one who had experienced other railway systems in the East—
but, like the railway itself a legacy from the Japanese, its bunks were of

well scrubbed wood, pleasing to look upon but hard upon the indulged western body. I was too restless to sleep. I went into the
corridor and there I stood at the window.

It was a night of the full moon. For hours we travelled along the
great plains. On all sides the moonlight shimmered over green shoots
of rice sprouting from the still water of flooded paddy fields.

Occasionally, as the engine roared on, I could obtain a glimpse of
the mountains in the distance, a long line of black velvet darker than
the night sky itself except where the wisps of white clouds played
around slopes and summits. It was a journey of rich enchantment, of a
profound solitariness unmatched in my experience. It was early
morning before I decided to try and get some sleep—to be aroused
by the squealing of pigs. I found we were standing at a small country
railway station, taking aboard a cargo of livestock. I finished the
journey after a long and very involved conversation with one of the
railway guards—a special force attached to the trains as a precaution
against saboteurs.

Equipped with an ancient phrase book—by the aid of which he asked
most politely after my cousins thrice removed and my aunts, uncles
and all other relations—my guard was charm itself. He was also
equipped with a massive Mauser automatic pistol—which he kindly
removed from its holster and loaded and unloaded with alarming
celerity and nonchalance, to demonstrate what an efficient weapon it
was. The train, despite his preoccupations, arrived, as usual, on time
and unmolested by bandits or communists.

This timekeeping is a matter of honour with the railway staff.
Trained by the efficient men of Nippon they treat their trains with
reverence and respect. When the engine whistles and the train pulls out
the porters line the platform and bow in unison to it. And at its destination it is again received by an assembled railway staff. A minute over-
due and heaven knows what would happen. Maybe the station-master,
or the engine driver, or the fireman or perhaps everybody would commit *hari-kari*? It is a subject on which I dare not speculate.

In Formosa they are the most extraordinary people. They send
runners to carry news from one village to another. Yet they have a
system of radio and wireless communications that is so efficient that a
cable sent to my newspaper arrived in London two hours after its
despatch! And the mainland soldier who, not so long ago, might have
viewed an occasional passing motor car as a minor miracle, now often
travels extensively by air.

Not that I can recommend the timid traveller to follow my example
and use the Nationalist Air Force. This is a strange experience to anyone used to the luxury of the PAL or CAT flights or even the clean
utility of an R.A.F. bomber. There are no safety belts. There are no

parachutes. The plane takes off incredibly crowded with a chattering swarm of soldiers creating a fog of acrid tobacco smoke. Each man has his inevitable "hold-all"—a basin which contains his soap, sweets cigarettes, mess tin and other scanty belongings roofed by fish net!

As fowls are much cheaper in the south than in the north, the Northern run means that every enterprising soldier going there brings with him, to supplement his salary, a bunch of unhappy looking birds, roped by the legs. I recall with horror an unhappy interlude where, stricken with mild dysentery, I could not reach the door of the toilet because it was crammed with livestock and the way to it was blocked by the merchandise of a man who had gone "poultry shopping" for an entire platoon!

Eventually, by a feat of skill a sergeant managed, while the plane rocked, to move his men around so that the cargo could be moved.

After this upsetting interlude the pilot, a veteran of the war with Japan, heard that I had not yet seen the precipitous cliffs that lay to the north east of the island. So he went sixty miles off course to show them to me. Life in Formosa is certainly not like life back home, although one would gather from some of the harsher criticisms one hears regarding its Administration that many people think it should be.

Yet how can one expect the perfection of our political system, a system that owes more to our traditional tolerance and way of life than to any imposed system of planning, to be grafted on to a place where everything else is so different!

6.   *The problems of Chiang and Mao Tse-tung*

THE sea surged in, on to the rocks at the harbour mouth and over and on. The sand was white, hard baked beneath the sun. The cliffs were lonely sentinels of silence, their tall tops circled only by strangely noiseless gulls.

Suddenly in screaming discord the Mustang fighter-bombers on morning exercise roared low overhead. The sun caught for a second the rustless places of the hooped barbed wire, hurled back the glint of steel from the crouching infantry behind.

Questingly the 75 mm. in the turret of the dug-in tank traversed the invasion obstacles of sharpened bamboo fire-hardened stakes that lay ahead of it.

And once again, while polite junior officers smiled their welcome, I wondered rather dismally at the conspiracy of fate which had so mocked the tranquillity of this lonely and idyllic Formosan cove.

It was a military exercise, one of several that I had seen on the island. The locale was Forbidden Territory. In large Chinese characters the notices at the top of the cliffs and along the dusty roads warned civilians to Keep Out. Patiently, outwardly uncomplainingly, the bowed Formosans had yielded yet another strip of their soil to the needs of "defence" and war.

Not that the exercise I was watching could be classed as purely defensive! It was in effect a test of the difficulties likely to be encountered by amphibious attacking forces when opposed by fixed defences. The irony of it, I reflected, was that over the water, probably in surroundings very similar to this, the communist forces were also alleged to be conducting exercises with an identical purpose.

Once again I wondered just why both the Nationalists and the communists should be so unanimous in this repeated desire to be allowed to get at one another!

For if Mao Tse-tung is willing to take all the risks of launching an attempt to capture Formosa then he must feel that the island is a menace to him! Yet, if that's the way that Mao feels, why should Chiang worry? Why should he in fact be so anxious to alter the *status quo* when the *status quo* apparently suits the other side so ill?

The question is by no means a novel one. It is one that occurs almost automatically to westerners who are forced to listen to the rival claims of these two most vociferous opponents.

If Chiang wants to attack the mainland, it is presumably because he feels he is badly off on the island, but if Mao Tse-tung wants to attack the island, then obviously its because he feels that the "defeated" Chiang is doing very well!

Who is right? Who is wrong? And why in this confused situation does neither side seem at present to think it is doing sufficiently well to forgo either the invasion of Formosa or, on the other hand, the invasion of the continent?

So apparently irreconcilable are the professed tactical objectives of the warring factions that many Europeans begin to doubt their sincerity. A belief is growing that both the communists and the Nationalists are bluffing.

A young diplomat – not in Formosa – expressed this view admirably when he said to me: "Owing to the Korean affair Chiang is doing very nicely thank you – and he knows it. He is sitting pretty, and he's talking big. He knows that he wouldn't stand a chance if he landed on the mainland. But he also knows that the Allies won't let him even attempt to land on the mainland.

"Therefore, he satisfies his own impatient supporters by alleging

that he is ready to go, and that it is only the Americans who are holding
him back.

"His repeated pleadings to be allowed to attack and the consequen
warnings–well publicised in the west–to go slow serve yet anothe.
purpose. They give the west an exaggerated idea of his following anc
status, and in the event of any big trouble between communist China
and America western public opinion becomes more likely to pin it:
trust upon him." From another source I heard this version:

"The Americans could leave the Straits tomorrow. Mao Tse-tung
just couldn't launch an invasion of the magnitude necessary to take
Formosa in the face of Chiang's mastery of the sea, thanks to America's
support in the form of arms.

"Mao Tse-tung's claim is propagandist–an appeal to be allowed to
do something he knows he cannot do, in order to get by frightened
peacemaking on the part of the west something which he cannot get
by battle.

"Probably all this stuff about 'resistance' on the mainland is equally
hooey–just an excuse to finish off opponents as 'plotters' and impress
the world that he's 'threatened' by Chiang's presence on Formosa."

Plausible though the "bluff" theory may appear to be it is not taken
very seriously in either Washington or London. As we have already
stated, Mao Tse-tung sees inherent perils to his régime in the continuation of the Kuomintang, while Chiang foresees that the Kuomintang,
cut off from the mainland, may perish by a form of atrophy.

But how serious are these perils? And what real hope does either
side–despite the boast of its leaders–have of launching an invasion
upon the other? In any consideration of the importance of Formosa's
threat to Mao, it is essential to consider the "indirect pressure" that
the continuing existence of an "alternative" government imposes
upon the dictatorship.

Ignoring the more spectacular claims of Taipeh, it is reasonable to
believe that at least 160,000 communist troops are in occupation of the
Fukien coastline, either as a precaution against an attack by Chiang or
alternatively as a striking force to attack the island. At Amoy a
strong communist garrison is permanently on the *qui vive* opposite
Quemoy Island. On the borders of Indo-China the communists
themselves admit the presence of Nationalist guerillas and "brigands"
who are preying upon their lines of communications and raiding
villages.

The French have reported the detention of Nationalist soldiers who
have crossed into Indo-China.

In the wild regions of Sinkiang astride the supply route of the Red
Chinese garrison in Tibet; out on the borders of Burma in the forests
of Yunnan, fragments of the Nationalist army have still never surren-

lered if Reuter reports from Rangoon are to be credited.* Waging a
constant guerilla warfare they are assisted by gangs of bandits—
inspired by motives more dubious, but with aims temporarily similar.
In all it is probable that over one million men are "contained" by the
Nationalist threat—men who could be employed in Korea, Indo-
China or elsewhere.

But even more serious considerations for the Peking régime than
the immediate military operations arise from the continued immunity
of the Kuomintang. Mao Tse-tung can indeed draw from his own
experience when seeking parallels of the present.

Back in 1927, when Chiang was the man in the saddle, he appeared
all powerful. The uneasy coalition of Nationalists and communists
had been dissolved, and the circumstances of its dissolution had been
accompanied by the "liquidation" of most of the prominent communists.

This happened when Chiang's Soviet advisers, headed by Michael
Borodin, were discovered to be involved in plots to wreck the government and bring in a Bolshevik régime.

With dramatic suddenness Chiang ruthlessly smashed the conspiracy. Those whom he did not execute he deported. The communist
armies were defeated in the field.

But it was then, when the trouble was officially over, that the real
trouble began. For seven years a desultory war flamed and flickered
over the long suffering mainland.

And by 1934 this warfare against a not too popular minority had
caused Chiang to march seven times on seven different campaigns,
while, when he had finally conquered the Sovietised provinces based
on the Kiangsi the communists staged their famous 8,500 mile long
march to north-west Shensi which they reached in 1935.

By transforming their "hideout" to an offensive base—as Chiang is
using Formosa-they maintained a nation-wide guerilla activity, and by
persistently refusing to be drawn into open battle, were able to train
and equip new and relatively efficient armies.

Their persistent efforts imposed an unbearable strain upon the resources of the government.

Even when the Japanese—seizing the infamous affair of the Marco
Polo bridge as an excuse to launch their long prepared attack upon
China, even when the Nationalists and their enemies made common
cause to beat the new invader, there was always a strong undercurrent
of resistance to Chiang that was fostered not only by the communists
but also those who had accused him from time to time of being too
autocratic.

*Two Muslim generals visited Formosa whilst I was there and one with whom I
talked had recently been in Yunnan. See also The Times 31.12.1951.

It is commonly said in the west that the Kuomintang lost the battles of 1945-50 through its own inefficiencies and corruption. It is generally admitted and already noted that this criticism is in a large measure justified. But, and this can never be far from Mao Tse-tung's mind, those corruptions were by no means the biggest single factor in the Nationalists' eclipse.

The eclipse was the culmination of the slow process of exhaustion to which, by warring feuds and factions, China had been subjected since the collapse of the empire. And corruption accompanied this process rather than caused it.

For when the Hsing Chung-Mui, the forerunner of the Kuomintang, took over from the Manchus, it inherited a territory that was insolvent, industrially non-existent, and, as regards the masses, politically unconscious!

Sun Yat-sen and his followers – their difficulties almost unnoted by a west busy with the first World War and its aftermath – had subsequently to cope with powerful War Lords, whose armies marched and countermarched throughout north China spreading chaos while adding to their private coffers.

In the course of a few years a dynasty was overthrown, the North and South, each with its own haphazard government, waged bloody war upon each other, and Russia attempted her communist *coup*.

The revolution – and it is important to remember this – was successful against the Manchus because the people were tired of the system under which they had previously been governed, not because the people understood, or even bothered to try and understand, the democratic principles for which their new leaders urged them to fight. Moreover, they revolted at the chronic weakness of their Imperial masters in their dealings with the European concession grabbers.

So, similarly, did the Kuomintang subsequently fall as a result of "tiredness among the People". It had failed to do what it had promised to do. The People were weary, and although richer than before, the People were poor. Chiang, who had been given no chance to organise his country in peace, fell victim finally to the very men who had deprived it of peace. Today Mao Tse-tung must be thinking of these things, but without any particular satisfaction.

For, like his predecessor and opponent, he has inherited a nation wherein the difficulties of administration, monumental even by reasons of geography, have become nightmarish by reasons of history.

As in 1927-34 there exists for China an armed opposition directed by an alternative government, a government that is, so far at any rate, beyond the reach of its enemies.

This "government" is receiving in abundance the aid of a foreign power. Yesterday Russia sent to the comrades of Mao, over the land frontier, the munitions of war. Now America–operating over a sea frontier –is supporting Chiang Kai-shek, and, while the army on the island trains and equips, the guerillas become more and more active on the mainland.

Mao Tse-tung has of course one weapon at his disposal that the Nationalists, even in their hey-day did not employ, for despite their brutalities and atrocities they had always preserved at least the semblance of a "democracy" in China. They possessed–before the coming of Chiang Cheng-kuo–nothing like the comprehensive Soviet police system that, unhampered by inhibitions as to what "the rest of the world" may think, can reorganise, purge and kill as ruthlessly as it likes.

Mao Tse-tung, less merciful or less hypocritical than Chiang, is using this weapon to the full. But the very ruthlessness of its use, may in the end, prove a handicap.

The more Chiang's followers hit back the more drastic the reprisals become. But reprisals can reach a point where they cease to affect the vigorous minority against whom they are aimed and instead, by their impact upon the normally placid majority, create the very opposition they are designed to prevent!

The Chinese are an orderly, peaceful people. They do not willingly expose life or limb for purely idealistic purposes. They will fight against something they dislike rather than for something they like. And it is the sad fate of the huge majority to be bewilderingly involved in conflicts by the few!

Paradoxically it is this very reluctance on the part of the masses that presents Mao Tse-tung with one of his biggest problems.

Should the political weather turn foul then it is probable they will be as lukewarm in their support for the communists as they were in their support of the Nationalists.

And if the strength and scope of communist reorganisation reaches a point where the average peasant feels his land and life is menaced anyway then, in self-preservation, he will espouse the cause of Chiang Kai-shek.

The Taipeh Government is indeed a thorn in the side for Mao. It provides every malcontent with a natural rallying point. It organises into a national force what would otherwise be the suppressed discontents of a weak and divided people. Therein lies one of the most potent of Chiang Kai-shek's arguments for the maintenance of his stronghold in Formosa.

If the Nationalist Government are ever forced from Taipeh into non-Chinese territory to set up an *émigré* government there, then the Kuomintang and Chiang would most certainly represent an irretrievably lost cause.

Obviously Mao has one short answer to all his difficulties – a success-ful invasion of Formosa and the destruction at its source of the instru-ment from which his troubles spring.

For "democracy", therefore, the continued presence of the U.S. sea and air forces in the Formosan Straits may be said to be providing bumper dividends.

We have already discussed some of the things that are worrying the Generalissimo, but there are others less obvious to the layman.

Tall, grim faced General Pai Chung-hsi, a senior member of Chiang's Strategic Planning Board, minced few words, when he told me: "We are fully aware that our resistance here is giving the com-munists a bad time. But, unfortunately, we cannot afford to be content with that resistance".

This blunt, uncompromising man, something of a curiosity among Chinese because of his lack of eulogistic eloquence added: "Morale is higher than ever before. But you cannot maintain superlative morale for ever.

"The more fighting fit your troops become, the more disciplined they are, the greater the perils arising from inactivity.

"You cannot tell the soldiers that you are just training them to remain on the defensive. You have got to give them some hope of attacking. In Europe you have summed up in the term 'Maginot Line mentality' a state of mind which we realise, just as you did, is a poten-tial disaster."

Chiang's gravest problem is man-power. General Pai Chung-hsi said of this: "Apart from a few odd refugees here and there we have little opportunity of obtaining replacements. It is not practicable to conscript Formosans *en masse*, nor would it be politic to do so.

"They do, of course, contribute to local defence and while they would naturally defend their homes, to expect them to fight on the mainland raises other considerations and issues.

"By the nature of things", he added, "our army must, after a while become a wasting asset. Without a shot being fired we are suffering natural wastages, the casualties of disease and sickness. Our soldiers are already five years older than when they came here."

General Pai drew an apt comparison between overtrained horses and overtrained troops. "What", he asked, "becomes in Europe of a horse who is trained to steeplechase and then confined to his stable ?"

I was tempted to reply to this by telling him of the unfortunate reactions of inactivity on the first batches of Canadian troops to land in England in World War Two.

Another worry for Chiang's men – although they will not readily confess it, is based on a rather unpleasant suspicion of the west.

They are undoubtedly concerned in case any sudden apparent

"change" on the part of Mao Tse-tung on Korean or other problems would be greeted with such relief that the democracies would stage "a Munich" over Formosa and hand over the Kuomintang to the tender mercies of its enemies!

This fear, needless to say, has been well played upon by the propagandists of Peking. And it is a fear that, due to the Western Powers approval of President Truman's policy to facilitate the island's ownership being decided "without prejudice" in a general Far Eastern settlement, it is extremely difficult to dispel.

General Chiang Kai-shek has declared repeatedly that he is confident that, once the new American equipment has been distributed, Formosa can be held against attack, and implies that he would welcome the opportunity of putting his confidence to the test.

Certainly the defeat of a communist invasion force would be a tremendous fillip to his followers, a formidable prestige raiser for him in the west, a tremendous loss of face for Mao on the mainland.

Theoretically the communists could probably muster an invasion force that would outnumber the Nationalists by three to one, and the "hard core" of that force would consist of the tough and seasoned "invincibles" who have been serving against the United Nations' forces in Korea.

Despite the inhospitable aspect of the east coast the western plains of the island provide an abundance of suitable beaches. The distance from the mainland is less than fourteen hours by motor junk, and the attack could be launched almost anywhere along some hundreds of miles of coast line.

The Nationalist navy—although still in a position to exact heavy punishment—could probably be obliged by feint attacks, to distribute and dissipate its force.

Nor are the Red leaders lacking in imaginative techniques to cope with the new tactical problems arising from amphibious operations. During one phase of the Quemoy battle for example, they employed triangular shaped buoyant rafts constructed of bamboo. Each raft held two or three soldiers and, used in extended order, they were undoubtedly effective in preventing even heavier casualties occurring from the fire of the defenders.

The main problem that besets the Red planners is the problem of the logistics of any such invasion—the technique of getting so many men to so many places over so many miles in so many hours.

With the solitary exception of Hainan—where the garrison was weak and the Nationalist leaders were divided on the wisdom of resistance—they have had little experience of this sort of work.

What ships have the communists available for an invasion attempt? It is known that a few warships and submarines have been transferred to the communists by the Russians. Should they prove to be as well handled as the jets of the Chinese Red Air Force in Korea (until Korea it was almost non-existent), or as intrepid as, but a lot more efficient than the E-boats supplied to the North Koreans, they might, with the backing of the small portion of the navy that is now in their hands, be able to lessen the impact of the Nationalist fleet. But otherwise, apart from the useful, but very slow motor junk, their sea resources are not impressive.

At the height of the invasion alarms of late 1949 and early 1950 it was said that about twelve coasters, each displacing little more than a thousand tons or so, were being fitted with armoured plate.

About thirty large tugs and other vessels were also commandeered and stationed at various places opposite the island, as also were a few motor launches and other small craft.

In all, it is extremely doubtful whether the Reds could move a "first wave" of attackers more than eight to ten thousand strong. And it is estimated that these would have to hold out for at least twenty-four to thirty-six hours before the transport could return with reinforcements. The Nationalist defence on the other hand is disposed in a way that is, on paper at least, impressive.

First there are the garrison troops and volunteers, dug in to contain the initial landing force. Behind these at various strategic points along the island are concentrated the "mobile groups"—picked soldiers whose job it is to launch a counter attack. And the cities and towns themselves have their garrisons and fortifications.

Notwithstanding these preparations for a hostile reception, it is exceedingly probable that Mao Tse-tung would attempt a show down should the Seventh Fleet be withdrawn.

Chiang's mission of attacking the mainland would be fraught with problems vastly different to those of the would-be invaders of Formosa.

He can be assured of little serious opposition from hostile naval forces. He has officers on his staff who have trained in the American schools of amphibious warfare, and, in some instances have served with the Americans in the classic "island to island" campaign of the Pacific War, and he has General Sun Li-jen whose ability in a war of movement is established.

Chiang has hopes that the existing shortage of landing craft, and amphibious vehicles, besides guns, tanks and heavy mortars may yet be remedied by the U.S. Aid proposals. The plausible argument one hears is that despite the neutralisation policy of President Truman it is no simple matter to draw a categorical distinction between offensive and defensive weapons or war machines. After all, a tank landing craft or a "DUKW" may well be required to land defending troops at points along the coast to facilitate contact with the invaders.

But–and it is a big "But"–General Ho Ying Chin, head of the Invasion Forces and Chairman of the Strategical Advisory Council, has estimated that 300,000 men is the minimum required to secure an initial tactical success.

Furthermore, it is believed by many military observers, that even a force of this size would have to rely on a mass defection from the communists before it could even hope to consolidate. The implications of a Nationalist reverse would be catastrophic.

The loss of such a large proportion of Chiang's army would, it is pointed out by the more cautious of the Nationalists, destroy at one stroke all the prestige they have so carefully constructed over the past twelve months.

It would cause the collapse of mainland resistance to the communists. It would leave the island dangerously unprotected and maybe prey to internal disorders, for no matter how tranquil the Formosans are now, the islanders have an aptitude for attempting to kick over the traces–a characteristic no one would be better than the communists at exploiting.

In any invasion attempt the Nationalists would have to ensure also superiority in the air. And there are indications that this superiority, unquestioned two years ago, will no longer exist unless the American jets arrive a lot quicker, and in greater quantity than has so far been visualised. During my stay I had an opportunity of paying two prolonged visits to the Central Flying School of the Nationalist Air Force at Kansan.

The Commanding Officer, Major-General Shin, Colonel Han, Colonel Ying and Major Yeh could not have been more co-operative. I mention this in particular because their very frankness seemed an eloquent argument of self-confidence, which to me, although very much a layman in military matters, seemed amply justified.

In red brick buildings ranks of Link trainers were occupied by eager young recruits directed by American trained officers and N.C.O.s. On a cinema screen the latest types of Russian aircraft roared to attack while Chinese gunners fired electrically equipped "guns" that registered "hits" upon the screen. There were also schools of navigation, a meteorological training centre and a school of radar. Formation drill was up to the best western standards. Major-General Shin told me that an average of 2,000 air crew a year are passing out. The period of training is spread over two years during which time the cadets have no leave other than an occasional week-end. About 35 per cent of all cadets admitted pass the final tests. The selection system is based on American practice–as is the general method of training. It was interesting to note that English was a compulsory subject and that tuition was in the Mandarin dialect.

As in naval and military establishments, austere living conditions and strict discipline were obviously enforced. No "pin-up girls" in the barrack rooms, no lounging about after duty—but on the other hand every centre I visited had swimming baths, playing fields and tennis courts, in every case built by the cadets themselves. I have never seen more enthusiasm displayed by audience and players than at the basket ball matches I attended. This is apparently the favourite game among the armed forces. It was at Kansan where I first noticed the results of the scheme to augment the rice ration by the use of military labour.

Not without natural pride in achievement, Major-General Shin explained that almost half of the total vegetables and pork consumed was produced by his "boys" and that both vegetables and pork figure in the main meal each day.

It was here also that I was introduced to the "814" brand of cigarette made by the Air Force, but the sale outside is prohibited. The "814" represents the 14th day of August, a date specially significant to the armed forces. These cigarettes were excellent and sold at about one shilling for a packet of ten. Several days later, in conversations I had with another officer of higher rank than Major-General Shin, I learnt that all was not so well as first appeared.

This General emphasised that all of his aircraft were of obsolete World War Two models—piston engined fighters and light bombers such as the Mustang, the P.51 and the Mosquito.

Now that the Reds have an air force of their own—equipped with MIG jet fighters that are as good as the very latest American models, the Nationalists are feeling understandably anxious about the results of any renewal of air fighting.

This anxiety is thoroughly shared by the officers. There is complete confidence in the men. But no responsible Ministry wishes to see them flying 350 m.p.h. aircraft against enemies operating at 675 m.p.h.

Major-General Claire Chennault—illustrious in the history of China's battle against Japan as leader of the famous Flying Tigers—is also anxiously looking for prompt implementation of American implied promises to supply jet aircraft to Chiang. I was present and cabled my newspaper at the time that the supply of jets was first hinted. And in conversation he told me that there was a serious shortage of fuel, spare parts, maintenance equipment and anti-aircraft guns. Squadrons of Mustangs, he said, were at half strength. Ill omens indeed for a successful invasion.

Yet, like Mao Tse-tung, Chiang says he is determined to place the difficulties of the attempt second to the consideration of forcing a decision. After listening to various Nationalist officers I feel that —if they are allowed to operate —the first phase of "The Return" will be con_ fined to the securing of limited objectives off the mainland, coupled with commando raids on the mainland itself. Should this be so it is a pretty fair guess that the first target will be the island of Hainan and the Chusan Archipelago. The recapture of these islands would be doubly advantageous to the Nationalist cause.

First, it would be good militarily. The Chusan Archipelago dominates the approaches to the Yangtse River and Shanghai. Before its evacuation it was the naval air base for blockading the north China ports.

Hainan island with three million people is situated off the border of Indo-China and could provide facilities for strangling the coastal trade of the south China ports.

Hainan would also be a great economic asset. It has immense reserves of iron ore easy to work as well as, so I was told, important deposits of tungsten. Also sugar grows well there and matures in twelve months as against eighteen months in Formosa, in other words three crops to every two.

The full weight of the Nationalist forces could be thrown in against each point separately without being committed to a battle against superior numbers or a campaign from which there could be no retreat.

The second advantage from Chiang's point of view, is that the operation would be a splendid rehearsal for the main attack, and in addition, possession of the islands would force the communists to deploy their forces more widely than at present as the invasion threat could come from three quarters instead of one.

A more personal reason too would probably influence his choice. I was told by a friend that Chiang against the advice of most of the Nationalist leaders, wanted to hold on to the islands and only agreed with the greatest reluctance to their eventual evacuation.

In actual fact the return of Hainan to the Nationalists would be by no means looked at too unkindly by certain influential circles in the west. For this is what it has cost the west since its occupation by the communists.

The French in Indo-China, scrupulously abstaining from intervention, have now found the island used as a supply base for the armies of Vietminh. The short sea route, operated at night by motor junks, and launches, is now belligerently alive with the traffic of war. Fighters, propagandists and equipment are pouring in to help the rebel forces, and the unfortunate French, already sufficiently hard pressed, have discovered they have yielded to their enemies a vital advantage.

In the Philippines the communist Huks, suspiciously well equipped, have launched yet fresh attacks upon the Manila government, and their raids are becoming increasingly daring, so much so that public opinion was loud enough in August to protest effectively against

President Quirino visiting the States to attend the signing of the defence treaty between the Philippines and the United States.

This protest by the Opposition followed the most serious attack by the Hukbalahaps on Samal, a town in Bataan. There is no doubt that this Huk menace is very real to the continued existence of constitutional government. Hainan island is undoubtedly a source of material support.

Even in the Cold War the behaviour of the Reds upon Hainan—(significantly the Nationalists left there only a few days before the outbreak of the Korean war)—provides an ominous foretaste of what might happen in the event of a communist success in Formosa.

The recapture of Hainan would be of benefit to Hong Kong by providing a base for an air "umbrella" over the port's approaches and anchorages for convoys.

There have been repeated reports of Russian built submarines having been sighted in waters off Hainan, and these reports have been repeated rather too often to be discounted entirely.

Meanwhile, whether his objective will be Hainan, the Chusan Archipelago or the mainland, Chiang, despite all previous unfortunate experiences, seems to place considerable trust in the fighting spirit of the men he commands.

For otherwise there is no accounting at all for his offer of 30,000 troops to the United Nations for service in Korea. It needs little sagacity to realise how serious it would be to the Nationalists' standing vis-à-vis the west if their forces in Korea meet with unjustified reverses. By the same token, perhaps mistakenly, he seems confident that Formosa itself will remain well behaved in the absence of the army. Mao Tse-tung – after the performances of his forces in Korea – must be at least equally confident in the valour of the Chinese Red Army. Each has his own good reasons for disliking the "neutralisation" of Formosa. Each has well founded fears arising from the continuation of the present situation.

7. *Formosan personalities: past and present*

IT IS entirely in the picture that this Formosa which has produced such colourful figures in the past should now be a sanctuary for adventurers and idealists, politicians and carpet baggers. At the moment, it harbours many men whose careers have been strangely checkered, whose pasts and whose destinies make one feel rather humble from contemplation of their courage, often blind, that has led them to this strange place. Several whom I met have no need to live there, cut off from either the sophisticated or the cultural spheres whence they came or were driven. They all have either the academic or mercantile qualifications which would ensure a comfortable livelihood, either in Hong Kong or the Occident. I submit that this is *prima facie* evidence of their goodwill and sincerity because even the most ardent admirer of Chiang Kai-shek, the greatest optimist and the most rabid anti-communist alive, does not rate the Kuomintang's prospect of survival in its present form very high. The salient factor is, that apart from Generalissimo Chiang Kai-shek, only two men are sufficiently outstanding as possible leaders and there is neither evidence nor reason to suppose that either have even contemplated rivalry.

There is much loose talk about a "Middle Way"–a "Third Force"– but desirable as that may be to the Chinese themselves and those in the west to whom Chiang Kai-shek is distasteful, it is no more than an idea and must remain so simply because Chiang still has a greater personal following than any other Chinese. Not until the personal fate of Chiang Kai-shek is settled is another leader likely to arise–unless to the accompaniment of several nights of "Long knives".

Formosa's most historic figure, of course, of whom mention has already been made, is Koxinga. He takes pride of place. To the Formosans, he is Tseng-cheng-kung, "National Saint" or "National Saintly Prince". This half-cast son of Nicholas Gaspard, inherited the driving force that enabled his father to become the admiral of 3,000 pirate junks with which he controlled all the traffic along the south China coast. Forty-two temples in Formosa are dedicated to Koxinga and the annual feast in his memory rivals the picturesque Moon Festival in splendour and meaning.

When the Japanese capitulated in August, 1945, and Formosa reverted to China in accordance with the Cairo Declaration made twenty months previously, Koxinga suddenly became the symbol of the freedom of Formosa and his soul an object of mass adoration. It was a phenomena which is interesting if for no other reason than that it is an example of how a whole people can be captivated by an idea.

It is to George Psalmanasar, however, a European of doubtful origin who hoaxed Oxford University, the Church and the English people, that credit must be given for the most imaginative and audacious capitalisation of Formosa's physical remoteness.

Psalmanasar started life as a confidence trickster but he sought fame rather than riches and reformed himself early enough to write an excellent *History of the Art of Printing*, as well as contributing an immense amount of work to the *Universal History* in sixty volumes and to the *Geography of the World* of which he seems to have written the bulk. He mastered the Hebrew language and became one of the most accom-

F

plished Hebrew scholars of his time. He earned the highest praise of Gibbon and, according to Boswell, Doctor Johnson declared that Psalmanasar was the only man whom he had ever set himself the definite purpose of meeting. He also told a friend that he would "as soon think of contradicting a Bishop as Psalmanasar". On another occasion, Johnson described him as "the best man I have ever known", and told Mrs. Piozzi that "George Psalmanasar's piety, penitence and virtue exceeded almost what we read as wonderful even in the lives of the Saints".

Psalmanasar was born somewhere in the south of France in 1690 and died in Ironmonger Row, London, in 1787. A Catholic, he was educated in a local school by the Franciscans and then at a Jesuit College. He was outstandingly clever but apparently found nothing to hold him—so took to the road and set off in the guise of an Irish student of theology on a pilgrimage to Rome. For more than a year he wandered over the face of Europe, suffering every privation to which a tramp is liable. He tried to join the Dutch army but was "under age" so he became a waiter in a Cologne billiard saloon where he remained until his employers became insolvent.

Perhaps he changed his career in desperation, or perhaps his early studies in philosophy at the feet of a Dominican friar convinced him that a bluff had a good chance of success if it were bold enough. Psalmanasar certainly did not lack imagination and from Irish theological student and billiard table attendant he appeared overnight as a Japanese convert to Christianity, brought to Europe by the Jesuit Fathers. The Jesuits had long been established in the East and were *persona grata* with the Court in Peking. In Japan they were highly respected until it was discovered that they were intervening in politics at the highest level, whereupon they were ignominiously expelled and their converts persecuted. Fleeing to the Portuguese settlement of Macao in 1620 after nearly eighty years in the Japanese islands, the Jesuits concentrated on China. In 1714-15 the Ming Emperor despatched three of these Jesuits, de Mailla, Regis and Hinderer to Formosa to map the island and report on it. They confirmed that Formosa was an earthly Paradise. But Psalmanasar anticipated the Jesuit explorers by several years. By 1714, Psalmanasar had established himself in Europe as an "expert", not only on Japan, but also on Formosa which he now claimed to have been his birthplace.

A second attempt at enlisting in the Dutch army had been successful and while still in the ranks, his strange background, as invented by himself, reached the ears of Brigadier Lauder, the Officer Commanding a Scottish battalion of mercenaries. Fate was specially kind to the impostor because through Lauder he met a rogue of a different kind, a chaplain called Innes, attached to the Scottish unit.

It was a case of a thief setting himself out to catch a thief. In order to test Psalmanasar's veracity, Innes asked him to translate a short passage of Cicero into the Formosan language which he did with amazing rapidity. The cunning clergyman "lost" the transcription and begged Psalmanasar for another. The unsuspecting George fell into the trap and when Innes compared the two "translations" his suspicions were confirmed.

Warning Psalmanasar to be more careful in future, Innes determined to use the "Formosan" for his own aggrandisement in the clerical field. Innes promised that if he would be baptised into the English Church, then Innes would introduce him to the Bishop of London, which would certainly ensure Psalmanasar a fashionable and academic career. Innes, of course, would receive great credit for the conversion. In fact, Henry Compton, Bishop of London, had already written commending Innes on his great zeal and even went so far as to suggest that if Psalmanasar could be persuaded to come to England, a Chair would be found for him at Oxford University so that he could teach the Formosan languages to future missionaries.

Psalmanasar was duly "converted" for the second time in his life and went to England with his army discharge papers safely in his pocket. According to him, his baptism was a great spiritual "ordeal" which much impressed the witnesses.

His Lordship welcomed Psalmanasar warmly but to satisfy himself regarding Psalmanasar's *bona fides*, requested him to translate The catechism into Formosan. The Bishop and his scholarly friends congratulated Psalmanasar on the speed and ability in which he carried out his little task, expressing wonderment and satisfaction. This seems to have been the signal for a gullible press to launch the impostor on the even more gullible society sets of London.

Publishers vied with each other to secure a book from Psalmanasar's pen and, with the unscrupulous Innes at his elbow, the impostor completed such a book in two months which is now regarded as among the most celebrated literary forgeries of all time. It was published in 1704, ten years before the Jesuit geographers visited the island of Formosa.

It was a tremendous feat of applied hallucinations and was described on the title page as:

"An Historical and Geographical Description of Formosa, an island subject to the Emperor of Japan. Giving an account of the Religion, Customs, Manners, etc. of the inhabitants. Together with a relation of what happened to the Author on his Travels, particularly his conferences with the Jesuits and others in several parts of Europe. By George Psalmanasar, a native of the said Island, now in London."

He included a description of the Formosan alphabet and coins.

There were illustrations of public buildings, costumes and religious ceremonies such as a funeral procession headed by a rotund elephant, such as are peculiar to nightmares and, by hearsay, chronic inebriates.

When it came to describing punishments imposed on certain types of offenders Psalmanasar excelled himself. A slanderer had his tongue bored with a hot iron–an idea which Psalmanasar might have had reason to relish in case the critics should receive his works unkindly and, vouched the author, "Anyone who strikes the King or any of his Ministers is hung by the feet and then four dogs are fastened to his body which they tear to pieces". As for anyone who strikes a priest, the Revd. Innes and the Bishop learned that the punishment was the cutting off of both arms followed by burial alive.

In fact, however, such punishments as horrible as they read, were no worse than those meted out in contemporary Europe, so Psalmanasar was not unduly straining the credulity of his public in this respect.

But he made a few stupid blunders. He asserted that classical Greek was taught in the University of Formosa, a country in which, according to his own account, the people mostly lived underground. (Incidentally, it was because the Formosans habitually lived underground that Psalmanasar's skin escaped the Oriental pigmentation.) Then, for good measure he gave an account of an annual religious rite during which eighteen thousand children under nine years of age were killed, their hearts being torn out as a sacrifice. One of his most influential supporters, the Earl of Pembroke, found these "factual" reports much too difficult to reconcile with his common sense and withdrew his patronage accordingly. Nevertheless the book became a best seller, causing a tremendous amount of heated controversy.

Psalmanasar survived the accusations of being a Jesuit in disguise or, alternatively, as alleged by the Catholics, a tool of the Protestants who had bribed him, and his fame as a raconteur spread.

He confounded many of his critics by living on raw meat and on vegetables that were uncooked. Often, he left a lighted candle in his study so that among his neighbours he gained the reputation of being industrious while all the time he lay in bed thinking up new fantasies. Other times, he would sleep in an arm chair for nights on end to the admiration of the servant who normally made his bed.

He reached Oxford under the sponsorship of the Bishop who financed him and remained there for six months. This is according to Psalmanasar, but research has not established this although it probably is true.

It matters nothing now whether Psalmanasar was the devout man whom Johnson admired or just a hoaxer. It has never been seriously suggested that he was anything more than exceptionally vain and having created an aura of make-believe it was not a simple matter to smash it.

As for the infamous Innes, he became Chaplain General to the forces in Portugal and I can find no record of his compulsory retirement though plenty of evidence of his "insurmountable propensity to wine and women, and when fraught with the former, fell immoderately foul of the other".

No one has ever secured so much publicity for Formosa as George Psalmanasar. The only reference I could find about him on the island was in the University Library and some pages of Blackwoods which were lent to me by Mrs. Jacobs-Larken, wife of the British Consul at Tamsui. However, the Dictionary of National Biography has a full account of his amazing career and there is a reference in Chambers' Encyclopædia. Paradoxically, some of the most interesting men seem even more so when one is out of the island, presumably because one expects to find the extraordinary in such an incongruous setting.

One of the first men I met was Major-General Claire Chennault. He gathered around him a band of American volunteers who proved that, man for man, and plane for plane, the Americans could shoot the Japanese out of the air.

The noses of their aircraft were painted to represent snarling tigers and he named his force the "Flying Tigers". Madame Chiang Kai-shek called them her "Flying Angels" while the Generalissimo rewarded each pilot with $500 for every Japanese plane destroyed.

In addition to the fighter force, Chennault organised a transport service over the Himalayas – or the "Hump" as his pilots nicknamed it. They carried supplies to the beleaguered Nationalists and, if rumour is correct, not a little in the way of luxury goods for Chiang's rich hangers-on, the parasites who have contributed so much to his downfall. Now, the aircraft of the Nationalists' Transport Command have as their emblem a camel painted on the fuselage to remind them of the "Hump" over which their service was born.

Major-General Chennault looks very much the tough soldier he has proved himself to be. His face and forehead is bronzed and wrinkled and when he expresses a viewpoint he is dogmatic. Twice married, he now lives with his charming Chinese wife and two small children in a small house a few minutes from the centre of Taipei. His house is also his office.

No longer a combatant officer, he now directs the Civil Air Transport of which he is Chairman. As a civil airline, it has a magnificent safety record and operates daily scheduled services within the island and regular flights several times a week to Bangkok in the south and Tokyo *via* Okinawa in the north.

It is characteristic of his airline that the chief maintenance depot is based on a converted L.S.T., moored at Tainan in the South of the island. In the past, the headquarters of C.A.T. had to be as mobile as the aircraft it flew and evacuated from the mainland with the Government. There have been occasions when, but for the willingness of his key men to waive their salaries, the airline would have had to cease operations. It is difficult to pay higher tribute to a man who can engender such demonstrative loyalty.

True to type, Chennault is modest and not a natural talker. He prefers, nowadays anyway, to interest himself in his airline's operations and to ponder the fate of the forty-one aircraft grounded at Kai Tak, Hong Kong airport, which have almost consumed their value in legal costs. But there is no one in Formosa who has a better knowledge than he of the fighting qualities of the Chinese air force. Therefore I sought him out.

Fortunately, a few days before I left London, one of those incredible things happened and I met Commander S. J. Swetland, R.N., European Director of the Philippine Air Lines, an old friend of Chennault's. Armed with a cordial letter of introduction, the General answered every question I put to him without reservation.

As a proven friend of China, he is held in the highest esteem by the Nationalists. He emphasised, as has already been mentioned, that the Air Force, starved of vital replacements is keeping planes in the air only by mechanical cannibalism, a process which must ultimately defeat its own ends. This discounted the extravagant claims I had heard before I left England of the immense size of the Chinese air force.

From my conversation with him I gathered he was a supporter of what one may now call the MacArthur policy in Korea and certainly he vehemently advocated the bombing of Mukden and other communist bases in Manchuria. It also seemed apparent that Chennault would have approved the use of Nationalist troops in Korea.

It was the proud boast of the "Flying Tigers" that their escape routes were so well organised that any member shot down by the Japanese over enemy occupied territory had more than a ninety per cent. chance of reaching safety.

The organisation of this underground movement was another of Chennault's accomplishments and it is reasonable to suppose that the nucleus of his organisation remains. I asked him what was the strength of the reports of sabotage and guerilla activity on the mainland. The General told me that it was considerable and given a little more all round support, could easily be extended. No doubt his views on this were supported by first hand information. Chennault believes that the guerillas could overthrow the communist control of the mainland if given adequate support. He estimated their numbers at 1,600,000 including communist deserters. However, whether or not supplies and reinforcements are flown over to the mainland or whether they reach the guerillas by other means it is extremely difficult to find out. If such assistance does not reach them, then the Nationalists are dissipating their most valuable asset—which is absurd; if it does, then the Truman edict of neutralisation is being ignored, but with the utmost tact.

With the Straits patrolled by radar equipped units of the Seventh Fleet, perhaps one would not be far off the mark in suggesting that a Nelson's eye is applied to the screens. The nearest I got to finding out anything definite was when I pleaded to be allowed to go on a reconnaissance flight over the mainland or on a flight with a plane carrying supplies. The refusal could quite easily have been—"No such flights take place", but the answer was worded quite differently—"Sorry, No. If you happened to be in such a plane that was shot down, it would be most embarrassing." I argued that the communists had no aircraft along the coast, but was told (quite without solid grounds), that this was no longer the case and that it was suspected they even had jets. It is apparently true that "rice planes" sometimes fly over and drop grain and propaganda material and that the communists do not, apparently, interfere.

My next was a courtesy call on my old friend, Doctor George Yeh, whose fortunes I had followed closely since he left London where he had been in charge of the Chinese Ministry of Information until he was appointed Foreign Minister. The reference books give space to his academic achievements at Harvard and afterwards at Cambridge, but it is not within their province to describe his privations in the service of his President nor of his escape from Hong Kong in the best thriller tradition.

He is a brave man, a scholar and exceptionally shrewd. It would be unjust to impute that there was any ulterior motive in his generosity, but one act of his contributed greatly to the creation of Anglo-Chinese goodwill a few years ago. That was his gift of "Ming" the panda to the London Zoo. "Ming" gave pleasure to a million people and must have cost a considerable amount of money to buy and transport to England. By accident, I came across another gift he made to the British people— where it is now I cannot find out. Whilst in London he bought from an antique dealer off Fleet Street a beautifully engrossed scroll; a letter of accreditation from King James and addressed to the Emperor of China requesting trading facilities for the bearer. This document he presented to Lady (Stafford) Cripps for the United Aid to China Fund, a well meaning organisation which died ignominiously and whose death rattle one so often hears linked up with Chiang Kai-shek's fall from favour.

With the demise of the Fund I made a tentative bid for the scroll but was told that the views of Doctor Yeh quite properly would have to be sought. I meant to mention it to him but we talked of more important matters.

He struck me as a tired and disappointed man–not bitter but certainly sorrowful that the gallant fight which he and men of his calibre had consistently put up against the Japanese and against the communists had earned them, not the gratitude of England, but rather the opposite. I could not help wondering whether we had lost his friendship for good.

It was about mid-day and extremely hot when I left the Foreign Office and I went straight back to the Friends of China Club, a stone's throw away. I had not quite recovered from the effect of the flight from London only forty-eight hours previously. I decided, therefore, to spend an hour or so in bed and this gave me an excellent opportunity to ponder over what Doctor Yeh had told me and what he had implied–all of it full of significance and innuendo. Maybe I am hypersensitive, but I wondered in my drowsiness if ever the opportunity will be given to Britain to make amends and for the individual Englishman to regain the respect in which he was once held by the average Chinese. Even in my time as a boy in China we were "Foreign Devils" and in modern parlance, "Imperialists", a term which the Fabians have distorted into something disreputable. For all that, there was mutual respect and affection while now there is suspicion at the best and hatred and contempt at the worst.

I remembered the fine office with its thick carpets and Adam fireplace which George Yeh occupied so modestly in Bentinck Street and compared it with his sparsely furnished room in his Ministerial Office, with worn linoleum and the floor showing through in patches.

Some days later I heard that in order to meet his domestic obligations (he has a family abroad), he has had to sell portions of his art collection. To the realist this may mean nothing more than making an intelligent use of material possessions, but I know from bitter experience what this can mean. I once had a bronze head from Ife and to which I became intensely attached because of its associations and æsthetic qualities. Just before the outbreak of war, I was compelled to realise my few assets as I was rejoining my regiment, and I sold my bronze to the British Museum. I doubt if I can ever become reconciled to its loss, even though it is appreciated where it is and at least I can see it whenever I wish.

How much greater must be Yeh's sacrifices? He is one of the men whom I had in mind when mentioning those whose only *raison d'être* for remaining in Formosa is one of loyalty to a man and a cause.

Like every other civil servant and Minister, irrespective of rank,

Yeh receives a monthly ration of rice and vegetables and coupons to purchase a limited amount of household necessities at a controlled price. Transport is provided and a very ordinary house not outstanding even by Formosan standards. Their salaries are so low that it seems almost indecent to quote the figures. The Chinese have a degree of pride Hispanic in its quality and I refer to the privations of the few as being typical of the hard core around Chiang.

The house next door to Chennault's is occupied by Admiral Charles M. Cooke who formerly commanded the Seventh Fleet.

In his spare time he runs an orphanage in Taipeh and it was indirectly through this orphanage I came into contact with the Admiral and was invited to his house. Like all public men, he is sometimes the subject of gossip and is accused, unjustly, of being "anti-British". In my interview with him I gained no such impression. So far as I could ascertain, he has rendered great service to the Nationalists as an adviser and operating on the government's behalf in the United States as a general agent. He is, I understand, partly responsible for the stimulation of public and official opinion in his own country as to the importance of Formosa to the western Allies.

It is largely as a result of this awareness that the Nationalists have gained so much public support in the States, thus preparing the way for vast monetary and military aid now available to the Chiang Kai-shek government. Given an opportunity, Admiral Cooke is quick to debunk the malicious fallacy that the Nationalists were entirely responsible for the uneconomical use of the sums of American money poured into China after the war.

"It is frequently charged", said the Admiral, "that billions of dollars were poured down the rat hole to help the Chinese fight the communists but it didn't do any good. Included in the claim of 'billions' is UNRRA. UNRRA went to relieve the destitution left by the War, and also to feed the hundreds of thousands of refugees that moved ahead of the communists' advance, wherever it took place. I helped feed 300,000 in Tsingtao. When the Nationalists advanced there was no movement ahead of them. When the communists advanced many were driven out and much of the UNRRA supplies had to go to feed them and feed the famine districts. Some of it actually went to feed the communists. With my planes I dropped a million pounds on the communist area—with the Nationalists' permission. It was all taken by the communist armies and did not, any of it, go to the destitute for whom it was intended. We know that. The State Department knows that."

In fairness to the Nationalists against whom sweeping accusations are so common, it is good to have this testimony of a man who was on the spot. We were discussing how, during the War, the Americans had armed and supplied thirty divisions to fight the Japanese.

"They were the best Chinese divisions," said Admiral Cooke—
"then Chiang Kai-shek whilst actually winning against the communists, was persuaded to stay his hand.

"We then declared an embargo on ammunition to the Nationalists."
(This was part of the move by the Americans to make the truce
effective in the hope that the Nationalists and communists would be
able to settle their differences.)

"General Marshall, himself, observed to me, at the time we declared
the embargo, that we had armed the Chinese and then we had disarmed
them." It was obvious they could not obtain ammunition elsewhere
for their American guns. These factors had a decisive effect on the
situation during the critical years of 1946 and 1947. General Chiang
Kai-shek has said of this period when he let up on the communists,
'I have made many blunders, but that was the greatest blunder I have
ever made'."*

In putting two and two together one only wants to make four, but
on the strength of General Marshall's and Admiral Cooke's statements
perhaps the divisions armed by the Americans who put up so poor
a resistance to the communists were not quite so disreputable as we
have been led to believe. The communists had the pick of the surrendered Japanese arms and equipment and in the light of Admiral
Cooke's assertions, the balance was very heavily weighted.

It is said in Formosa that the very efficient Marine Corps which I
watched carrying out landing operations owes a great deal to Admiral
Cooke's inspiration and guidance.

By chance I met him one evening at the Naval Officers' Club at Tso-
Ying, two hundred miles south of Tamsui where we had met only two
days previously at the British Consulate cocktail party in celebration of
the King's birthday. By an unhappy coincidence quite unrelated to the
Consul's party, the Admiral had slipped into an open drain in Taipeh
and injured his leg.

It was a pleasant surprise, therefore, to meet him again, although he
was limping badly. Such a journey in these circumstances could have
only been made for a very good reason. Also, in Tso Ying was Major-
General William Curtis Chase—he too had arrived that day by plane
from the north and was at that moment the most talked of man in the
island. He had just arrived to take up an appointment in Formosa as
Chief of the United States Government Military Assistance Group
(MAAG for short). He had told me in Taipeh that his mission would
soon number over two hundred, which so far as I could recollect,
would make it the second largest military mission to leave the U.S. in
peace time. If this is correct it is surely full of significance.

General Chase's war record is of special interest; in World War Two

* See footnote, page 128.

he commanded the reconnaissance force which landed on Los Negros in the Admiralty Islands. He took his brigade into Leyte on D-Day and subsequently captured Luzon. He personally led the two famous "Flying Squadrons" into Manila on February 3, 1945, and in July assumed command of the First Cavalry Division which was the first American Division to enter Tokyo.

The meeting of these two veteran experts in the strategy and tactics of amphibious warfare in Formosa's naval base so close to the Marine Corps headquarters was an incident upon which it is interesting to speculate.

In September, Major-General Chase said that his mission's programme was gradually being expanded to make the island impregnable from attack. He also said that although President Truman's "neutralisation" policy still stood, the United States fully realised that Formosa was of high strategic importance in American Pacific defence. "By making the Nationalist forces capable of success against all attacks, the United States was forging a stronger defence system of its own", said Chase. Concerning the amphibious training which I have mentioned, Chase said: "If the railway should be cut in the first phases of any attack, amphibious operations would be the sole means left to the defending forces to move from one part of the island to another". That seemed just a little naive. I wonder if the ultimate objective of the Chinese Marine Corps is not in fact to be the spearhead of an invasion force?

If I were asked who impressed me most among the civilians I met in Formosa, my mind would immediately turn to Dr. K. C. Wu, Minister without Portfolio, Governor of the Taiwan Provincial Government. True I only met him twice, and on both these occasions in his office, but they were long interviews. The second, which lasted for two hours, took place on the eve of my departure for Hong Kong.

I would venture to guess that no Chinese is better known or more highly respected by westerners than K. C. Wu. He was educated in the United States, is a graduate of Princeton and speaks the most fluent English with a pronounced American accent. He has a distinguished appearance, does not look his forty-eight years, is of medium height and wears wide horn rimmed spectacles. Never have I met anyone in high office so easy to talk to after a short acquaintance. He struck me immediately as being frank and his mannerisims and speech reflect his dynamism. Foreigners learned to appreciate his ability for getting things done and his highly developed faculty for governing was particularly exemplified during his periods as Mayor of Shanghai. The task of administering the most complex city in the world is no sinecure and K. C. Wu's performance of it was remarkable. He has held other offices, including those of Mayor of Chungking, Minister of Information, and Vice-Minister of Foreign Affairs – in all he has excelled.

He told me a lot that was disturbing, coming as it did from a man in whom British and Americans have unqualified confidence. He quoted one little matter then in the process of being worked out to a not very satisfactory conclusion. Two British subjects resident in Singapore had applied through the British Consulate in Tamsui for permission to pay a prolonged visit to Formosa for the purpose of learning the Fukien dialect.

Dr. Wu, as the Provincial Governor, was about to sanction the necessary permits, whereupon subordinates reminded him of the consistent obstructionism of the Hong Kong Government in all its dealings with Formosa. There was, unfortunately, no possibility of denying this. It was common knowledge and a continual source of embarrassment to the British Consul and Vice-Consul, that the Immigration authorities in Hong Kong make it extremely difficult for Chinese resident in Formosa to obtain even temporary visas to enter the Colony. This unhelpful attitude applies equally to Chinese of impeccable character.

As a result of representations made to K. C. Wu, he felt compelled to pass the responsibility of admitting the would-be Fukienese students to the Foreign Office. This was mentioned in general connection with the residue of Chinese goodwill towards Britain and K. C. Wu summed up the position by warning that this goodwill was "wearing a little thin". He gave me a sidelight into his character when he told me how, when Mayor of Shanghai, he sometimes had leading communists awaiting trial on charges of treason brought to his private room. He would dismiss the guard and interrogate them in his own manner and his conclusions on communist theories and practices might be of great value to those whose business it is to combat them.

It was "K.C.", as he is commonly known, who pleaded with leaders of the British commercial community in Shanghai to withhold recognition of the communist régime. He recounted the main points of a two hour conversation he had had with the generally accepted leader of British interests whom I met a few days later. In vain he had stressed that China under the Reds could only mean the complete loss to Britain of her vast financial stakes whereas under Chiang Kai-shek, there would be some sort of a guarantee for the sanctity of private property and investments.

Therefore, Britain could not possibly gain by recognising Mao Tse-tung. "K.C." did not bandy words regarding the continuance of trading by British owned ships (as distinct from British registered ships) into north China ports. "The sole purpose of their owners is the profit motive, such actions will be remembered".

We also referred to the unforgivable secret clauses of the Yalta Agreement which "sold Chiang Kai-shek down the river" and put Russia back into the position she had been in before she was driven out as a result of the Russo-Japanese War of 1904-5. "K.C." agreed with that thesis so far as it went, but added that in his opinion, Russia would have found some pretext to occupy Port Arthur and Dairen, in order to implement the fundamental object of her foreign policy from the time of the Czars–to have access to and control of warm water ports without which Siberia cannot be fully exploited. Moreover, Russian strategists require these ports, as well as Korea, as defensive outposts against Japan and her economists and industrialists have long had their eyes on Manchuria.

K. C. Wu is a realist, young for a politician and he will inevitably figure prominently in China's future. As Governor of Formosa he has applied his energies and gifts to reconstruction and reformation in that island. There is much evidence of his success in working with the Premier, General Chen Cheng, in land reform which is discussed later.

I also met General Chen Cheng, described as one of the Generalissimo's "strong arm" men. Apart from the highly successful land reforms which he introduced, it was he who took the almost totalitarian steps to halt inflation and stabilise the currency in the nick of time. As Governor of Taiwan, he deposited adequate quantities of gold to cover the note issue and countermanded instructions which would have released millions of banknotes already printed.

The Taiwan dollar is now relatively stable and officially pegged to the U.S. dollar at the rate of one U.S. dollar to fifteen Taiwan. There is no "black market" in currency dealings in Formosa in so far as "black market" implies moral turpitude. But there is a market in which the U.S. dollar is worth eighteen to nineteen Taiwan dollars. The fact that a brisk trade is done fairly openly seems to show that the Taiwan dollar is sound. How this reasoning stands up to economic theory I have no idea, but I do know that in Manila where the peso is officially quoted and linked to the U.S. dollar at two pesos to one dollar U.S., there is immense competition to buy the American dollar at three pesos. By comparison, therefore, one may assume the Taiwan dollar to be at least as sound as the Filipino peso. I might add, that foreign currency dealing is unlawful but to try to deprive the Chinese of money changing facilities is somewhat impracticable.

It was General Chen who first had the Herculean task of reorganising and training the demoralised and defeated units evacuated from the mainland in 1949. To the amazement and displeasure of several high ranking officers and administrators, he had the courage, and the sagacity that went with it, to dismiss a number of generals and disband more than twenty undesirable units.

This occurred, it will be recalled, at a time when Formosa was seething with hatred against the Chinese mainlanders. He was the General chiefly responsible for the victories which led to the expulsion of the communists from Kiangsi Province in the 1930's when they commenced their epic march. In World War Two he was Commander in Chief of the Chinese Expeditionary Force (known to us as the "Y" Force) in 1943-44 serving with both General Joseph W. Stilwell and General Albert C. Wedemeyer. Finally, as Director General of Military and Political Affairs of the South East (Formosa, Fukien, Chekiang and Kiangsu), he was responsible for the spirited and immensely important tactical and military defeat of the communist attempt to capture Quemoy.

He is another of the stalwarts who has chosen to throw in his lot with Chiang Kai-shek and there is certainly no doubt in my mind that he is actuated by the same high motives as George Yeh, K. C. Wu, General Sun Li–jen (pronounced Soon Lee Wren) and a number of equally well balanced men of outstanding achievement.

Unfortunately, Premier Chen Cheng had to undergo a serious major operation three years ago and although it is claimed that he has made a complete recovery, the high colour in his cheeks and his gentle but persistent cough made me wonder how long it would be before his health might necessitate a less strenuous life.

He seemed much less sophisticated than either K. C. Wu or George Yeh and his almost saint like appearance and his smile belies the evidence of his unbending will of iron.

If I only refer to one more man who convinced me that Chiang Kai-shek has some first class men around him, it is not because they are limited to the few I have mentioned. I have selected the few with whom I spent most time and of whose past history I have some knowledge.

In a humble house tucked away in a back street in Taipeh I called on Mohammedan General Pai Chung-hsi. He is tall with a fine figure and pride and strength of character apparent in every feature. Apart from his profound knowledge of military matters he is interesting as a man. From boyhood days his bosom friend has been General Li Tsung-yen, until recently Vice-President of China, who lives very comfortably in New York. Li has always been the politician and Pai the soldier and at one time they were the most influential partnership in China. (I understand Li is to be impeached.)

It was these two who persuaded Generalissimo Chiang Kai-shek to "retire" in 1949 in order to facilitate peace negotiations with the communists whereupon Li became President until Chiang resumed office. General Pai, when he realised that his good intensions had been spurned by the communists, went to Formosa uncoerced by anything but his conscience and loyalty to the Generalissimo. But his friend, the erstwhile President, Li Tsung-yen, hastened to the United States for medical treatment and as soon as he recovered his equanimity and health launched a vitriolic attack on Chiang Kai-shek which was fully reported in the press at the time. It was sometime early in March, 1950. Li pulled no punches; Chiang was a "dictator"; Chiang was a "would-be usurper representing nobody but himself and a small *clique* in the Kuomintang". And so Li fumed and cursed until finally at the end of March having boasted that he would return to Formosa to overthrow the Generalissimo "by force if necessary" Li ended up by announcing that he would return to China within six months (September, 1950), to assume command of "more than 500,000 armed resistance fighters" in his native province of Kwangsi and in adjacent provinces of south China.

The unfortunate General Pai was not unnaturally under strict surveillance during the Vice-President's fulminations.

Two points occurred to me after my interviews with General Pai. Considering his many years of friendship with Li, surely it says volumes for Chiang Kai-shek that Pai was not "liquidated" as he would most certainly have been had he lived behind the Iron or Bamboo curtain.

I think I can understand General Pai and can well imagine him paying his respects to the Generalissimo on his return and explaining that he had but done his duty as he conceived it to be and I can equally understand that the Generalissimo would accept this because it came from General Pai. But it is beyond my comprehension, why with the regularity of clockwork, Li Tsung-yen until recently received a salary cheque, and expenses, as became his office, through the New York branch of the Bank of China. It is just another of the riddles to which I know no answer but makes one feel that the virtue of mercy can be extended to astonishing lengths by those who themselves are large minded.

8. *Chiang himself: a personal interview*

AT THE end of the old fashioned board room table the slight looking, unobtrusive man in the sober uniform of olive drab murmured quietly: "I have pledged myself to return to the mainland. There is no argument possible about that, I have given my word to return, so I shall return".

Thus, in a few telling sentences did Chiang Kai-shek re-emphasise that, for him, there could be no final solution to the Chinese crisis except a solution obtained by arms.

It had not been an easy matter, this task of obtaining an interview with the Generalissimo. Owing to the British Government's attitude towards Peking they said – and "they" after all were members of his immediate entourage –British visitors were by no means welcome in the Presidential Building officially. For over three years Chiang had refused to speak to a British journalist; while, infuriated by what he regarded as "persistent betrayal" by an ally, his attitude, it was hinted, was one approaching that of anglophobia!

At the time of my arrival in the island the "Gisimo" was holidaying with Madame in a mountain hide-out of which, for security reasons, even his top ranking officers did not know the exact location. For similar reasons the date of his return to Taipeh was also un-announced, while the suggestion that I might be flown to see him was smiled away as being quite without precedent.

When Chiang eventually did get back his intimates reported him to be in a towering temper. The time could not be worse to apply for an interview they protested, it had just been confirmed that the Nationalists were to be denied the opportunity of even becoming co-signatories of the Japanese Peace Treaty and of the resultant recriminations Britain had indeed been granted the lion's share, with the United States a close second for "yielding to Whitehall pressure".

The situation was subsequently in no way improved by the resolution displayed by President Chen Cheng and Foreign Minister George Yeh. Both of them tendered their resignations to Chiang as a gesture of protest; both had their resignations firmly declined.

However understandable, such resentment augured ill to one who was attempting to persuade the Generalissimo to break the precedent, and for a time even the affable Dr. Shen Chang-huan, who with the unusual title of Government Spokesman is very close to Chiang indeed, seemed a little despondent over my chances.

I had seen Chiang when I was a boy, but had never spoken to him. I could recall, as an adolescent in Tientsin hearing my father, then a newspaper editor, discuss his meteoric career. And I could still remember – all too vividly – the names of the people who, in those days, were Chiang's enemies – the legendary war lords Wu Pei-fu and Chang Tso-lin. Hadn't I had to run from them once?

Eventually of course Chiang had triumphed over these men, and lesser rivals also. What belief, I wondered, did he have in eventual triumph over Mao Tse-tung?

My suspense had a speedy termination. Chiang eventually surprised his supporters by deciding to see me, although I received due warning from Job's comforters that I would find him remote at the best, and openly hostile at the worst – a prophecy that, in view of his just having issued his strongest protest to date at the behaviour of the western powers – did not appear unduly far fetched!

At first, on entering his unpretentious and rather depressing office – so cold and shadowed after the glare and bustle of the streets outside – one is a trifle surprised at the apparently unimpressive appearance of the man, so unlike the usual Nationalist portrayal of the "Man of Destiny", and equally so unlike the Tammany Hall character portrayed by the West!

Chiang does not strike dynamic poses. To his visitors at least he does not demonstrate his undoubted talent for rhetoric. And, after the "build-up" given him by his admirers, it comes as rather a shock to find him gentle and almost shy in his initial greeting.

Only the eyes of Chiang – undimmed by age or adversity – portray something of the steel that lies concealed in his almost fragile body. They are expressive eyes. They can soften to tenderness when he speaks of old friends and cherished memories, or they can, I was to notice, assume a frozen implacable hate when the discussion relates to communism. Why, I asked, did he feel so confident of eventual victory on the mainland?

With a grim smile he advised me to study Peking's own official "treason trial" announcements. If they were so anxious to punish, he inferred, then things were indeed troubled across the water!

In addition, he added, his army now know not only what it was fighting for, but also *what it was fighting against*. The stories of the communist régime that came from the mainland today were vastly different from the stories with which the communists had so cleverly primed the soldiers when the mainland battles were still on! The fighting forces regrouping on Formosa, said Chiang, were the pick of the Kuomintang, while, in China proper, resistance grew from day to day. Did he really believe it, I wondered, as an attendant gravely proffered glasses of fragrant Soochon tea?

Chiang would, of course, be other than human if he did not claim that his cause was bound to prosper, but there are grounds for crediting him with honestly believing his claims to be founded on something more than wishful thinking or political manoeuvring.

This is by no means the first time that Chiang has endured a political eclipse. It is even true to say that his present situation has certain advantages compared with the past.

It is often forgotten that Chiang has resigned high office on three occasions, yielding to pressure from those who either accused him of being a dictator, or alternatively claimed that there would be a better chance of coming to terms with the enemy, or of unifying the country, once he was out of the way.

G

Today, he is opposed by an infinitely more powerful foe than hitherto, but, correspondingly he says, he can boast of far greater resources.

Despite the misgivings of my friends, I found that on all questions except his opinion on Britain's Sino policy, he gave me shrewd and speedy answers. But on British policy he adroitly side-stepped, and those replies which he did give I was later asked by one of his personal representatives not to publish.

The closing of the Burma Road in 1940, when Britain, absorbed in the European War, tried to appease Japan by cutting China's sole remaining "life-line", had a profound impression upon Chiang that even his subsequent alliance did little to eradicate.

He is much inclined to typify this as an example of what he regards shortsighted British policy, and to elaborate it as an awful warning of what happens to those who proffer appeasement to a remorseless foe.

Nor is he slow in pointing out that Britain's policy of recognising Peking appears to have produced nothing but the Korean war, and that, while British lives are lost in battle, our government is still embarrassedly waiting for the communists to condescend to send an ambassador to London. The Peace Treaty is, indeed, a sore point!

The subtle niceties of western diplomacy; a diplomacy that, seeking to find a way out of openly deciding between the claims of Mao Tse-tung and himself has excluded China from the Treaty are (apparently) lost upon him.

Chiang argues that, by his decision to continue the fight in 1942, despite tempting Japanese offers to negotiate, he not only rendered to the west services of incalculable value, but equally, left the Reds free to prepare the civil war.

In insisting that the Nationalists should be consulted on this and other matters as "the only legitimate government of China", he is adamant.

In actual fact, I do not think that he considers a split between the western powers on this point could be anything but disastrous to his cause and, I feel, he anticipates that in any case the communists will prove so unresponsive to western tact that, sooner or later the entire world will eventually be forced to back him.

Beneath the glass top of his desk is a map of the world. On top of the bookcase is a golden globe, its place names are in Chinese.

The cynical say, "A pity that the 'Gisimo's' view is merely restricted to the park and its sentinels outside!" Whatever the talk about his "isolation" and "narrow opinions" Chiang can claim to have had more experience of the Asiatic World than any of his critics.

His intimate knowledge of Japan is rivalled by his familiarity, as a young man, with the tenets of Marxism and the practice of Soviet Imperialism. He was sent to Russia by Sun Yat-sen in the 1920's, and there was a time when my elders in the European community used to describe him as "That Bolshevik".

I think they then respected Chiang infinitely more than any other Chinese personality although they preferred the marauding War Lords – who after all were understandable enough in their quest for loot and gain, and could usually be "bought off". Chiang learned his lessons in a hard school and it is probable that he has more experience of brute force, and the tortuous paths of subtle plotting than any of his contemporaries.

First and foremost, he is a soldier. His military career began in an orthodox enough way. He trained in military academies in China, and later in Tokyo, where he graduated and became a trooper attached to the Japanese field artillery.

In the course of this training, however, he joined the Tung Meng-hui, a revolutionary secret society which drew its inspiration from Dr. Sun Yat-sen, "The Father of the Chinese Republic", who, incidentally, received part of his medical education at the British University in Hong Kong. On October 10, 1911, the tenth day of the Tenth month, favoured by astrologers for this particular project, Chinese Imperial troops mutinied at Wuchang.

It was the signal for a revolution which spelt the violent doom of the Manchus after nearly three hundred years on the Dragon Throne. It was the birth of the unstable and ill-fated Republic of China.

Chiang Kai-shek's part in the days that immediately followed the events of the "Double Tenth" was inglorious. Sun Yat-sen's Party was outwitted and Chiang was forced into "exile" at Shanghai.

Here, the "toughening up" process of this young man was continued. In the unsavoury underworld of the city he became a member of the Green Gang, a collection of those thugs and mystics who are the evil appendages of all revolutions, and it was not until later that he saw the more respectable side of life as a clerk in a stockbroker's office.

After 1913, he renewed his acquaintance with Japan and not until ten years later as Sun Yat-sen launched a second revolution to oust President Yuan Shi-kai, did he return to a career of soldiering and politics that soon brought him from obscurity to fame.

Chiang, I noticed, wore no decorations, although in 1942 the British Government had shown their appreciation of his services against Japan by knighting him and bestowing upon him the G.C.B. (Military Division) for "outstanding achievements to the Allied Cause". Political considerations or not there is no doubt that an excessive ostentation in dress, or love of ornament, is certainly not a trait of this so called Dictator, and the austerity of his garb would satisfy the requirements of the most exacting of Cromwell's Puritans.

His shoes are shining. His slacks are neatly pressed, but they are shoes, not jackboots, and the slacks are unadorned by any stripe. His tunic is of an old-fashioned high necked style and when he goes out he adds to this ensemble a perfectly plain Chinese cavalry cloak. Again and again when in Formosa I came across references to the "Whampoa Clique", an allusion dating back to when General Chiang Kai-shek founded the Whampoa Military Academy in 1924 and became its first President.

Speedily it acquired the hall mark in China of a Sandhurst or West Point. It generated an *esprit de corps* which still remains very evident and active. The "hard core" of the Nationalist officers today are among its products. For although young in tradition Whampoa has been intimately linked with Chiang's tumultuous career.

There exists among Chinese a bond between teacher and pupil as deep as the fraternal loyalty among comrades in arms, plus a strong element of a filial quality.

In Whampoa they developed this tendency to the full. Cadets were picked for their personal qualities–fidelity and courage–as well as for their potential military attributes. Subtly the revolutionary idea was inculcated into their training and when they had completed their course they formed the nucleus of a coterie devoted to Chiang's cause–then the unification of China and the destruction of the power of the War Lords. Chiang's protégés still recount how, although the Academy's President, he was up at five every morning after making his own bed and cleaning his humble quarters. He used to take the early morning parades as well as instruct, inspect and plan for the "Great Day". By 1926 his chosen followers were in key positions in the army and then Chiang struck. Within eight months his armies occupied Hankow and Nanking while Shanghai was almost under his control. By 1928 the National Government was overawed by his troops and he had conquered north China.

Further military successes were gained, but in 1931 he yielded to those who accused him of extreme autocracy, and sought solace and rest in his mountain birthplace.

He did not stay there long before the Japanese swarmed into Manchuria and Chiang returned. His earlier sojourn among the Japanese stood him in good stead in the years that followed. He negotiated, he compromised, and he built up the Chinese forces to prepare for the second attack which he knew would come.

When in 1937 their mechanised army was hurled at Chiang its task was not as simple as the men in Tokyo planned. Chiang's armies reeled, retreated and here and there they were routed. The main forces fell back steadily, and stabilised a front along 2,800 miles, behind which, at Chungking, far up the twisting Yangtse, Chiang made his capital. He held that line for nearly four years while his commanders perfected themselves in guerilla warfare and infiltration tactics. At one crucial stage he had to make a decision whether or not to destroy the dykes along the Yellow River, "China's Sorrow". To do so would hold up the Japanese advance, but it would mean death to thousands of peasants and misery to many more. Chiang, the soldier, gave the orders that resulted in the Japanese halt, and a position of virtual stale-mate with the immobilisation of many divisions. Militarily Chiang's act was a classic piece of "scorched earth" tactics.

Never had things looked so black for China—the Japanese had been stopped but they were only 300 miles from Chungking which they bombed day and night. The French (it was during the summer of 1940), had permitted the Japanese to occupy Indo-China so that the enemy was now at the back door. Finally came the British decision to close the Burma Road. Unofficial peace overtures were made but Chiang stubbornly refused to treat.

Chiang, rejecting the advice of his advisers, lashed at them with his tongue. They had argued that mathematically it would be wiser to compromise and Chiang replied in a voice which became high pitched with emotion.

"You count how many men we have, how much ammunition and cry about our small reserves of petrol. But I care nothing about that— I do not count. When I started fifteen years ago I had only 2,000 cadets in a military school. England, France, America and Japan were against me and the communists were more powerful than they are now. I had no money. But we marched north and we beat the War Lords and the country was united. Today we have 3,000,000 men and half the country. We have powerful friends. Let the Japanese come on, let them drive me into Tibet—I will return and I will conquer all China again."

This is what Sumner Welles had in mind when he wrote in *Where are We Heading?*—"He has been untiring in the pursuit of his country's interests as he has seen them. His resiliency has been superhuman."

It is also presumably what Chiang meant when he reminded me that "past examples" proved the value of standing up to the overwhelm-ing. The enemies of Chiang say that beneath his "smooth" exterior is a terrible ruthlessness. I subscribe to that theory, although without accepting all of its implications.

The Yellow River decision was one that could only be made by a ruthless man. So also was the decision in the Borodin Plot—where those of the Russian's followers who were not executed were deported.

Chiang could never have risen to power in China without possessing this quality. He might not have lost power, say his friends, had he exercised it to a much larger extent than he did!

It should, I feel, be emphasised that Chiang's particular brand of ruthlessness–however much we may deplore it–is of a much milder and understandable quality than that of the communists. It is a controlled ruthlessness–displayed only when all else fails.

To old foes in fact Chiang can be surprisingly generous, once they cease to menace him. He has been known to award pensions to those who have shown good faith in their subsequent behaviour and have not erred for personal gain. On the other hand the scope he has afforded Chiang Cheng-kuo is not, as we have seen, a happy augury for a truly democratic China should the Great Return prove successful!

Chiang's Taipeh office has been called "the heart of a fortress". After preliminary "checks" at two separate guard posts and a conversation with an army officer whose smiling courtesy is backed by bayonets, you are duly "approved" and conducted to the Presence.

At the foot of the great staircase and along the corridors soldiers stand alert–so many of them that to an Englishman they create an air of melodrama.

Here, you may think, are all the trappings of a dictatorship, the signs of a public figure who is afraid to stir among his people outside the circle of his guards. Yet once again you encounter the contradictions.

Chiang travels to Taipeh early each morning in a sleek black Cadillac. From his "home", a simple Japanese style bungalow in the folds of Grass Mountain, to the office there are ten miles of lonely winding road.

Recently, in peaceful Antwerp, I had the opportunity of observing that military officers above the rank of Colonel could be heard approaching a mile away. Their cars were preceded, and followed, by posses of soldiers on motor cycles. The soldiers carried tommy guns across their chests. Yet Chiang, the man who is so badly "wanted" by his foes, travels the lonely road alone, except for his chauffeur and an A.D.C. There are no armed outriders. There are no wailing sirens. There are no jeeps, no motor cycle escort.

Chiang's car is well known to all on the island. It is known not on account of the pennants on its bonnet or the identification papers on its windscreen, but because of the total absence of these formalities with which only General Officers can dispense.

This morning ride of Chiang's–and the return trip in the evening– have given his counsellors considerable anxiety. Although he will concede the necessity for posses of guards on buildings that belong to the State he insists on being unescorted when on the highway. This scarcely appears to be the action of a frightened man.

Then there is the speech made by Chiang Kai-shek on his fiftieth birthday. It was a public speech and 100,000 people in Nanking listened.

"For seventeen years", said Chiang, "from the time I was nine when my father died, until I was twenty-five, my mother never spent a day free from trouble. Though often anxious about my fugitive life she remained calm and self-confident regarding the re-building of the home as her care. She taught me how to behave myself. She taught me manual labour. She told me that misfortune, danger and suffering were a daily occurrence in every corner of this world and that only self-reliance and self-betterment would find a way out.

"She taught me that from the family is built the nation. She said a good son does not merely fulfill his obligations to his parents, he must devote himself to the nation. No man can ruin others unless he ruins himself. No other nation can ruin us unless we first ruin ourselves.

"We lived, widowed mother and fatherless son, in the shadow of cold realities; yet my mother gave all me these good counsels to guide my life. She showed me that injustice and oppression might disappear from human history. Such is the debt I owe my mother.

"During all my years I know that what I ate, what I wore and all the things I needed daily were provided by the State. In other words, from the sweat and toil of the people. All this I owe my country. The difficulties that concern the State and the misery of the people are great. I am ashamed to think I have let so much time go by without fulfilling my duty. Now, while the trees by the grave of my mother have grown tall and thick, I realise how little I have accomplished".

I have quoted his speech at length. These are not the words of a despot – but rather of a poet. He has had the powers of a dictator and has acted as such, but a megalomaniac or a "crook" does not speak this language nor cultivate this philosophy! No picture of Chiang Kai-shek could, of course, be complete without a reference to the celebrated and spectacular Madame Chiang.

When Chiang arrived at an allied conference during the war he was accompanied by only a handful of advisers. The British had brought along two hundred, but Chiang had his wife with him and he counted her as "worth ten divisions"! I am afraid that few of the Generalissimo's followers would whole-heartedly endorse that panegyric today.

Rightly or wrongly Madame, far more than any other single influence, is being blamed for much of Chiang's present difficulties. Her very affection for him, coupled with her ambition, is said to have led him to make stupid political blunders on the mainland.

It was in December, 1927, that Chiang married Mayling Soong, the youngest of a famous family of sisters, the eldest of whom married the banker, H. H. Kung, now living in America and reputed to be one of the world's richest men. Another became the wife of Dr. Sun Yat-sen so that by either a happy accident or astute arrangement, General Chiang Kai-shek became related to his mentor.

Father Soong, who laid the foundations of his fortune by selling Bibles, imparted much of his business acumen to his beautiful daughters. It could be that Chiang was chosen as a desirable son-in-law after his firm dealing with the Russians which obviously marked him as a man out of the ordinary to whose star one's wagon might profitably be hitched. Thus the most powerful man in China married into the most influential family.

It is painfully true that nepotism and a tremendous rise in the fortunes of Chiang's relations by marriage occurred when he was in a position which could be used to the advantage of those closest to him. That they did so is notorious but there is another side to this medal. No one has said, much less proved, that General Chiang Kai-shek himself was a beneficiary of the stupendous graft that permeated the Kuomintang. His modest tastes in living and dress belie any suggestion of avarice. That the country was robbed and that China's benefactors were bled for the benefit of a few scoundrels is correct, but I believe it was not until he was away from the scene that Chiang Kai-shek was able to appreciate the full extent of the depredations of his trusted friends.

There is no point in blinking the fact that General Chiang Kai-shek's name in the western world is synonymous with graft. It is almost impossible to converse on the situation in Formosa without the allegation being made that Chiang Kai-shek betrayed his backers in the past and should not be supported in the future.

It may be infinitely nearer the truth if it were said that his failure on the mainland was due to misplaced trust.

There was a time when no newspaper in China would care to risk publishing anything derogatory about anyone connected with the Generalissimo by marriage, but I saw such a reference in a Formosan newspaper in June, 1951. That is a healthy sign.

A cause of offence to many of the faithful are the political pronouncements of Madame. It is said that her heroic style of public address has sometimes given offence to the policy makers of the Kuomintang, and certainly she has often alienated by her excessive candour what might otherwise have been the sympathetic reactions of the world outside.

On October 1, 1949, Dr. F. T. Cheng, the Ambassador in London (a Bencher of the Middle Temple) was told of Britain's intentions to recognise Red China by Mr. Hector McNeil and before the end of the year diplomatic relations were broken off. Madame Chiang Kai-shek, in her inimitable and spirited way had a lot to say and on January 8, broadcasting from New York, she attacked Great Britain as a "moral weakling who has bartered her soul for thirty pieces of silver" and then said she would go to Formosa to join the Generalissimo, who was already there, and continue the fight against communism to the death.

Madame Chiang's eloquence was a sign of her distress and anger as she prophesied in the same speech: "One day these pieces of silver will bear interest in British blood, sweat and tears on the battleground of freedom. Shame on Britain". Eleven months later on November 5, detachments of the Royal Ulster Rifles disembarked at Pusan, in Korea.

Madame Chiang's prophecy was all too correct, but her interpretation of Britain's motives had done great harm to Chiang's cause among the indignant British.

In one of his more excitable moments the communist General Chen announced to the world, "Under no circumstances will my army, charged with the sacred duty of liberating Formosa, allow the American aggressors to occupy Formosa nor will they allow traitors and bandits to remain in occupation".

Madame Chiang Kai-shek's answer to the General did not mince matters. The Generalissimo's wife addressed the soldiers and as a Joan of Arc she threw back this challenge: "I tell you we hope to be well on the mainland by the end of the year".

That was in January, 1951, five months after General MacArthur had paid his unheralded and momentous visit to the Generalissimo, after which he described Formosa as "an unsinkable aircraft carrier" and submarine base, essential to America's Pacific defence system.

Madame is now unwontedly quiet and, significantly away from the limelight, devoting her energies to the job of organising working parties to provide clothes and comforts for the troops.

In this less flamboyant role she appears to be doing extremely well, and I saw for myself the well to do and the humblest working side by side on the project in complete harmony.

Despite her naughtiness in politics and the undoubted shortcomings of her family I must confess to still retaining a certain admiration for this extraordinary lady's defiant spirit. I went out to see her at the bungalow in the Grass Mountain. In her deceptively simple Shanghai style frock –the buttons were of solid gold –in her nylons and Parisian shoes, she looked thirty-two rather than her fifty-two years.

She spoke in English, with a slight American accent and was in a conciliatory mood. "The British are a realistic people. Everyone expects they will eventually see how foolish they have been to offer a compromise with the Reds. With the Reds there can be no compromise."

In this statement at least she was at one with her husband's present advisers. They also are not of the type that yields lightly to reverses. They are, for once, men after the Generalissimo's own heart.

They are men who have looked to see what they could give rather than what they could take, and they have provided an example of loyalty that would indeed have been a phenomenon in the hierarchy of the Kuomintang before the disaster.

It is not possible to assess with justice the character of a man of Chiang's stature, only in the light of history can this be done, and then he must be judged according to the lights of his people, at the time in which he lived. But there are some who have placed on record their opinions of Chiang Kai-shek, and among them was Mr. Anthony Eden then Foreign Secretary.

Mr. Eden was fresh from the momentous Cairo meeting when Mr. Churchill and Mr. Roosevelt made their famous declaration in which the Generalissimo joined. To a crowded House of Commons the Foreign Minister said this of Chiang Kai-shek: "Under the outward gentleness and gracefulness of this remarkable personality, there is a core of supple steel. His is the strength that you feel cannot be broken; it can only be bent and then strike back again with even greater force".* Can yesterday's hero really be the villain of today?

9. *The economy of the island*

THE geo-politician would most certainly find in Formosa an absorbing subject for objective study. The history and economy of the island illustrates every tenet of Haushofer and the orthodox geo-politicians.

Its geographical position, dominating the sea route along the south China coast, was exploited by pirates and utilised by the Dutch as an outpost for their trade with Japan. They yielded to Koxinga, who made the island into a rallying point for his defeated forces just as has Chiang Kai-shek. The Japanese converted Formosa into a fortress with a strategic railway, an extension of that brought over by the Chinese from Woosung in 1878. They laced it with airfields and air strips in furtherance of their notorious "Greater Asia Co-prosperity Sphere" in which they were to be the masters. As recent history has recorded, Formosan bases enabled the Japanese to raze the better part of Manila to the ground and made Hong Kong and Singapore untenable.

Precisely because of its geographical position American and Chinese

* *Hansard,* Col. 1426, 14. 12. 1943.

armed forces are pledged to deny Formosa to the communists. From Red Formosa not only would the whole of south-east Asia and Australia be threatened once more but its occupation by a hostile power would smash the continuity of America's Pacific defence line. Okinawa and the islands to the north, including Japan would be under continual menace no less than the Philippines to the south.

Geographical accident, therefore, has put Formosa into the same category as Iceland, Malta, Cyprus, and even Gibraltar so that she has become, not a pawn in international politics, but a piece of major importance.

It is of little more than academic interest now to look back and recall that both Commodore Matthew Perry and our own Admirals and later the British Consul General, Robert Swinhoe, all vigorously advocated the acquisition of Formosa. These genteel opportunists wanted Formosa's indifferent bituminous coal for the ships of their nationals so that their trade would flourish. Indeed, the coal might have meant to Formosa what gold did to the Transvaal Republic. It is true, of course, that the remarkable and erudite Robert Swinhoe also urged the acquisition of Formosa because he was satisfied that its dense forests and forbidding mountains inhabited by murderous head hunters, in conjunction with its tremendous cliffs along the east coast, endowed the island with the most desirable qualities for a much needed British convict settlement. Australia was no longer amenable to her shores being made a dumping ground for criminals. At the Cape an effort by the Home Government to land miscreants almost led to rebellion so that even the convicts who were landed there preferred to escape to England and their death.

Swinhoe's impassioned appeal was written from his club in Royal Avenue, Chelsea, and addressed to the Foreign Secretary asking for permission to contribute to a correspondence on this vexed matter then running in the London *Times*. Apparently the Minister's permission was not forthcoming and Swinhoe's suggestion that Formosa might be bought from Peking has ended up in a bound volume of letters in the Public Record Office in London.

Politics having fortuitously made Formosa important, nature has added a more intrinsic value; small mineral deposits including the coal, a little gold, some oil, sulphur and pyrites. The Creator, by placing her directly under Cancer (the Crab of the Zodiac), so that the Tropic splits the island right through its centre, has ensured a humid, sub-tropical climate and one of the world's heaviest rainfalls. At Keelung it rains 200 inches a year over 219 days. Its great mountain ranges include forty-eight peaks which exceed 11,000 feet, many of them extinct volcanoes. Great torrents of water rush down these mountains to collect into lakes, notably the Sun and Moon Lake, and to form rivers which have been harnessed to produce as much electricity as the island can consume and which is sold at less than four-pence per kilowatt-hour. (The maximum generating capacity is now 273,395 kw.) The broad rivers wend their several ways into the Straits of Formosa, to the west, thus watering the vast coastal plains of alluvial volcanic soil.

From the time of Queen Elizabeth, sugar and rice have been grown on this coastal plain but only since King George V ascended the throne of England has man put back anything into the crop-weary soil. For in the north the characteristically industrious Chinese farmers wring two crops of rice a year out of the near exhausted earth while their brothers in the south, two hundred miles nearer the Equator, force a third crop from the tired land.

The story of the systematic rehabilitation of the soil by fertilisers is one of politics no less than economics. Between June 1950 and June 1951, the United States through the Economic Co-operative Administration supplied no less than U.S. $13,246,000 worth of fertilisers while another 58,675 tons valued at U.S. $3,295,770 were produced by the five Formosan factories.

During the later part of the Japanese occupation about 30,000 tons were produced locally and the balance of the annual requirements, estimated at from 150,000 to 175,000 tons, was imported from Japan. This fitted in perfectly with Japan's overall colonial policy which was to force Japanese services and goods, ranging from fertilisers to patent medicines and clothing, on Formosa. No secondary industries of consequence were permitted and the island's economy, including currency, was rigidly geared to Japan's.

A good example of Japanese exploitation was the sugar industry. In the year 1938-39 Formosa produced 1,400,000 metric tons of sugar and 95 per cent of the crop was exported to Japan. Taiwan Seito, the largest individual company in which the Japanese Imperial family was a principal shareholder, showed an annual average profit of 44½ per cent and paid a dividend of 12 per cent. The company owned nearly 100,000 acres, thirty miles of railways and great refineries in Japan.

Three-quarters of the sugar cane was produced by 128,000 small farmers who owned an average of one acre and they were able to produce the sugar at less than the big corporations. There was no official compulsion to produce the sugar and the farmer was paid a fixed price set by his overlords and was adequately financed during the eighteen months between planting and cutting. It was a hard life but had the virtue of security. Here it is interesting to note that further south, in Hainan Island for instance, in Malaya and in the Philippines, sugar cane matures in twelve months.

The Japanese financed modern research stations and imported special varieties of cane from the Hawaiian Islands and Java but apart from increasing the net yield they were unable to produce a cane that would mature in twelve months. Again, even this apparently uneconomic factor which is basic, fitted in well with Japan's political economy in that the sum total involved coincidently wiped out the ten per cent deficit in her balance of trade payments which she suffered when the flag of the Rising Sun was first hoisted as that of the conqueror. It did not matter one iota to the Japanese economists that sugar could be bought cheaper elsewhere—what did matter was that sugar produced in Formosa could be paid for in a currency linked to her own, or better still, in goods and services at whatever price the Japanese chose to charge. The Formosans had no opportunity of benefiting by foreign competition because all her imports and exports were virtually for "Japanese only".

The result was that Formosa became "Japan's India" on the one hand and her granary on the other, just as one hundred years ago Formosa supplied sugar and rice to the poorer regions of north China.

It was an eloquent criticism of Japan that the Formosans who produced the sugar could afford to consume only slightly over half that consumed by the Japanese at home.

In 1951, as in Japanese days, sugar is by far the most important of Formosa's industries and represents 82 per cent of her total export trade and it is responsible accordingly for her vital foreign currency earnings. It is not sound politics or economics for a country to be dependent on any one crop, specially when subject to the vagaries of international supply and demand. That is obvious, but under the Japanese there was no question of Formosa having to conduct her national finances as an entity—she was merely an integral part of a large and complex organism.

When the Chinese returned to Formosa, thirty-four of the forty-two factories which had belonged to four Japanese companies had been smashed to ruins by American bombing. Acreage was reduced by four-fifths, most Japanese thought rehabilitation was impossible and American experts estimated that at least U.S. $30,000,000 would be required to put the factories in working order. Apart from the point of view of the national finances, the bulk of Formosa's farmers depended on sugar for a livelihood, which was a serious consideration.

The Government appropriated all the assets of the Japanese sugar companies, public and private, and the sugar industry became duly "nationalised" as part of the National Resources Commission. On VJ Day they found only 3,000 tons of fertiliser in the island which was a very small fraction of what was needed. Moreover, the new Government was without sufficient funds to finance the farmers to enable them to tide over the eighteen months growing period.

I had an opportunity of visiting the rebuilt mills and the Chinese engineers have accomplished the "impossible". The productive capacity of the Taiwan Sugar Corporation is now over 1,000,000 tons a year but the supply of sugar had dropped as farmers have turned from sugar to rice. In terms of revenue the picture is not quite so dismal as was feared but only because the world price reached a particularly high level and offset the loss that was expected for the lower output. It is freely admitted, and not without apprehension, that the position is not satisfactory and from 600,000 metric tons in 1949-1950 the crop has fallen to perhaps 350,000 tons in 1950-51. This can only have the effect of increasing the unit cost of production. The target figure for 1952-53 is back to 600,000 and it would be a bold man who would assert that it is impossible of attainment.

The Formosan sugar industry has had many vicissitudes since it first shipped sugar to Australia in 1873 and sold sugar to a representative of the Robinet Company of America in 1856. The obvious customers in the near future are Japan and the British Ministry of Food which in 1950 bought 50,000 tons. But Mr. Cheng Tao-yu, Minister of Economic Affairs, was careful to remind me that China's annual sugar consumption in normal years was about 1,000,000 tons—a *per capita* consumption of less than two kilograms as against 50 kilograms in the United States and Great Britain; the ultimate ambition of the Taiwan Sugar Corporation, therefore, is to be China's main supplier which would be the natural position if Formosa becomes, as Chiang Kai-shek holds out, a province of a United China.

Against the rather worrying background of the sugar industry with so much hinging on its earning capacity, Mr. Cheng Tao-yu had some encouraging facts to report.

Apart from sugar, Formosa's other main products broke all the peak records achieved during the Japanese occupation—rice, electric power, petroleum, fertilisers, cotton, coal, salt and cement. During the first six months of the year there was a favourable trade balance of nearly U.S. $21,840,660 which, although there has been a slight recession, will probably end in a favourable surplus at the end of the year 1951.

The Minister certainly had cause to be optimistic.

Early in June, the week before I left, 10,000 tons of cement were being shipped from Kaohsiung to Melbourne. I don't suppose there is anything startling about this but it seemed a strange sort of commodity to take from Formosa to Australia. The price offered was satisfactory and I gathered that forward contracts could be made if the Chinese were agreeable—which they were not. The explanation was simple. "We will require all the cement we can produce as soon as we arrive back on the mainland for war purposes and reconstruction", was the answer so full of hope and determination.

Already a pre-war trade has been reopened with Japan in salt. Two hundred and fifty thousand tons were sold in 1950 at U.S. $16.80 per ton and another 100,000 is about to be shipped.

The Government has many other grounds for satisfaction in the economic field, not as spectacular as the sugar industry but revenue earning nevertheless. In the first six months of 1951 sugar had yielded U.S. $30,000,000 (£12,000,000) approximately; 239,000 cases of tinned pineapples as fine as I have ever seen or tasted, had been sold to the United States, Japan, Denmark and Britain, whereas in the past this prosperous little industry involving 20,000 acres of plantations was only known to the Japanese. At U.S. $6.40 a case another U.S. $1,529,600 was added to the national income.

Tea, the commodity which first attracted the attention of Robert Swinhoe and which was the crop responsible for the arrival of the early British traders, still flourishes and alongside it a complementary industry, the growing of tons of jasmine, oleacear and gardenias which are dried and mixed with the tea to scent it, after which the sweet perfumed, shrivelled blossoms are mostly removed. One British firm had recently built a very fine tea factory and had, according to reports, intended to go into the financing of tea growers in a fairly substantial way. Unfortunately, when I was in Formosa, the factory had little prospect of working to capacity because the owners had second thoughts on locking up more money in an industry from which it could not be recovered if Mao Tse-tung's threat of invasion is implemented. It is a popular legend in Formosa that it was Formosan tea shipped through Amoy which enlivened the Boston Tea Party. Before Swinhoe left the island, ten British firms were established there mainly exporting tea and importing opium for re-export. In 1893 the island was producing 21,000,000 lb. a year, a figure which it has never greatly exceeded.

Then there is a banana industry. The tree is indigenous to the country and under the Japanese 45,000 acres were set out in plantations and it is capable of re-establishing its former Japanese market. Natural sulphur, aluminium manufactured from bauxite ore mainly from Indonesia and a quite considerable paper industry all contribute in a small way to make the island less dependent on imports. There is also a textile industry which produced something over 3,000,000 yards of cotton cloth, which is quite inadequate, of course, to meet the local demand. However, it provides work for some skilled labour and a market for the little cotton produced in the island.

There are two heavy industries that struck me of being capable of great development. The first was the dockyard at Keelung started by the Japanese in 1899 and now taken over by the Taiwan Shipping Corporation which operates three modern dry docks owned by the Harbour Bureau. The Manager,* who is a Cambridge graduate, went to considerable trouble to show me round. The biggest dock can take a 20,000 ton ship and major work is being carried out at Keelung in competition with Japanese dockyards. I was told by a shipping agent that in some instances the quotations from Keelung make it worth while towing a ship all the way from Tokyo, 1,500 miles away for repair. The time of turn-round, which used to average seven days, has now been reduced to three including time of entry, unloading, loading and leaving. There is little unnecessary delay in the warehouses –usually less than seven days. On an average a vessel of more than three hatches can load or unload 1,000 tons of general cargo per day. The record cargo discharge was 255 tons of bagged fertiliser per hour from a five hatch ship.

Work was being completed on an outer breakwater and four big piers with all modern facilities in the outer harbour, additional railway and highway connections including several tunnels and elevated bridges have been planned as well as dredging to a depth of twelve metres. Warehouses now having a total capacity of 150,000 tons are being extended.

It is a beautiful harbour, surrounded on three sides by mountains with its entrance facing the north. The water depth at the entrance is twenty metres and even at low water the fairway is navigable for any Pacific going ship. Anchored in the harbour, on both occasions when I visited the city, were American destroyers with their radar in restless action twenty-four hours a day. The town itself is gayer even than Taipeh twenty miles away.

A small luxury liner, the S.S. *Kiang Ning*, captured from the Japanese, serves the purpose of a hotel and is moored alongside. It is also the "smartest restaurant in town", although I must confess the enormous hoarding of a competitor–"Harbour Café–It's so cosy and so gorgeous" from which dance music blared, enticed me away from my floating hotel from time to time. It had a competitor equally fascinating, with the delectable name of "Intoxicating Moon".

The Japanese spent very great sums in developing this natural harbour for strategic as well as commercial purposes. Like every other such venture sponsored by them in Formosa, Keelung was efficient and typical of the Japanese genius for orderliness. But to the great credit of the Chinese, they have maintained and even improved on the docks and its services even if the same cannot be said of the cleanliness of the city. The Chinese took over a derelict harbour and once again performed "miracles".

* Mr. Wellington S.T. Tu.

The other heavy industry, with a host of subsidiaries, is the great oil refinery at Kaohsiung. It was built by the Japanese Navy in 1942 but has never worked to capacity. It is set in beautiful surroundings at the base of a small mountain which the Japanese studded with anti-aircraft batteries and honeycombed with air raid shelters. A hundred battered blast walls, and burnt out plant and buildings bear witness of American bombing. The Japanese estimated that at least eight hundred bombs fell on this target.

There is a strong temptation to eulogise the Chinese engineers for putting the plant back into partial production in little over a year. It would not be praising their achievements too highly to compare the results of their reconstruction work with the best in devastated Europe. In the first instance they sought the advice of Dr. Gustav Egloff of the Universal Oil Products Company of Chicago who spent some time at the refinery. The Chinese Petroleum Corporation took over in 1946 – by April, 1947, they were processing 6,000 barrels of Iranian crude oil per day.

The second stage of the reconstruction programme was the rebuilding of the No. 1 Topping Unit which had a designed capacity of 7,500 BPSD. This plant was about the most heavily damaged; the pipe still received a direct hit practically demolishing the heater area completely. The unit was put on stream in the beginning of March, 1948, and processing 10,000 BBLS per day of Iranian crude oil on a two-stage flush operation. The whole job was done by Chinese engineers and local contractors.

Since 1948, a great deal more work has been done and Kaohsiung refinery now has a capacity greater than any other between Japan and Indonesia. Apart from petrol, paraffin, diesel oil and fuel oil, nearly 4,000 tons of asphalt was produced in 1950.

Unfortunately the purchasing capacity of Formosa is strictly limited so that the refinery has never been able to operate fully. However, it must be of considerable consolation to both Formosa and the United States that such an installation is available in the event of war in the East. Half an hour's drive from the refinery on a first class road is the ammonium sulphate works now capable of producing 7,000 tons a year.

The reconstruction of the plant itself is an epic and a monument to Chinese fortitude and tenacity of purpose. During China's War with Japan, the plant was purchased from America under lend-lease. It was destined for the arsenal caves of Szechwan, but with the tide of war against the Nationalists, the crates containing the machinery were manhandled over thousands of miles, back and forth between China and northern India.

Whenever the equipment rested long enough in one place, its

Chinese guardians unpacked, dismantled, removed rust, re-greased and repacked. Finally after years of wandering it reached Formosa – still legally the property of the Nationalist army. Recently it was sold to the National Resources Commission and once in full operation, will save US. $1,260,000 in foreign exchange.

It is hard to come to any conclusion other than that the energy and faith plus the proved skill of Chinese engineers is justifying the growing American assistance.

Without this American assistance Formosa could not possibly have staved off the communists nor could internal order have been maintained except by military means.

Fortunately for Formosa and the Government, rice grows in superabundance so that there is even an appreciable surplus available for export. This means that at least the people are never in danger of starvation provided always that there is fertiliser. Also the country produces all the vegetables and fruit necessary for the population to have a reasonably balanced diet.

As has been emphasised, without fertilisers Formosa could produce no more from the land than would maintain its population at a subsistence level. This essential commodity has to be bought from other countries with foreign currency. Without the sugar which earns this foreign currency there could be no fertiliser and this dangerous and vicious circle would have in fact been set up excepting for the Economic Co-operation Administration—an integral part of the Marshall Plan.

It is a simple fact that without aid Formosa would have been a chaotic, impoverished and unhappy land with just that very setting of general distress which would have made it receptive to communism or any other political organism that thrives on misery and unstable conditions.

The mere action of the United States in having funds made available was not sufficient to ensure that the Formosans would benefit thereby and so stave off hunger and evil. What is equally important is that every dollar that has gone into Formosa in the form of either money or goods has in fact been utilised for the purpose it was intended. Thus, history has not been allowed to repeat itself. In Formosa a job has been done which, when it is fully recounted, will be of unbounded credit to the anonymous Americans and Chinese who put General Marshall's noble and imaginative scheme into operation with such success in this remote part of the world.

Before ECA could operate satisfactorily in Formosa there was some cleaning up to be done simultaneously with the importation of fertiliser and the hundred and one other agricultural commodities. Help was by no means limited to farmers, but to every aspect of the island's economy, from the financing of a great railway bridge, rolling stock for the railway and road-making machinery. As an adjunct to ECA, the Joint Commission on Rural Construction (JCRR) went into operation to supply everything from livestock for improving the breed of poultry, pigs and cattle, to financing irrigation and rural health schemes, in fact, everything to help the farmer attain his legitimate aims by guiding him and providing the necessary supervision, expert assistance and funds.

The quotation of money figures can mean little or everything, so much depends on the use to which the money is applied, but pre-supposing, as is correct, that no money was channelled off for unauthorised purposes, between April, 1948 to June, 1950, $30,000,000 was spent in ECA assistance to Formosa. From June, 1950, to June, 1951, the figure jumped to $53,765,000. Of this $13,246,000 was allocated to fertiliser, $10,185,000 for raw cotton for the textile mills, $6,278,000 for industrial projects, $411,000 on public health and so on. The list is long and impressive and the coverage broad.

Other vast sums so large that the layman is inclined to dismiss the matter as much too big for anyone not an accountant to appreciate, have been allocated in the form of military aid grants for the armed forces. In June, 1951, for instance, a sum of $20,000,000 was granted in the form of military aid through ECA quite apart from a sum five times as big a few months later. As I toured the island I saw the evidence of ECA in operation in a hundred different ways and I also visited the administrative offices on many occasions. One specially healthy aspect of ECA is the complete absence of self righteousness. Doctor Raymond T. Moyer, Chief of the ECA Mission in Formosa put the function of ECA very fairly when he said to an audience of Formosans and Chinese:

"The importance of a strong military defence is generally recognised. But military efforts alone cannot assure that this island will remain outside of a Russian-dominated communist bloc. Healthy economic conditions also are necessary."

This statement at once removes any feeling that Formosa is in receipt of charity. Its economy was saved and has now been put on a sound basis because it is in the interests of the west that it should be so. Conversely, it is against the interests of the communists that a prosperous island should be close enough to be a show window for the power of the west.

In accomplishing its primary aims ECA is naturally spreading the benefits of modern science and performing a wide number of humanitarian services but it is not a missionary effort in other than a political sense.

ECA retains the service of the J. G. White Engineering Corporation which has provided the technical advice and labour for such enterprises as a steel works at Kaohsiung; a power project; a calcium cyanide plant and a paper mill and several other industrial undertakings. It is very important to note that the funds for these enterprises are not entirely American. Local currency costs for labour are met by "counterpart funds" which are derived from payments actually made by farmers in cash or kind for goods and services but instead of being remitted back to the United States these payments remain in Formosa for use in further ECA projects.

In effect, then, the money paid by the farmer for say fertiliser or bean-cakes may very well be ploughed back into Formosa in the form of benefits through the JCRR programme. Moreover, everyone shares in the successful outcome of efforts to maintain stable economic conditions and gradually to improve these conditions. The creation of employment, giving people a chance to work for the money they need, is only one of a number of examples that might be given illustrating this point.

Economic Co-operation Administration has helped Formosans to mobilise their own resources of initiative and creative energy by this ingeniously contrived system of self help which is a curative rather than a palliative, and is the most dignified method of lending assistance to another country, completely taking the wind out of the sails of those who would raise the bogy of "imperialism".

But before ECA could begin to fulfil its objects the rapacious landlord had to be brought under control which has been done. This is not only a matter of concern and interest to Formosa but also to the mainland because land reform has been a catch cry of every political party for decades and its appeal is to the vast mass of Chinese, the majority of whom, after all, are agriculturists.

I spoke to the two men primarily responsible for the introduction of land reform in Formosa and then to Mr. Wolf I. Ladejinsky, an eminent American agricultural economist attached to ECA who had made it his business to study land reform in operation and later, whilst I happened to be in Formosa, to report on results.

Land reform had, of course, been attempted years ago by the Kuomintang on the mainland but generally speaking whatever benefits were promised seldom seemed to materialise. What has happened in Formosa is a most desirable contrast.

The first measures were introduced by Premier Chen Cheng when he was Provincial Governor. When he became Premier the task was carried on and put into operation by Dr. K. C. Wu. It would have been difficult to find two men more able by sheer force of character to push forward these reforms which quite understandably were resented by the Formosan landed proprietors.

It is axiomatic in the non-welfare state that incentive is the motive power of industry and enterprise and he who does not work and who has no capital resources becomes an unwelcome parasite. With the departure of the Japanese and the threatened collapse of the sugar industry the Formosan farmer was faced with the worst prospects in living memory.

Ladejinsky explained the situation as he saw it in September, 1949, and I quote verbatim from my notes.

"At first glance, Formosa appeared prosperous; agriculture its mainstay. On more than 2,000,000 acres of arable land, rice, sugarcane and citrus fruits are produced in abundance. The people are hard-working and their carefully tilled fields stretch away on all sides of the west coast of the island. But this look of wealth is illusory. The tenants of Formosa, who constitute two-thirds of the island's people, suffer from undernourishment, disease and poverty. Many factors have contributed to these conditions, but the principal one is that Formosa, though to a less degree than any other regions in Asia, has too many farmers and not enough land. A total cultivated area of two million acres is worked by 530,000 families, less than four acres per family. As a matter of fact, more than half the farmers cultivate no more than an acre or two."

But it was not only the small holdings that contributed to the low economic standard of the average farmer. It was also a fact that so much of the land in Formosa was owned by so few that the amount of land a farmer cultivated had little relation to the amount he owned. Only about 33 per cent of the farmers were owners; 27 per cent were part owners and part tenants; and 40 per cent were tenants who owned no land at all.

The rents have been far above the level justified by the productivity of the soil. Usual rents were 55 per cent to 60 per cent of the crop; but rents as high as 70 per cent were not uncommon. And, when the tenant's other expenses were included—high priced fertiliser, seed and equipment, and the buildings on the land—his total costs had been as much as 75 per cent of the crop. He also had to pay the landlord a large deposit for securing his leases and what was termed locally, "iron rent", *i.e.* a minimum rent payable irrespective of the crop yield in the event of any natural or domestic disaster. The deposit alone was enough to prevent many a farm labourer from becoming a tenant, much less an owner.

Ladejinsky confirmed what I had already been told: that a great many farmers had little or no rice to carry them from one crop to another; in the principal rice growing areas more than 30 per cent of them fell into this category and in the southernmost part of the island, in the village of Shin-Lin, approximately 70 per cent did so.

One interesting result was that over generations every community in Formosa was split by a form of class distinction so that they could be classified as sort of first class and second class citizens with the landlords obviously the first class. This discrimination was apparent not only at public meetings but extended to the attitude of officials wherever public business was transacted.

It is quite obvious that so long as such conditions persisted there could be no political stability in urban Formosa and land reforms were an urgent necessity if political extremism and civil dissension were to be avoided.

Under the Japanese the credit system was well organised as part of the network which was responsible for agricultural education, the distribution of fertiliser and catered for the other day to day needs of the farmer. So long as the farmer could obtain a loan at a reasonable rate of interest he was, all in all, very much better off than his brother on the mainland and certain of a fixed price for whatever he produced. With the collapse of the established channels of farm credit, the usurer came into his own and he advanced money at the rate of from 150 to 200 per cent interest per annum.

The land reformers went into action with complete disregard to the implied threats of the politically powerful rentiers and the warnings of the timid Chen Cheng had extremely painful recollections of the Nationalists' defeats in China and the measure that the failure of promised land reform had in bringing that defeat about. He had all the qualities necessary to force the measures through and every impelling reason to smash opposition. In one of my interviews with General Chen Cheng he told me what he had planned to do and it sounded rather like a military operation which was not remarkable in view of his background.

We sat at a small table – no interpreter was necessary as his English is excellent. Our only interruption was the manservant who came in first to hand us the customary hot towel which had been wrung in slightly perfumed water and the inevitable glasses of hot tea of the famous local variety in which as like as not, the petals of jasmine or gardenia floated. I mention this unimportant sidelight merely to show that the conversation was informal. Moreover, the Premier was now in the happy position of one who has successfully launched an ambitious scheme upon the success of which much depends. Throughout the conversation he paid generous tribute to his successor, "K.C." and to the unstinting Americans. His natural pride was associated with the certainty that not all Chiang Kai-shek's 500,000 troops fighting with a will and efficiency could do more towards the re-conquest of China than the genuine hope of the peasant millions that the land reforms would be applied to them as in Formosa.

General Chen Cheng made three main points:

(i) No society can attain economic and political stability so long as it is hopelessly divided into the "have's" and "have not's".

(ii) Had the landlords not made concessions they might eventually have had to pay the grim price demanded of landlords in communist China:

(iii) his programme of land reform would give the peasantry an economic and political stake in their country.

In a nutshell, legislation was passed putting a "ceiling" on rents limiting payment to 37.5 per cent of the crop. Tenants were given security of tenure which has made it almost impossible for the landlord to eject excepting by Court order which is only granted if the landlord proves serious default. Together Premier Chen Cheng and Governor Wu prevailed upon a willing Nationalist Government to put considerable areas of public land on the market and to make it available to farmers on generous terms. Land is let to farmers at 25 per cent of the crop.

The results were electric in their effect. Whereas in the past landlords were unwilling to sell, they now grumble that there are no buyers. The explanation is two-fold, the farmers still have insufficient capital and those who have would prefer to take advantage of the government terms of sale. In the first six months after the introduction of legislation farmers only bought 537 acres from private owners. In the meantime the price of land has fallen steadily from six ounces of gold per acre in 1949 to three and a half to four, or even less.

After a full year of operation very few instances of landlords seeking to circumvent the provisions of the Land Acts have been reported and there is no doubt that the peasants have suffered too long to have any inhibitions about reporting suspected offences for which heavy prison sentences are the penalty.

Over emphasis of the repercussions of the reforms is impossible. They have not only more than counteracted the atrocities and excesses of General Chen Yi and his assassins, there has been built up a real foundation of respect among the Formosans for the Provincial Government in which they are taking more and more part from Ministerial posts down.

This is not to say that the few who hope for eventual independence or that Formosa will come under UN trusteeship have reconciled themselves. But, as has been pointed out, even if such persons holding these aims are in fact an organised body, they are inaudible in Formosa and no responsible Formosan organisation exists outside the island advocating Formosan independence in an orderly or articulate manner.

From talks I had with some very politically conscious Formosans, I gathered that they recognised that whereas Formosa might be in the position of a reluctant host, it was quite obvious to all but the blind and the bigoted that the Nationalists want nothing more than to be back in China and to leave Formosa as a loyal and prosperous province with a liberal degree of local autonomy.

The days when the island supplied ninety per cent of the world's natural camphor, mostly to Germany, have gone – the time when it performed the entrepôt function of transhipping opium to the mainland and re-exporting silk from Japan is now only of historical interest.

Japan's policy of absolute exploitation was not a hundred per cent evil but it was economic cynicism *in excelsis*. However, Formosa cannot escape its geography. Its rainfall and its plains, its humid climate and its industrious people, hereditary rice growers, must be taken into consideration in conjunction with the virtually insatiable demand for rice and sugar in Japan and China. Formosa has an important part to play in respect of both these countries and so long as she is not free to trade with her mother country, then no doubt she will with Japan, who though never a fairy godmother was not the evil witch.

It would, however, be unrealistic to disregard the potentialities of the great oil refinery at Kaohsiung, the fine dockyards at Keelung, the cement factories and the forests with the unlimited water and the power generated from the fast flowing streams. The aluminium industry commenced by the Japanese may be extended, also the paper industry can be built up and who knows, the "hush hush" drilling for oil may yet yield handsome dividends. Small quantities of oil have been produced for many years and some say it is only because of the inadequate machinery and failure to tap lower levels that more oil has not been produced.

But in the meantime the man-in-the-street grumbles that 800,000 spindles are not in full use; that 600,000 bottles of beer were imported in one year with the limited supply of foreign exchange; and that seventy per cent of the island's revenue is earmarked and spent on a huge army so that more is spent by the islanders proportionately than any country in the world.

I shall always remember, however, the observations of Mr. Koh Chung-tsui, most respectfully introduced as "An aged economist". I am not suggesting that his remarks should be taken to indicate that a general state of inflation exists, but because he echoes the thoughts of everyone of his, and the present, generation from Piccadilly to Times Square.

"When I landed at Keelung from Shanghai on May 26, 1949," lamented the precise Mr. Koh, "I took a common meal in a small restaurant on the bund there and the price was $5,000 Old Taiwan

Currency equivalent to 12½ cents New Taiwan Currency. What is the price now? I think it at least equivalent to $3 NTC. This shows the price of food has increased by twenty-four times in as many months." Mr. Koh added that the price of public transport had increased seventeen times and finally he hoped that ECA would put a further stop to any further depreciation in currency.

Mr. Koh's experience differed from mine in restaurants but we suffered neither more nor less than Formosa's other residents and it would be unjust to suggest that Formosa's currency at the moment is unstable.

10. *The strategic importance of Formosa*

AFTER all is said and done, is Formosa worth all the hundreds of millions of dollars which are being poured in by the American taxpayers? Is America's interest in Formosa likely to precipitate a war?

The answer to the money question is undoubtedly "Yes". Since so much of the "money" is, in fact, in the form of American goods and services which ultimately reverts to those who subscribe it. Whether Formosa is worth the risk of war is quite another matter.

Dismissing for the moment any questions of prestige and the moral and legal rights of the Chinese protagonists, let us set down Formosa's strategic assets and liabilities and then apply these considerations to the interests of the west.

There are three main factors to be weighed before judgment can be passed. These are military, which in the strategic sense includes all branches of the fighting services; economic and political.

Whether or not Formosa is politically reliable and an asset from the Western point of view is a matter of fact rather than of opinion and from the evidence adduced in this book one can only come to the conclusion that Formosa offers no scope or comfort to communists of any hue.

Economically as has been seen, Formosa is of value to the west in peace and war. She is an internationally important producer of sugar and was the "Sugar Bowl" of Japan. She is likely to become so again. Rice production which is already great, can be increased and there is now a valuable exportable surplus.

These sugar and rice exports place Formosa in a position to purchase consumer goods most of which can be supplied by Japan. As the sugar is urgently required by Japan, their trade is complementary.

Reference has already been made to the refinery at Kaohsiung –

built by the Japanese Navy for strategic reasons. It might be important in any future war and must be protected and at the same time denied to the enemy.

There is also the dockyard and floating docks at Keelung which, in event of a Far Eastern War would also have to be denied to the enemy. Hong Kong's dockyards would probably be put out of action and there would be no others available between Japan and Singapore.

These are sufficient reasons (and there are several others), for stating categorically that from a politico-economic point of view, Formosa is strategically important to the non-communist nations both in peace and in war.

Finally we come to the more direct military considerations. Military strategy, until put to the test, is always arguable and even after the event it can often be shown that this or that advantage was not exploited properly by one side or the other; thus the course of battle may be altered to the confusion of the experts.

In "the Cold War" Formosa is fundamentally important because of its proximity to the China coast to which it lies parallel for 240 miles thus forming the Formosan Straits through which ships must pass if trade is not to be stifled. Midway are the Pescadores, with an important naval base, which are under the control of the Nationalists. These Straits can be effectively patrolled from bases in Formosa and the Pescadores as has been amply proved. Patrolling Chinese and U.S. aircraft are in constant communication with naval units and radar is playing an ever increasing part.

If an all out blockade of the south China coast became necessary it could be imposed from Formosa and this would be extremely damaging to China which is so dependent on imported war materials.

It is a fact that a large army is based on the island and that it is supported by an air force which is increasing in strength as well as by the nucleus of an efficient navy which has the personnel if not the ships. This deficiency can be remedied at a moment's notice. The fighting quality of the troops is speculative but those best qualified to judge believe the bulk of them to be good. The presence of these armed forces leaves the communists no option but to counter their threat by stationing at least a million troops along the Fukien and Kwantung coasts. This is still no guarantee that a serious invasion attempt could be defeated and it is certain that "commando" raids could certainly attain their objectives.

Putting aside logistic disadvantages from which the communists suffer even more than the Nationalists, the communist troops which must be tied down along the coast cannot be used elsewhere, against the UN. in Korea, for instance. This is a negative argument but a very strong one in favour of Formosa's retention by militant Nationalists.

Let us now consider Formosa as a base for military operations. Its terrain could not be more suitable for air fields and there is an inexhaustible amount of coolie labour to increase the large number already operational. The island has an abundance of cement and by-products from the oil refinery for various installations if necessary. As already noted there are adequate harbours.

It is close to the mainland, an average distance of little more than 100 miles. This gives aircraft based on Formosa the advantage of being able to supply fighter cover for bomber raids as far south as Hong Kong and Canton as well as fighter cover for convoys proceeding to or from Japan. From Formosa the whole of the China coast from Shanghai to Hainan could be bombed with relative ease.

Should they be required, reinforcements can reach Formosa by air from the American base in Okinawa in the Ryukyu islands within a couple of hours and from Manila in the south and Japan in the north in less than four hours. Similarly, airfields on the island and meteorological services are available midway between Japan and the Philippines which could be very valuable. Obviously, therefore, Formosa could be invaluable to either side, which disposes of any doubts as to whether or not it should be held.

The question of its defence has been the subject of immense study not only by the Japanese but more recently by the Chinese and Americans. Both the Japanese and the Americans have had great experience in planning invasions and in amphibious warfare generally. The island is too long and the west coast too flat for it to be easily defensible. On the other hand the scales are weighted so heavily on the side of the defenders that it is hard to imagine a successful invasion except by airborne divisions which is not a serious threat at the moment.

One might have suggested infiltration and fifth column tactics were it not for the knowledge that the intelligence service is well able to cope with any such attempts. To me there is no doubt that Formosa should be held and so long as American help is available it should be possible to hold it.

The west is divided on the Formosan issue which is a pity. We have already, in Korea, seen what lack of policy leads to in terms of blood and material and the slaughter of innocent civilians in their thousands.

At the moment, America has chosen a policy of the "middle way"; a policy that seeks to keep out the communists and yet not provoke them into action; to aid Chiang Kai-shek and yet not allow him to employ that aid.

It is a policy that is pleasing neither of the "Chinas". It is confusing both, but it has the virtue of being an honest effort. So far it has not involved trouble but it would be wrong to imagine that it won't bring trouble later on.

Let us consider the implications yet once more:

By continuing to arm Chiang, by continuing the policy where, simultaneously, U.S. warships "seal" the Straits, resistance to Mao Tse-tung on the mainland will be increased. If Chiang finds that his troops are well equipped both militarily and morally, he may, as we discussed earlier, attempt a desperate blow himself.

By implementing the existing "neutralisation" policy we find ourselves – (a) involved in an all out shooting war with the communists, or (b) committed to a course of action against Chiang that would leave his enemies – and ours – the only beneficiaries. There are, of course, alternatives to the *status quo*.

From time to time the rightful concern of the west in Formosa has expressed itself in suggestions that the island should be placed under UN. Trusteeship or else be given independence. This has even been mooted in the London *Daily Mail*. It is unfortunate that such well-meaning suggestions have, despite their superficial attractiveness, little to commend them as ways of escape from the major problems.

From Chiang's point of view, agreement with the trusteeship proposals would mean political suicide. It would entail the end of the Kuomintang. Instead of being in command of an alternative order, equipped with its own army, navy, air force and all the machinery of government, "Nationalist China" would be overnight converted into a selection of talkative ineffectual exiles meeting in hired rooms. In view of this, such a proposal might, indeed, be tempting to Mao, but is it really so attractive to the west?

Just who would garrison Formosa? Neither Americans nor British would tolerate communists and at least on this issue the combined Chiefs of Staff might well disagree with the administration. Conversely, the communist Chinese fear the thought of the Americans taking over.

Personally I am convinced from discussions with the Nationalist leaders and from a study of the mainland's propaganda and policy statements, that the Chinese would never agree to the trusteeship proposal. Neither side can dare lose face with its suspicious followers. Both sides would point out that solemn international agreements had given Formosa to China and that there is no historical justification for severing Formosa from China. They would accuse the world of once again "cashing in" on the woes of their unhappy country in order to acquire an influence disproportionate to any benefits conferred.

Also the man in possession (Chiang) would first have to be persuaded to move, and the man who claims to be the rightful owner (Mao) would reserve the right to treat the new tenants – at some opportune time – as nothing better than a bunch of bandits who had cleared out a lodger he had detested and then installed themselves there instead.

What about independence? What hope is there of creating a Formosan nation? Unfortunately the island's actual and potential leaders were no doubt shot in the February, 1947, purge and massacre. Here again, the question arises as to how to maintain this independence without the backing of adequate defence forces—drawn from where?

We have also to ask: Would Chiang's men say "Yes"? And if they did not—as they would not—who is going to take the responsibility of forcing them out?

Let us face it: To be even installed, let alone effectively operated, the machinery of either a UN. trusteeship or an independent Formosa would have to have behind it the approval and goodwill of the world.

The recent history of discussions between the Powers—on subjects infinitely less controversial—does not encourage the belief that this would be readily forthcoming.

The plain fact is that the world is in a quandary about Formosa. At the moment it is not so apparent—the Korean War and the Japanese Peace Treaty have enabled the question to be temporarily shelved.

Someday, however, whatever the current preoccupations, this problem will have to be solved. This is going to be a most difficult task, for the British viewpoints have somehow to be reconciled with the opposition of the United States and the views of the Dominions of Australia, New Zealand, Canada and the Union of South Africa.

Countries will be wary about being pushed into a position where they may be portrayed as "Imperialists in occupation of Chinese territory".

Many Chinese I know sincerely believe that war with the communists is the only solution and responsible Americans are to be found in London, as well as in Formosa, who agree.

On the right, are the Nationalists claiming that they should be allowed to hit the communists as often and hard as they like. On the left, the communists demanding to get at the Nationalists. In the centre is America, backing one of the boxers (the one with a long record of defeats), threatened by the other, and, at the same time, attempting to act in the guise of referee and trainer, a difficult combination. The invidiousness of such a position needs small comment. But how to get out of it without suffering infinitely more than by remaining in the ring is quite another matter.

I pass on, for what it is worth, the typically Oriental suggestion of one of Chiang's advisers. We talked together in an atmosphere charged, as Hollywood would say, with "colour".

On one particularly flamboyant poster opposite to this man's office a picture of Chiang Kai-shek appealed for a return to the mainland.

On the street corner nearby the long barrel of a gun was craftily concealed beneath a mass of camouflage – the gun of a tank that had been "dug in" to a trench of its own to help resist any communist invaders.

I had been discussing with him the reiterated demands of the Nationalists to be given "a free hand" in choosing the time and place to attack the communists. I had observed that America could hardly be expected to agree to a Nationalist assault – an assault made possible only by reason of the weapons she had herself provided.

Any such step, I argued, might implicitly place upon America the responsibility for "intervention" in the affairs of China and provide an opportunity for the Russians, if they wished to pose as champions of "a free China" or if the terms of the Russo-Chinese Treaty were invoked. Furthermore it would split the west, already sufficiently divided over the question of Chiang Kai-shek, to a degree that could only be of profit to the communists.

My friend smiled and suggested that the west should study the technique of the communists in Korea and adapt it to its own purposes. "You do not", he remarked, "defeat evil by evil, nor do you defeat evil by being careful not to offend it".

"In Korea", he said, "you have the anomaly of British soldiers being killed by the soldiers of a foreign Power and yet, with that foreign power, you are in a state of diplomatic relationship although in its territory your foreign office representatives cannot function in a state of official normality, indeed they remain in China on sufferance!"

How can this situation exist? It exists because of a legal fiction, which is accepted by both sides because neither side is willing, by exposing its falsity, to take the responsibility of calling the other's bluff. "What part", he asked significantly, "does 'Big Business' play in the ignominious scene?"

The fiction is that the Chinese Government, as such, is not involved in hostilities in Korea. China instead has sympathetically permitted "volunteers" to aid a people with whom Britain is not even officially at war. "Why", he pointed out, "should not Nationalist volunteers go to the aid of the French to repel communism in Indo-China?" (One reason, of course, is that France does not want "Free Chinese" volunteers.)

"Let the west permit our Government to choose its time to return to the mainland. Let the west also sympathetically abstain from the quarrel. America need not be involved at all – not unless Mao Tse-tung has decided the time is ripe, and thus incurs the odium of precipitating a conflict.

"America's role is a simple one. She could supply arms to us as the Government of one country can always supply arms to the organisation that it acknowledges as the Government of another. Britain does not acknowledge the existence of a North Korea. China does. China does not acknowledge the existence of a Nationalist Government. The United States does.

"America could supply the arms. She could also provide the volunteers—only this time they would be real volunteers—as she did under the gallant Major-General Claire Chennault of the 'Flying Tigers'.

"Then she could leave the rest to us. If we emerged victorious the Formosan problem, the North Korean problem, and all problems in north-east Asia would be solved. If we lost the position could not be much worse than it is today.

"In any case, victory or defeat, and looked at by your governments simply from the point of view of expediency alone, your enemies would be much weakened." I would like to have heard more. One may indeed be shocked at such blunt and frank avowals of subtlety and craft. One may also wonder just when straight dealing ceases to become a social duty and instead, in the face of those who would cheat, develops into a liability for the honest.

The argument so freely voiced that day I was to hear reiterated in many parts of the island before I left. Already that argument is being echoed in the world outside.

"Let us stop trying to appease. Let us stop trying to make friends with a thug who repays our bows with blows. Let us arm Chiang, and unleash him, and then keep clear of trouble unless we are pushed into it." It is advice that should be seriously considered. It has all the weight behind it of our past experiences of the "reasonableness" of the people now opposed to Chiang, it possesses the appearance of logic, and it certainly is backed by the emotions.

Most westerners, although perhaps not very sympathetically disposed towards the Nationalists are, at least negatively, opposed to the spread of communism. As a result they need little convincing that Chiang, as the only Chinese who could possibly provide an alternative to Mao Tse-tung would be better home than in Formosa.

There is, one obvious flaw in the argument. It presupposes that the Nationalist forces would be efficient enough to maintain themselves at least short of an immediate military disaster.

If they were not, the west would either suffer its biggest loss of face or else be reluctantly committed to "pulling the chestnuts out of the fire", and of pulling chestnuts out of the fire, especially the chestnuts of the Generalissimo, America has had a considerable and bitter record of experience. Outside the windows of my hotel in Taipeh the braying of bugles in doleful disharmony daily saluted the rising sun.

The bugles were loud and strong. Whatever the heady history of the night before this unrequested, resented reveille pulled one angrily out of bed.

Even the claims of the propagandists of Chiang are varied in character and strident in delivery, but like the buglers, the propagandists are new recruits. The raw style of their address arouses one's initial interest, but fails in the end to inspire confidence. The Americans after all have had sorry recollections of the difference between Kuomintang promises and Kuomintang performances.

American policy in Asia at the close of World War Two received a terrific rebuff as the armies of the American equipped Nationalists slid from defeat into catastrophe in the "phoney" battles of the mainland.

In August, 1948, a White Paper on Sino-American relations – covering a thousand pages, it was surely the longest White Paper ever to be printed – was issued in Washington to explain it all and to condemn. (Since then I think it has been shown that some of the judgments were not quite equitable.)

At the same time Secretary of State Dean Acheson wrote a historic letter explaining the causes leading to the breakdown of the National-ist Government. In a nutshell, Mr. Acheson's thesis was that the Nationalist Government had sunk into corruption, into a scramble for place and power; and a blind reliance on the U.S.A. The General-issimo, he emphasised, had made little true effort to correct the situation, despite repeated American representations followed by unfulfilled assurances. From the political side the story was sorry enough, but on the military side Major-General David Barr went even further, and Mr. Acheson quoted him as reporting: "The complete ineptness of high military leaders, and widespread disruption and dishonesty throughout the armed forces."

Said the Major-General who–together with Generals Hurley, Marshall and Wedemeyer had made, and failed in, monumental efforts to bring about the end of the Civil War in China: "A complete loss of the will to fight". This, he said, together with the world's worst leadership had caused the débâcle. Since his arrival no battle had been lost through lack of ammunition or equipment.* In the battles in Manchuria of November, 1948, the White Paper commented, the

* After Germany's surrender General Wedemeyer arranged to ship quantities of captured German small arms and ammunition to China of the type already in use. These were stopped on the personal instructions of Lauchlin Currie. It is also a fact that Lease-Lend war material for Chiang Kai-shek was destroyed and dumped into the sea. This material had been assembled in India for despatch to the Nationalists. After raising the ban on arming Chiang (see page 90) in December, 1947, Colonel Moody, a U.S. army ordnance expert stated that the Nationalists had only 22 days supply of ammunition for their German type small arms and 36 days for their American type. By obstructionism the April 1948 grant of $125 million for military aid in form of equipment did not reach Chiang until the communists had virtually won the day. There was also graft somewhere along the line because the supplies were valued at 30 times more than similar supplies to other countries at the same time! The fallacy that the U.S. gave unstinted military and financial aid to Chiang Kai-shek which was dissipated is historically untrue but has been assiduously propagated by communists and fellow travellers in high places in the U.S. until now it is blindly accepted.

Nationalist Forces lost eight divisions, eighty-five per cent of whose equipment, including a hundred thousand rifles, came from the U.S.A. It was said—and very truly—that the armies were not beaten in the field. Instead they just disintegrated! Nor did the subsequent record of the Nationalists appear, to American eyes, any more encouraging. Despite General MacArthur's enthusiasm for the fighting men of Chiang, despite its own decision to supply "aid", the U.S. Administration remains watchful and wary.

Basically it does not share the optimism—now apparently so current among the Nationalist leaders—regarding the outcome of a counter-attack, but on the broad issue of whether or not it is a good thing to maintain Formosa free from domination by the mainland there are no such reservations. There can be no reservations. The original Nationalist reverses entailed a complete re-orientation of America's defences in the Pacific.

From having a powerful ally of 450,000,000 people; from possessing a place "on the doorstep" of the Soviet Union, and possessed of all the advantages of abundant airfields, ports and strong points, America found herself suddenly faced by a new and truculent enemy, and her strength confined to a weak and half trained garrison in an enigmatic Japan. Within a year the British territory of Hong Kong, always prosperous and so strong—was besieged; a place where a thin line of trenches and pill boxes manned by a handful of troops, looked bravely formidable to the layman, and to the intelligent soldier heroically pathetic. The Republic of South Korea was the only democratic representative on the whole of the north Asian land mass, and even it, on closer examination, took on the appearance of a frightened hostage and perhaps not so democratic after all.

In those grim days—let it not be forgotten by the publicists who blame today's unhappy events upon American "interference"—the Truman policy was cool and temperate. It persisted in what these same critics today demand, *viz*: "an effort to get a new understanding with Mao Tse-tung" in fact the attitude of the west was desperately appeasing.

President Truman issued a directive to State Department officials (referred to elsewhere) that wherever they were serving to "soft pedal" Formosa and, indeed, play down arguments purporting to show that Formosa's disposition was of any great concern to the United States.

Chiang Kai-shek, bewildered and infuriated by the storm of criticism and abuse that had broken so suddenly upon his last remaining roof, appealed in vain to the west to supply his forces with instructors, equipment and finance.

In September, 1949, a conference was convened by the triumphant

Reds in Peking, and the People's Republic was proclaimed by Mao Tse-tung before a crowd of 200,000 in the square of the Gate of Heavenly Peace. While the trumpets were blaring across the continent of China, Washington remained pacific. Far from assisting a "reactionary", "corrupt" and "discredited" government to cause further bloodshed on the mainland, the United States, or rather the Administration of the United States, seemed almost anxious to ensure that the last traces of that government were interred as rapidly as possible. Time did nothing to lessen the friction between the former "friends".

It is not commonly known that Chiang Kai-shek, in the extremity of his despair, brought into the island former officers of the hated Japanese army to do the job the Americans had refused. I met one of them in Formosa, a General who had served his country with distinction.

He was General Nimoto, one time Chief of Staff of Japan's crack Kwantung Army. I was taken to his little Japanese house not without some trepidation on the part of my guide. My friends in the Government were not at all pleased that I had even heard of him, much less met him, and it was surprising to learn that his presence in the island was a revelation to every European to whom I spoke. His views were most informative and I gathered he had no intention of returning to Japan.

Someone close to the White House has since told me that the revulsion of feeling throughout the United States towards the affairs of the Kuomintang was so intense that President Truman was at one stage considering how he could best follow Britain's example in acknowledging the Government of Mao Tse-tung.

Then came the bombshell; the invasion of Korea precipitated a political somersault in Washington. Practically overnight the status of Chiang rocketed. Formosa became appreciated in its true and obvious rôle, an integral part of the defence line of the west and MacArthur came into his own, even if only for the period of a swan song.

By his executive action in ordering the Seventh Fleet to deny Formosa to the communists on the one hand, and to contain the Nationalists on the other, President Truman tardily, yet dramatically, admitted the importance of Formosa to American security, and at the same time, made the last effort of the west to prove "impartiality" towards the warring Chinese.

The authors of the January directive no doubt blushed and felt a little uneasy—but at least they had tried to be honest.

This appreciation of Formosa's importance, in spite of the previous reluctance of the politicians to acknowledge it—could never have been far absent from the minds of the United States General Staff. Certainly there had been no doubts in the mind of General MacArthur.

MacArthur was the best man in the world when it came to implementing the President's policy towards the North Korean Commu-nists. He was the worst man in the world to be "impartial" regarding the claims of Chiang and Mao to the island.

For MacArthur, with his memories of Luzon and Corregidor, knew from bitter personal experience just how important Formosa could be. Consider the facts.

The first defence line of the west in Asia today curves from North Japan through Ryukyu Islands to the Philippines and Borneo. At the forward extremity of the curve is Formosa, to the south is the isolated outpost of Hong Kong, to the north there is Korea.

If Formosa should fall, the capital of the Philippines would be placed within an hour's flight of modern bombers. Hong Kong would no longer be able to hope for air support. And the sea route connecting the British bases at Singapore with the Americans in Japan would be cut asunder. Even the most simple of strategists could conceive of no better place to harass the China littoral than Formosa.

It is no exaggeration to say that many American military leaders believe the fall of Formosa would eventually entail the complete "pull back" of the U.S. forces across two thousand miles of sea and island to the Second Line that runs from Alaska, through Guam and the Solo-mons to Australia.

To this school of thought the impressive events in Korea and the continued intransigence of the communists take precedence over purely political considerations in the uneasy days ahead.

I think somebody may be a little too frightened or is there near-panic in the Pentagon? Is somebody forgetting or deliberately ignoring the fact that the Japanese, to effect their conquests maintained a large Fleet a hundred times the size of the odd ships of Mao Tse-tung?

I asked the question when in conversation with a member of the American military mission. His reply was indicative of the misgivings of certain U.S. leaders. He said: "The plain facts are that it would not matter whether the Reds had a large surface fleet or not once they had achieved possession of the island.

"The main mission of the Japanese was to contain the American fleet, to keep it away from the first area of invasion – the Philippines and Hong Kong, and safeguard Japan from reprisals.

"In this they succeeded. If Formosa were to go Red and war followed, the triangle Amoy–Formosa–Hong Kong would soon be free of American warships.

"For war would presumably entail the entry of the Soviet Union. The Soviet Union possesses at least ninety submarines in the Far Eastern Squadron. The possession of Formosa would extend their range and scope enormously. There would be no spot on the 'triangle's fringe' where they and supporting aircraft could not operate. The northern Philippines would become untenable within a month."

Was this an exaggeration? I do not know. But the principle of denying Formosa to the communists is supported by the test of what happened as a result of the island not being denied to the Japanese!

In allied hands Formosa could ensure, with its network of airfields and air strips, and its ports and anchorages, "cover" for the movement of allied forces by sea between the island outposts, and at least some degree of support for the British in their precariously held territory of Hong Kong. It could protect the Philippines. And it could also threaten the Chinese mainland, for the MacArthur phrase of "unsinkable aircraft carrier" is an apt one to describe the utility of the island.

While–despite the loss of Hainan, and the Chusan Islands, the islands dominating the Yangtse, the firm possession of Formosa could still cause the paralysis of the coastal route of South China.

So much then for the purely strategic considerations of Formosa's value in the event of a war which nobody is confident will never happen. But what of the comparative difficulties of Chiang and Mao today? Is there not a danger that this very insistence on maintaining hold on the island because of its potentialities in war may not in turn, help to precipitate war?

The answer is that we cannot afford not to take the risk and the best way of lessening the risk must be the subject of very careful examination. Unity must be obtained at all costs among the western powers with regard to this most urgent affair.

11.   *The situation in Hong Kong*

JUST four hours after leaving Taipeh Airport in the north of Formosa, the Civil Air Transport plane circled Hong Kong Island and Kowloon, the little strip of British territory opposite.

There are fewer more entrancing sights than the barren little islands around Hong Kong, set in an azure sea dotted with fishing vessels. Everywhere were the stoutly built single masted boats of the Hakkas, with their hulls high out of the water and the flimsy little boats that can be either rowed or sailed and which are favoured by the Cantonese for their greater speed.

The Hakkas have been migrating from Fukien for over two hundred years–the same people who went to Formosa long before that. With the Cantonese they have settled in the New Territories which form by far the largest part of the the colony, 356 square miles out of a total of

391, leased in 1898 to Great Britain for 99 years. Across the boundary stretches Communist China.

They are important people in the economy of Hong Kong, these 60,000 farmer-fishermen, Hong Kong's primary producers. In 1950, they sold 32,729 tons of fish; lizard fish, croakers, mackerel, scad and anchovies, through the Government to five markets where the catches are handled for a mere six per cent of the selling price. I was quite prepared to accept that Hong Kong has the largest fishing fleet in the Colonial Empire.

Tai Pak, Hong Kong's airport, is becoming as busy in its way as the harbour. It nestles between sharply rising granite hills so that the approach is unusual and from the window of the plane (there were no vexatious regulations about drawing the curtains), I saw the forty-four aircraft concerning the ownership of which there has been so much litigation and whose fate has not yet been decided. They are claimed by General Chennault and his Civil Air Transport on the one hand and by the Peking controlled Chinese National Aviation Corporation on the other. In the meantime the planes are protected by the Hong Kong Government. In neat rows, minus their engines which have been removed to safeguard them from the mischievous hands of saboteurs, this fleet awaits the decision of the Judicial Committee of the Privy Council.

A service runs between Taipeh and Tai Pak six days a week carrying mail, newspapers and the oddest assortment of freight imaginable including orchids and tinned pineapples from Formosa and a frequent cargo of fish fry from the mainland for Formosan fish ponds. The fry come from the river regions of Kwantung and are shipped from Hong Kong in four gallon petrol tins three-fifths full of well water and two-fifths full of oxygen. There are from 500 to 1,000 in each tin and they average one inch in length in summer and up to two inches in winter and spring. In Formosa, as in China, a fish pond is as frequent an appendage to a country household as a chicken run in a small holding.

Leaving Formosa was an unhappy experience. I felt rather like a deserter, because Formosa's crisis, be it tribulation or triumph, has yet to come and in either case she will need friends. I would liked to have remained there.

Hong Kong, however, plays so many strategic and economic parts in the sinister game of high politics, that a visit was a "Must". If I was sad at leaving Formosa, there was some consolation in the sight of Hong Kong which is always exhilarating. An uneventful trip from Formosa was made interesting by the excellent view of the Pescadores naval base (Mako) with three foreign merchantmen lying in the lagoon under the lee of the watchful shore batteries. A small Nationalist gunboat was nosing her way into the Straits, possibly to apprehend another blockade runner. Two days before, I had been told in confidence that a ship was known to have left Singapore with strategic materials for Tsingtao and that she was registered in Hong Kong which meant, of course, she would be wearing the Red Ensign. This news was disturbing because I also knew that Hugh Moffat, *Time*'s Far Eastern correspondent and a *Life* staff photographer had, that very day, joined a gunboat at Kaohsiung which was going out on patrol. It would have made a wonderful news story of the wrong sort if they happened to be present when the ship was apprehended and my professional interest made me just a little jealous, while my patriotism made me feel guiltily uncomfortable. I never found out whether their expedition was successful but I did learn that one of the Nationalists' most zealous informers was an American citizen in Hong Kong.*

There was no question of his abusing the hospitality of the colony although I imagine he would have been *persona non grata* in the clubs most frequented by the ship owners and brokers who form so important a part of Hong Kong's commercial life. The basic fact that Hong Kong ranks among the world's greatest ports gives it paramount importance, not only in imperial affairs but also in international commerce. Its main function is that of an entrepôt port where every conceivable type of cargo is brought from all the corners of the earth for transhipment here, there and everywhere, but mainly to China.

The final trade figures and general statistics for the year 1950 had just been issued. Even a superficial study of them explains the self-satisfaction of the people of Hong Kong, particularly the 10,000 British who regard the colony's prosperity as their handiwork. It also explains why 25,000 British troops, besides units of the Royal Navy and Air Force are there to guard this valuable heritage.

During 1950, 27,350,520 tons net of shipping cleared the port, a record according to the "book of words". Exports from Hong Kong to China totalled £91,000,000 and another £13,000,000 went to Macao which, in effect, meant China. The main commodities shipped were textile fabrics, chemical and pharmaceutical products, vegetable oils and rubber. The imports from China were £54,000,000 giving the Colony a favourable balance of trade with China of £37,600,000. It was significant that £41,000,000 of the remaining total of £120,000,000 of Hong Kong's imports were from the United States as against £25,000,000 from the United Kingdom and £19,000,000 from Malaya.

During the heated debates in the Houses of Parliament and Congress when the morality of the Hong Kong merchants and shippers who were dealing in goods of any kind for communist China was being challenged, it was characteristic of Hong Kong that the cry of

---

*Several months later I learned that the ship was the *Taikinshan* (2,284 tons), *vide The Times*, 8.1.1952. She was seized on June 25th, 1951. The vessel was wrecked in the South China Sea a few weeks after her release.

"Well, who is supplying the goods, anyway, and in what proportion?" was not audibly heard. The Hong Kong business man is very
much of a rugged individualist.

It was characteristic because the traders of Hong Kong are the
legatees of a tradition of free trade in which hard bargaining, shrewd
judgment on the proposition in hand, matter rather more than ethical
or political considerations, a tradition in which success meant kudos
as well as profit.

It is interesting to recall that in 1857 a British Government was
defeated in the House of Commons by sixteen votes and in the House
of Lords by thirty-six because of the high handed action of the Governor of Hong Kong in support of British "rights" against the Chinese.
Members took the stand that national honour was more important
than individual gain. Palmerston bowed to the storm, and the Government went to the country. In the meantime, the unfortunate Governor,
Sir John Bowring, and most of the other British subjects in Hong
Kong were poisoned by arsenic. None died and the Chinese baker
accused of being responsible was brought to trial and acquitted. However, military reinforcements arrived from Madras and within a few
weeks, Canton was blockaded. The Chinese fleet was destroyed by
Admiral Seymour and Commodore Kepple and the luckless Commissioner of Canton, Yeh Ming-ching, was deported to Calcutta where he
died. He had already forfeited his fortune to the Emperor who by
some tortuous reasoning held that Yeh had been weak in his opposition to the "Foreign Devils". Yeh was certainly a remarkable man. He
hated the British venomously and offered high monetary rewards to
anyone who killed a "Foreign Devil". To his own people he was also
extremely harsh and according to Palmerston, was responsible for
70,000 executions in one year in Canton.

That year of 1857 was a difficult one for England apart from the
unfortunate campaign against the Chinese. She was at war with Persia
and the Indian Mutiny was in full swing, while the peace with France
was an uneasy one.

Not that the national affairs of the United States were very tranquil
at that time either. Troops had to go to the support of the Governor
of Utah; there were serious riots in New York and Washington against
the Irish electorate on account of changes in the police arrangements;
an insurrection in Kansas had to be arbitrarily quelled; there was commercial panic in New York and the unpopular judgment in the "Dred
Scott" case caused the greatest dissatisfaction. (Two judges of the
Supreme Court had declared "Dred Scott", a slave, to be emancipated
in a free state but seven other judges on the bench ruled otherwise.)

Therefore, remembering that Napoleon was still within living
memory when Hong Kong was acquired and that the international

attitude towards national violence was one of tolerance, it speaks volumes for the integrity of the British people that they reacted as they did to what they considered to be unfair treatment of the Chinese, despite the opposition of the traders in Hong Kong and the "money-bags" of England and Scotland.

The broad minded man can understand the mentality of the other-wise kind individual who enjoys blood sports, which is not condona-tion. He can even more easily understand the millionaire remaining in business because of the profit motive. In both cases there is something of the spirit of the hunt. No doubt the stag at bay goes through the same emotions as a U.N. soldier facing an overwhelming number of Chinese "volunteers" who have come part of their way down the Korean peninsula in trucks which have component parts transhipped through Hong Kong, whether they be tyres or magnetos. There is little room in these circumstances to sympathise with an urge to make money or to kill but the trouble is that these arguments are usually overlooked by those who are at the benefiting end. K. C. Wu ex-pressed the opinion that Hong Kong shippers resent the embargo that had been placed, firstly, on American goods from going to Hong Kong and, much later, the British embargo against goods destined for the mainland because they hate the loss of opportunities for "doing deals". He was voicing the beliefs, not only of the Nationalists but of many others who are intimately concerned in combating communism.

Hong Kong has a defence and it is not merely plausible. "We live by our trade with China, they say (not that they are peculiar among commercial communities), and if we are prevented from trading with China then we must face bankruptcy. If the harbour is empty then business must come almost to a standstill". That is axiomatic. It would, indeed, be a very doleful sight to see seventeen square miles of wonderful harbour, one of the finest in the world, with thirteen deep water berths empty, to say nothing of 860,000 tons of godown space unoccupied. It would be enough to drive many an honest Hong Kong stevedore to drink, the very thought of it. The tears of a British or American woman whose son may have died in agony in Korea are even more pitiful but where the imagination does not extend is there guilt?

Expediency was not, however, Hong Kong's main defence for trading with an enemy with whom we were fighting.

The people of Hong Kong, with every justification, point out that this British territory is a "shop window" of the democratic way of life which all communist Asia can see in practice. It is the only foothold the free world has on the mainland of China and has become to China what western Berlin is to the Iron Curtain. Its loss would be irreparable in the propaganda war and of that there is no doubt. No one would wish to detract from the force of this argument but it is reasonable to ask is such loss likely? Could Hong Kong fall into communist hands without a major war? Would China risk such a war for the sake of Hong Kong, even though it is the richest prize in the Far East?

China would not instigate such a war against Great Britain and her Allies with Hong Kong as the main objective because she would lose, ultimately. It is no reflection on the British garrison to say that it could do little more than fight a delaying action. It could not be adequately reinforced soon enough to combat the "Human Wave" tactics of the communists if they should be applied. Korea has proved, once again, that command of the sea and air does not guarantee the success of a heavily outnumbered land force. The presence of the Royal Navy and the Royal Air Force would have no effect on the fate of Hong Kong, although it might ensure the evacuation of the population and the military survivors.

It is not impossible, however, that Hong Kong might become communist by internal pressure and it would be a temerarious man who sneered at that possibility no matter how remote.

The prosperity and safety of Hong Kong has always acted as a magnet to Chinese but since the defeat of the Kuomintang the numbers seeking sanctuary of *Pax Britannica* have been overwhelming.

The "book of words" says that twenty years ago, in 1931, the official census put the population at 864,117; in 1941 it was estimated at 1,600,000 and now it is cautiously estimated at 2,100,000 "allowing for a considerable margin of error either way". This rise in population has not been steady, the numbers have fluctuated violently with the fortunes of war. There is a great deal of evidence, some only too well known and the rest kept discreetly quiet, that a formidable number of the population have a greater affinity with Mao Tse-tung than with Chiang Kai-shek. No one with any knowledge of China and the Chinese would underestimate the efficacy of their secret societies nor their prowess at organisation. That many of them exist for charitable purposes as well as political is beside the point, they are a ready made media for fifth columnists.

For only one week during the whole of 1950 was there a period when police were not occupied in extraordinary precautions or operations. As one of them explained, a large number who have taken advantage of Hong Kong's sanctuary are unscrupulous men supplied with, and well versed in the use of, firearms. While I was there a policeman was shot and killed in broad daylight because his assailant wanted a revolver such as all the police carry. Again, the relationship between the Hong Kong and Chinese Governments which used to be cordial are now so strained that the patrolling of the border and mutual assistance in the apprehension of criminals hardly operates.

To maintain law and order this tiny territory has a police force of over 4,000 plus about 700 employed on administrative work. As colonial police forces go it is perhaps the best organised, with a marine section that has twenty-three vessels ranging from ocean going tugs to motor boats all fitted with radio telephones and co-operating closely with the Royal Navy in an effort to combat smuggling and illegal immigration. It also has four armoured cars besides all the usual appendages of a modern police force, a central fingerprint registry, a C.I.D. and a traffic section. Nevertheless, of the 161,959 recorded offences in 1950, 12,462 were for serious offences. As in almost everything else, these tell-tale figures reflected a record.

Crime, however, is as effectively combated in Hong Kong as can reasonably be expected but that is not to say that fifth columnism is equally well under control because it is an unknown quantity. It is a fair commentary that the Europeans in Hong Kong regard any prospect of invasion by the Chinese with something like contempt which I suppose has its commendable aspect, but I found them hesitant to dismiss as mere Nationalist propaganda what friends in Formosa had told me of the communist underground movement in Hong Kong. The communists, be they Chinese or European, have nothing to learn from the Nazis in peacetime infiltrating tactics. I imagine many a thoughtful European in Hong Kong sleeps easier in his bed in the knowledge that the predominantly Chinese police force can be reinforced at a moment's notice by the largest garrison Hong Kong has ever seen, under the command of a South African, Lieutenant-General Sir Robert Mansergh.* In our colonial experience, in Nyasaland, Kenya, Nigeria and the Gold Coast, and more recently in Malaya, it has been found that in times of serious crisis and internal stress, police recruited locally have been unreliable. In Hong Kong most of the police are Cantonese, blood brothers of the majority of the 2,000,000 Chinese in Hong Kong.

For a people who suffered for three and a half years under Japanese occupation and whose territory was forced to capitulate so quickly because of its relatively hopelessly placed position, they certainly have an air of detachment which strikes one as somewhat irrational.

With the embargo on the shipment of goods to China and the very strict control of import and export licences, I expected to find Hong Kong at least a little depressed. It might well be insulting to suggest that business was being carried on "as usual". I have no doubt that this was far from the case but it did not detract from the stimulating effect that Hong Kong has on one. A great deal of business was in fact being carried on. The harbour was by no means empty, the large European stores seemed to be doing a healthy trade and the hundreds

---

* He left Hong Kong 14.10.51 to become Deputy C-in-C., Allied Forces, Northern Europe.

of smaller Chinese owned shops did a steady turnover during the traditional fourteen hour day.

The money changers seemed as active as ever and I was told that there were 133 firms registered to carry on banking business as well as 23 major banks of which three are note issuing.

Nearly 90,000 Chinese are employed in small factories owned by their nationals which make goods ranging from rubber shoes to torches which, being entitled to carry the markings "Made in the British Empire", benefit by Imperial Preference tariffs where such apply. Most of these factories work a seven day week and in the textile factories an average of from ten to twelve hours. Labour legislation is designed, as far as is practicable, under local conditions, to conform with the International Labour Code. Wages range from 5s. 3d. per day for unskilled labour to 12s. a day for skilled workers and even more for piece work. The forty-eight hour week is standard. Bearing in mind that rice and fish which is the staple diet, are both very cheap, I doubt whether the ranks of the factory workers contain many likely recruits for communism any more than do those of the traders.

The pattern of the colony's trade, until the enforcement of the embargo, was rapidly reverting to its pre-war pattern and something like 30 per cent of the imports were from Commonwealth countries and nearly 27 per cent of its exports went to the Commonwealth while a two-way trade with Japan was going up by leaps and bounds.

Hong Kong's prosperity is naturally reflected in its budget which has shown a consistent and increasing surplus since 1946 in spite of the heavy cost of partially supporting more than a million refugees and maintaining extended social services. Its Public Debt could be written off out of its surplus revenue any year the Government chose.

If private motor cars are any indication of a standard of living, there were 16,028 cars exclusive of Service vehicles, and that in spite of a cheap and excellent public transport which carried 169,800,000 passengers in 1950. Taking into consideration the large number of taxis and the fact that there are only 426 miles of roadway in the whole colony, *i.e.* one and a quarter miles per square mile of territory, it was surprising to find that there were only 128 fatal and 601 serious accidents during the previous year.

Hong Kong's happy financial position is due to a combination of several factors. Firstly, its proximity to the great markets of China; Secondly: its political stability, making it an oasis of law and order in a desert of unrest, where the Law of England is administered in the traditional manner so that business men of all nationalities may enter into contracts which will be interpreted, should occasion arise, swiftly and with scrupulous justice: Thirdly, it has collected in its tiny area a tremendous amount of capital which remains in the hands of men to whom trade is the spice of life: Fourthly, it is favoured with one of the world's finest natural harbours which is also one of the most modern. It also has an excellent airport: Fifthly, it has a healthy climate which does not impose the strain of the tropics: Sixthly, it is almost a free port, which relieves the trader from a great deal of red tape and some of the autocracy that goes with it.

There is a duty on tobacco, liquor, hydrocarbon oils, toilet preparations, table waters and proprietary medicines, but the amount of these duties is low enough not to militate against the easy movement of goods.

It is idle to suppose that the future of Hong Kong was not well to the fore in the Government's considerations when recognition was accorded to Mao Tse-tung. Moreover, it is an open secret whose advice the Socialist Government finally accepted. No doubt the military planners also urged conciliation on the score that Hong Kong would be untenable against a determined Chinese army so long as British commitments in other parts of the world remained as onerous as they then were.

Another serious military consideration is the fact that Hong Kong draws its water supply from the mainland and the destruction of the pipes and reservoirs or their contamination would be relatively easy. In this gravely over-populated area this could only lead to widespread disease and chaos. It is, unfortunately, the most vulnerable part of the colonial Empire.

Mr. Dean Acheson during the MacArthur enquiry referred to Hong Kong as an "important point for observation" and went on to say that it must be kept out of communist hands. He also went on to remind the Committee that Hong Kong depended on China for food as well as water. These are serious handicaps.

The water shortage was brought home to me very forcibly. In my hotel bedroom there was a notice which I did not see until too late. It read that owing to the scarcity of water, the mains would be turned off at 10 p.m. I returned to my hotel after that hour and tried in vain to have a bath and went to bed a little disgruntled as a result. At daybreak I was suddenly awakened by a rush of "boys" with mops and buckets bursting through the bedroom door. To my horror I saw the floor was covered in water, the mains having been turned on at 5 a.m. Obviously I had not turned off the taps fully the previous night as the occupier of the room below was the first to find out.

If Mr. Acheson's statement implied that the United States would help to protect Hong Kong it could account for the self confidence of its citizens. However, it seems unlikely that the United States defence line would continue to run along the Sino-British boundary if Formosa were to fall. In pulling back Hong Kong would have to be sacrificed.

Hong Kong is a beautiful, hospitable and brave island, a great credit to a maligned Empire, a symbol of freedom and a monument to the energy and genius of the British race. By its precept it may, in the long run, do more than all the soldiers of Chiang Kai-shek to spread the revulsion to communism across its borders. I spent the greater part of the night before I left Hong Kong in the Red Lion, a very different place from the luxurious hotels in the island itself. The Red Lion is in Kowloon and the nearest equivalent to an English "pub" anywhere in the Far East. It is jointly owned by two charming Chinese landlords and an Englishman now retired and living in England.

At the thirty or forty tables sat a mixture of British soldiers in their green-khaki, tanned by the sun of Korea and Hong Kong, sailors from a cruiser which had arrived that day from Korean waters and perhaps ten ratings from a Portuguese gunboat paying a courtesy visit. In addition, of course, there were a number of pretty Chinese and Eurasian girls. I had wanted to spend this last night with friends at the Hong Kong Club when at the last moment one of my "contacts" offered to introduce me to a Nationalist agent and at my suggestion we met in the Red Lion.

He promised to tell me the truth about the smuggling racket as it was then being run. For all I know circumstances may not have altered. I pass on what he said, or a part, for what it is worth with only this observation; a trained liar does not lie unnecessarily and he minimises his chances of detection simply by avoiding the use of place names or figures that can be verified and shown as misleading.

We quickly passed from the subject of Formosan orchids and Kwantung fish fry on to the sins and pleasures of Macao.

Then Mr. "Wu" explained that the harder the British authorities tried to enforce the embargo and the more successful they were in doing so, the greater the costs of smuggling and the greater the potential profits. The smugglers merely added on their increased charges and the customers seemed willing enough to pay. "The Reds have all the money in the world", was how Mr. "Wu" put it.

According to published figures which I presume to be correct, the following contraband was seized in June: 60,000 gallons of petrol; 39,256 gallons of lubricating oil and 3,065 gallons of paraffin, large quantities of tyres, radio equipment and rubber.

Of course it may have been the gin talking but I am a great believer in the adage, *in vino veritas*. The smugglers, said Mr. "Wu", sometimes received armed protection and when taking goods by land had highly organised cycle patrols and a signalling system. Under the cover of darkness fishing boats in dozens, Mr. "Wu" assured me, made for one

or other of the little islands near Hong Kong where they made a
rendezvous with communist agents. He named two of these, Futai
and Changchiu. Doubtless they have served their purpose for the time
being and some other places have been substituted.

As for Mr. "Wu's" assurances that the hands of a few of the pre-
ventive officers were not quite as clean as they might have been, I
accepted these allegations with the greatest reserve but a visit to Macao
dispels any doubt that smuggling is going on. It was surprising to hear
from Mr. "Wu" the most circumstantial account of smuggling out of
the Philippines to the mainland.

12. *Macao: the city of spies*

I EXPECTED to find him in some furtive hide-out on a deserted wharf
side. Instead I met him in the extravagant, rather tawdry, setting of
a night club in Macao, the tiny Portuguese colony that is the near
neighbour of Hong Kong, just across the estuary of the Pearl River.

He was a resistance leader of great repute, establishing liaison in this
neutral territory with Nationalist officials from Formosa but, far from
being the sort of figure I had conjured up, he was a slight almost fragile
looking man dressed in the most conventional western costume.

Festoons of hand grenades and pistols were conspicuous by their
absence and only a slight bulge beneath this small politely bowing
person's armpit–a bulge that provided the only obtrusion into the
smooth and careful cut of his well brushed dinner jacket–betrayed the
profession of the man upon whose life a liberal price was quoted.

Around him also were four equally docile seeming *habitués* of the
club–a compact bodyguard that was as necessary as it was unobtrusive.

For the movements of this "cloak and dagger" man of Chiang when
restricted to the colony were all probably well-known to his watching
opposite numbers in the service of Mao Tse-tung.

In Macao, for the benefit of the Portuguese and to preserve all
parties from embarrassment, the convention of secrecy, false names,
disguises, etc., are maintained, but in actual fact neither side stirs far
without the other knowing all about it.

And although, in typically oriental fashion, many peculiar arrangements are conducted between the rivals from time to time, the ability
to dodge sudden death, whether ostensibly, accidental or blatantly
deliberate, depends in the final reckoning on the ability to command a
greater fire power than one's antagonist.

Colourful, busy, with the prosperity of a boom town, the curtailment of Hong Kong's trade with Red China has caused the place to be of number one significance to the communists – Macao, as already mentioned, is known as "Spy City" in the Far East.

And the vivid settings of the dramas that are enacted there would gratify the soul of an Edgar Wallace, attract the pen of a Joseph Conrad. Out on Pearl River, the brown-sailed junks labour home past a coast line that suddenly, incongruously, takes on the aspect of a medieval harbour of the Mediterranean.

Down to the water's edge marches the decaying lovely architecture of the great days of Portugal, church spires and battlements soar into the China sky. And the sun picks out the delicate pastel blues, the greens and white of shuttered villas. Such is the impression of one's first visit to Macao, militarily insignificant, yet politically so important. On closer view the elusive picture fades. The winding, hilly lanes are thronged with native costume.

Negro soldiers, Indian policemen, Chinese smugglers, spies and refugees rub shoulders with the colony's normal population.

Macao – all four square miles of it – is the oldest European settlement in Asia. That it stays so is apparently puzzling but, in fact, easy of explanation. Its soldiers, mostly negroes drawn from Portugal's east, and west African territories, Mozambique and Angola, have been "reinforced". Some sort of defence works have been prepared against attack.

But, as every "China Hand" knows, it is certainly not by reason of the armed might of its motherland that there still flies above the city the red and green flag of Portugal. Macao's immunity is due to the fact that Macao is of use to everybody, and it is worth nobody's while to eliminate it!

The peculiar position of the colony – incidentally, you meet few people who look like Portuguese but tens of thousand who claim proudly Portuguese descent – offers benefits to all.

To communists, Macao provides, it is true, a convenient place to spy on Chiang, but far more important, it offers a trade route, a link with the Western world at a time when such links are few and far between. It has the added advantage of being the possession of a power too weak to resist should it ever be considered desirable to attack.

To the Nationalists, Macao has all the advantages of an observation post on the very fringe of hostile territory, an area where the key men of resistance can contact representatives from the island, a *peste restante* for the mail of the "underground".

The toleration now extended to this city by both Reds and Nationalists is no new thing.

Even the Japanese, when they took Hong Kong and overswept the rest of Asia, allowed Macao to remain its usual pleasantly sluttish, thoroughly genial and totally Portuguese self. It provided them with a useful port preserved from bombing by its neutrality, while, for the Allies, it was the only loophole left in Asia.

The Union Jack flew over the British Consulate for the four years between Hong Kong's fall and the final victory and many ticklish and humanitarian tasks were fulfilled there by the then British Consul, Mr. J. P. Reeves.

In 1927, the population of Macao was meticulously established as 157,175. Since then, to this refuge came the victims of the two Chinese Civil Wars, escapees from Hong Kong when the Japanese attacked and many thousands of people who set their hearts on profiting from the colony's recent, and dubious trade boom.

Today, it is said that there are over 500,000 in the tiny territory and this sort of haphazard estimate by no means takes into account such "guests" as my acquaintance, the Resistance leader and his henchmen, nor, of course, the men who are detailed to watch them!

What sort of information do these fighters bring back from the territory that lies behind the hills that run like a saucer's rim round the harbour's hubbub? I quote, without comment, part of a report handed to me by Chiang's Ministry of Defence back in Formosa.

"*January to May* 1951. In this period, roughly seventy highway bridges were destroyed by our guerillas. The big ones among them included the Chanting Bridge on Sunkiang-Wukang border on the Hangchow-Nanking Railway, one on the Soochow-Kiashin Highway in Northern Chekiang, the Che-ho Bridge in Loshan district, Honan. On the highways linking Huichow with Tansui, Paihwa, Pingshan, Hoyanu and Chiking in east Kwantung more than thirty bridges were blown up."

To most of us a line through a large scale map tracing elusive Chinese place-names is, at the best, unprofitable, so I do not propose to list minutely the locality of the other "incidents" mentioned on the report. Nor, as Chinese communiqués are notorious for their optimism, do I necessarily advise a complete acceptance of the facts the report contains.

There are, however, in this and other messages from the mainland, certain factors that are worthy of consideration in assessing just how much of a myth and how much of a reality is the "resistance movement" of Chiang today.

Of particular interest is the fact that twenty-two of the thirty-two "major" bridges listed are situated in the Kwantung province, the territory whose 100,000 square miles embrace Macao and Hong Kong and has, as northern neighbour, Fukien facing Formosa across the Straits.

For communist "treason trials", although carried out in most of the big cities of China, have been far more numerous in Canton, the capital of Kwantung, than anywhere else, a fact so well advertised by the Peking Government that it really would appear as though Mao Tse-tung has a special concern for the area's security. Against this it may be held that any department circulating news that it knew to be false would locate the scene of the fictitious activity in some remote region from which details would be almost impossible to obtain.

As Kwantung is probably the most accessible, or least inaccessible, of the Chinese provinces today, it would be infinitely worse business than the very bad business that Nationalist propaganda made of the Nationalist cause in 1945-49 if Chiang were to tell untruths which could be easily refuted to the people who live nearest him and upon whom, therefore, he must be most dependent for future support.

In the night club at Macao, where the tobacco smoke hung like a cloud, dark-eyed girls, squired by paunchy gentlemen in "sharksin" suits, murmured of love, admiration and the cost of living. And very quietly, very courteously, the five men took their respectable, sober way to the door, the darkness and their return.

Not for the first time did I have a feeling of anti-climax, the strange sensation of detachedly watching a play in which the characters, having held one's attention throughout the first act, have lapsed into melodrama in the second and taken unconvincing exits after a "trick ending" in the third. And yet, although the setting is so bizarre, so improbable, there was little to bore the most blasé westerner in the tasks to which these men had devoted themselves.

For, like their opposite numbers in the ranks of the communists, the Nationalist secret agents and guerillas are neither nice in their methods nor merciful in the techniques that they employ. And in the fact that, perhaps for the first time, a communist régime has opposed to it an underground force whose knowledge of the game is equal to its own, may lie one of the best hopes of anti-communist mainlanders for the fall of Mao Tse-tung.

Always provided of course that the guerillas possess an ideological enthusiasm equal to their craft and continue to be supported by the moral and material aid of an organised force outside.

We have already touched upon the significance of this second proviso, but upon the fulfilment of the first there are some doubts.

Resistance to communism on the mainland springs from three main sources.

First, there are the organised military groups who come under the direct control of the Formosan Government and operate as part of the Nationalist forces.

Next, mostly in the more remote provinces, operate "no surrender" fragments of the Nationalist armies that, sometimes in touch with

Formosa and often not, wage a desultory warfare rather than surrender to the communist armies.

And lastly come those odd and purely temporary allies—groups of bandits and pirates who, always opposed to authority, earn their living by flouting it!

In many cases even the existence of these bands is unknown to Chiang Kai-shek. But, in so far as that any service they render in dislocating the affairs of Mao Tse-tung is of considerable use to the Nationalists, their profit making activities achieve a political and military importance.

My acquaintance of Macao belonged to the first group and, like several thousands of other "key men" he had been left behind deliberately when the main body of the army withdrew from the mainland.

He told me that he himself is known to the Reds only under a *nom de guerre*, his real identity must remain a secret because he has relatives still living on the mainland. Retaliation upon the relatives of prescribed persons, he said, was one of the most effective methods employed by the communists to break resistance, and one member of a neighbouring group had recently been executed by his comrades because he had attempted to betray them—to save the life of his brother!

The communists, I had been told, had now created a special "guard" system for railways and road bridges, but when I asked him what effect this would have upon guerilla activities, he smiled and said: "It will not make operations so difficult as you would think. At a rough estimate, some twelve hundred miles separate the start of the Peking-Canton railway from the terminus. There are probably thousands of road bridges, the sabotage of any one of which can cause confusion out of all proportion to the work involved.

The real Red soldiers cannot be spared to guard every place we may care to attack and very often the militia are very raw and very unwilling to fight whatever the oaths they swear to Red China!

"The main weapon of the communists", he told me rather grimly, "was the liberal use of gold. At the beginning of resistance many were betrayed because of the temptations of gold. Today", he added, "not so many. People who use treachery know they will be punished".

"The Korean War", he said, "has created a favourable situation for the guerilla movement. Before the communists intervened there, we had three armies stationed in our coastal provinces. They were the 2nd, 3rd and 4th Field Armies, the very best organised soldiers the communists had.

"Our activities were very much restricted as a result but now the troops who have gone to Korea comprise most of the 3rd and 4th and large sections of the 2nd.

"Before Korea the mainland had not really recovered from its illusions that the communists were out to benefit the peasants and would 'forgive' those who went over to them from the Nationalist cause. Very few people – except for the officials and the veterans of the Red Army – think that way now. And as we are much better organised and equipped now than we were a year ago, the strain upon the communists is becoming very serious".

The extent of these Nationalist "active" elements on the mainland is as much a matter of opinion as of fact. Their exact numbers are not known and the estimates are most secret. But even these official estimates, at which a guess can be hazarded, cannot be relied upon because loyalties become strained in adversity.

On the other hand, a military success would bring to the Nationalist followers by tens of thousands for although there is a tendency to scoff at the claims of Chiang, the communists in China are not so light-hearted.

Last February, Mr. Peng Cheng, Chairman of the Political Committee of the Administrative Council of the communist Government, told his department that in Kwangsi province alone more than 3,000 communist officials had been killed.

He said: "Counter revolutionary influences have madly torn away the mask of repentance and stretched their heads out of underground hiding places. They have indulged in sabotage activities and they have openly attacked the people."

"Accidents have occurred in which railways and bridges have been destroyed, factories and mines damaged, warehouses set ablaze. In one place more than forty members of a peasant's society were murdered. Whole groups of peasants moving military supplies for the army were also wiped out."

Peng Cheng then went on to gravely deplore "excessive magnanimity" – only two thousand Nationalist "traitors" had been executed in 1950 – and then came to the main business of the meeting.

This was to approve the draft of new security regulations; regulations which imposed the death sentence or life imprisonment for everything from active sabotage to offering resistance to tax collectors!

With a frankness that was indeed appalling, he said that in "democratic" China, the Government was being violently resisted by peasants who did not see the benefit of the land reforms. And then he pointed out that "if we do not suppress the wolves of American and Chiang Kai-shek's bandit groups, the security and victory of the people cannot be consolidated". "To be lenient towards them is to be cruel to the people."

The draft regulations were accordingly approved! Were Peng Cheng and the planners who had prepared the regulations merely trying to frighten the opposition, or did they mean business ? It was not long before an answer was forthcoming.

In Peking they celebrated Easter Sunday with a massacre. They made no effort to disguise the fact. Quite obviously they were out to impress "liberated" territories just what responsibilities that liberation entailed.

The *People's Daily* explained why. It said: "Only by developing publicity work on a large scale, by fully mobilising the masses and by careful leadership can the objective of liquidating counter revolutionaries be correctly attained. To suppress counter revolutionaries with Fanfares has now become the universal demand of the masses."

The trial was broadcast and, according to communist Canton reports (later quoted by the *Daily Telegraph*) the howls of the mob were actually heard by 500,000 radio listeners.

A little later, three Cantonese students showed the mettle of their new communist morality by denouncing their fathers of "counter revolutionary" crimes. The fathers they denounced were Generals Yeh-shao and Yung Kan-cheng and Dr. Chan Yun, former Chancellor of the Sun Yat-sen University!

For this they received the plaudits of the local communist daily which added that it had received 139 similar denunciations.

In June the communists announced the execution of 122 counter-revolutionaries in Siking and the sentencing of 284 in Shanghai. This followed the official announcement that 376 Nationalists had been executed in Nanking on April 29 and 50 in Hangchow on April 13.

In all these communist trials, the technique was similar. In many districts even the so-called "Peoples Courts" appeared to have fallen from favour. The new technique called for denunciation of the victim, his judgment by a howling mob and death by shooting or hanging in public.

Psychologically the process was designed to serve a twofold purpose: firstly, to terrify the average Chinese into acquiescence with everything the Government did; secondly to "blood" the crowd, to whip up a hysteria of denunciation.

Most of those who were killed at the beginning of the new Reign of Terror were former officials of Chiang, landlords and army officers.

But after the first two months, all sorts of people started to suffer.

The existing phase of the blood bath is a puzzling one. It almost appears that the very enthusiasm of the publicity given to the earlier executions may have defeated its own ends. So once again we may expect a policy switch.

This would seem to be borne out by the fact that the current (August 23) Peking *People's Daily* merely states that sentences on 418 "counter revolutionaries" were passed in Peking on August 22. It does not, for once, stress that the accused – 273 sentenced to death and 50 to suspended death sentence and life imprisonments – were tried at a mass accusation meeting. This was quoted in *The Times*.

Maybe, as Chiang's intelligence reports have hinted for some time past, the Reds feel they have succeeded too well in the "fright campaign", that fear itself may lead their people to rebel.

Or maybe on the other hand, they are just preparing the stage for an even bigger purge. But there is no doubt, whatever the procedural change, that the heads will continue to roll. But how hard have the Reds been hit so far by the operations of Chiang's men on the mainland? The answer must be considered in relation to their difficulties elsewhere.

The Korean war has already imposed an enormous strain upon the battle-scarred, rickety rolling stock of the railways. The coastal transport has been decimated by the Nationalist navy. Fuel supplies are becoming strained.

These difficulties explain the excessive preoccupation of the underground forces in damaging the Red lines of communications.

Very often the efficiency of a road depends at some point or other upon a flimsy looking wooden bridge – a bridge that can be easily destroyed by the Nationalists equipped with paraffin (one of their favourite weapons).

Even the destruction of one of these bridges entails the hold up of supplies, the necessity to conscript peasants to rebuild it.

In other words, by disposing of the minimum amount of man-power themselves, the Nationalists, repeating these simple little tricks of sabotage all over the country, force the communists to deploy forces out of all proportion to the work in hand or the strength of their enemies. Furthermore, when one bridge has been destroyed, the potent threat of others also being attacked places a yet greater strain upon the defenders. Railway bridges are rather more difficult to attack but the results from the point of view of the saboteurs are even more profitable.

Among the Nationalists left on the mainland to organise resistance were many skilled engineers. They had the specific mission of training dynamiters – one result of their activity being, it is said, the destruction of the new railway bridge across the Yung River between Nanking and Chennankwan.

This target, which the Nationalists claim it took the Reds a full month to repair, is of considerable strategic importance.

The Nationalist intelligence service has now issued a warning that the beautiful Kunming highlands in the province of Yunnan are being developed as a major base for future operations directed at Indo

China, Burma and Thailand and that the Nanking route is being used
to transport heavy artillery to the aid of Vietminh.

The word seems to have gone round among the resisters to concen-
trate on this war of communications and nerves rather than to risk
overt rebellions that would be crushed in the open.

A simple operation with pliers and a telephone wire is cut. What
happens next? The communists have not only to locate the break,
they have to provide their linesmen with armed escorts in case of
ambush. Then no sooner is the break repaired than another break
occurs further on.

It is significant that on Mao Tse-tung's long list of crimes for which
the death penalty can be imposed "bribing or suborning the civil
services or armed forces or militia to participate in rebellion" has a
prominent place.

The age old affliction of the governments of China – venality among
their underlings – is again making itself felt while a simple guarantee
of Chiang's that anyone "Returning to Righteousness" will be treated
like a long lost brother, is causing fresh harassment to the planners
of Peking.

The "Return to Righteousness" has a confusing sublety that it
typically Chinese. No mercy is shown to a Red who surrenders. But if
he "repents" and utters the laudable sentiment: "I wish to return
to righteousness", he is accepted (on certain terms) back into the
fold. He finds a second desertion back to the communists impossible,
for the partisans, it is said, make sure that his "repentance" is duly
recorded. Most gratifying recent return – to the Nationalists – was that
of the S.S. *Capella*. Flying the Panamanian flag, this 1,667 ton coaster,
laden with fertiliser, recently put into Kaohsiung.

Her Chinese crew had mutinied, and insisted that instead of proceeding as they thought to the mainland she should deliver her cargo
to Formosa. They were welcomed by a cheering crowd. The subsequent *fête* broke all records.

Apart from the purely operational rôle in the physical destruction
of communist communications and encounters with communist
troops – the guerillas, co-operate with those who are responsible for
collating information and intelligence.

Even in the days when the war on the mainland brought an ever
increasing toll of disasters for the armies of Chiang, the Nationalist
intelligence system was by no means insignificant.

Nationalist military intelligence reports shown me when I was on
the island referred to Russian technicians arriving in the South-East
coast to advise in the preparation of fortifications and air strips.

One naturally accepts with a certain degree of reservation allegations of this nature – so obviously of propaganda value. I had no

intention of inadvertently being used for that purpose. Now, however, reports have appeared to the British press quoting the communists as claiming that two hundred Russian experts have arrived at Swatow, opposite Formosa, for this very purpose.

On balance, I think the Nationalist military intelligence services can be acquitted of any charge of primarily working for the Government's propaganda organisation. In fact, if any Government ever lacked an adequate propaganda organisation, it is Chiang Kai-shek's.

If one may be so presumptuous as to plagiarise Mr. Winston Churchill–"Never has so little been done with so much"–a clever propagandist would find an inexhaustible fund of material in Formosa which could be capitalised, a radio station which is one of the finest in the Far East, and an exemplary communications service.

13. *Manila and the Huks*

IN the blazing tropical sun, appearing from the shore to be a mass of orchids and bougainvillea is an islet in a delicious cluster of colour out on the still waters of Manila Bay.

Yet behind the bush that crowds upon the flowers, tucked away in the green unstirring foliage of this most magical islet, is the monument of a battle that has probably done more to promote the United States' present attitude towards Asia than any other single factor.

For here, weed grown, flower decked, the erstwhile fortress of Corregidor–once so proud in name and now so neglectfully concealed –symbolises to many the fate of all efforts to appease a ruthless and unappeasable foe; epitomises the splendid defiance of those who fight on when the politicians fail.

Corregidor, perhaps more than the world has yet realised, was the tomb of U.S. appeasement. It was also the birthplace of "MacArthurism"–the policy that will not appease, the policy that projects the responsibility of "the white man's burden" into the twentieth century and into Asia; the policy that, condemn it how you will, brings something of the naive enthusiasm of bygone missionaries into the era of the technician and scientist.

It provides a faith. It also supplies the atom bomb!

For here in Corregidor during the torture of a community fighting against aggression, was born the American version of the Legend of the Leader.

As the multi-coloured lizards slide beneath your feet into the bomb-shattered, bush covered remnants of gun emplacements, you begin to understand some of the intense personal bitterness and suspicion that lies behind the *pronunciamiento* of this so much loved, and so much hated, so much trusted, so much suspected genius of flamboyant speech and gallant action.

And it is here, also, that you start to appreciate why the opinions of Asia regarding Chiang Kai-shek are even more intense and even more divergent than the views of the west about MacArthur!

It is important to realise this, and to appreciate that the question of Formosa's ownership is so vital to the average Filipino that it would be impossible for the Big Powers to give the place to Mao Tse-tung without encountering the archipelago's resistance.

There are 500,000 Chinese in the Philippines. There are well over one million Filipinos who claim, not without some pride, that they have Chinese blood in them.

But it is only when, from the north-eastern-most tip of the Philippines, the traveller sees the southern extremity of the disputed isle lie like some low, black threatening cloud; only when he recalls the horror that came from it upon that December noon ten years ago and sees the scars it left behind; only then does the import of Formosa's possession become clear.

For it is due to the memories of bygone battles alone that the Filipinos see danger across the north horizon, because the islands are in the throes of a cruel and pitiless fratricidal combat, none the less horrible for its being virtually ignored by the world outside. At first, the Philippine scene enchants, enthralls – if you arrive by night.

In Manila, the lights burn bright and long. Into the tropic skies the neon signs glare. The streets are alive with purring, shimmering cars, the restaurants and night clubs are full.

From nickelodeon to string band the purveyors of music ply a busy trade, and the near Castillian elegance of the women is matched by the expensive new world tailoring of the men.

The clubs are gay. Outside swing doors white shirt fronts glimmer. Inside is the pop of champagne corks, the laughter of lovely women.

For the European, the American and the rich Filipino – and there are very many rich Filipinos – life seems a thing of pleasantry and expense.

Night comes to Manila with all the grace of the tropics, the grace that conceals the treacheries and the perils; night is enhanced by the lights of Manila, the lights that show you what is meant to be shown and hide the wounds. It's all so pleasant, so attractive, you feel; so "well stocked", so solid, so pacific! And then you begin to awaken.

I soon discovered that my companions at the streamlined, chrome-edged bar of an exclusive night club carried pistols in the pockets of their tuxedos.

And when I returned to my hotel, I found that the man who drove me there was equipped with a Colt automatic; while behind the reception desk, beside a brochure advertising "scenic beauty" of the islands, lay a heavy carbine.

For today this versatile Manila–to certain income groups superficially so gay–is unique among "peacetime" cities in that it is living in a state of siege.

It is a siege maintained by a guerilla army called the Hukbalahaps (or Huks); a siege so intense that anyone driving outside the city boundaries at night is considered a suicidal maniac unless he is accompanied by an armed guard!

And when you appreciate that the threat that has come to this once so peaceful and well managed a territory is held to be sponsored by the Chinese communists, you will comprehend the aversion of its inhabitants to Mao Tse-tung and its sympathies for Chiang.

In Clark Field, the giant air base to the north of Manila, you see everywhere the flags and uniforms of the United States. While overhead, in steady sequence, bumble the long range aircraft of America, setting out for their constant patrol of the Formosan Straits and certain other destinations "unknown".

But otherwise–despite a treaty for a defensive alliance between the Philippines and the U.S.–the task of maintaining the archipelago's security remains in the hands of the Filipinos themselves, and they are by no means happy about it.

This collection of seven thousand isles and islets–in which live 19,000,000 people–does, indeed, present a promising field for communist exploitation. And, as in other places, the path of the Reds has been made easier by the ravages of war.

For the bombs and shells did not destroy Corregidor alone. The splendid Old City of Manila–with its latticed, white Spanish style houses, its magnificent cathedral, and its noble wall–is today an expanse of tumbled brick and debris, of smashed homes and gutted offices. The New City–before the war a rightful source of pride to both Americans and Filipinos on account of its well planned, modern streets and buildings–is, in the light of dawn, a place where only a hurriedly patched façade reminds one of the prestige that has departed.

In Taipeh, I have remarked, there are no beggars, no starving children. But in Manila, there are slums and poverty, tucked away on the outskirts. It is heart rending. Thousands of them today have no other home but the wreckage and the ruins. And it is so that there is probably not one family in Manila that has not suffered, through the War, the loss of at least one near relative.

The wrecks of 366 ships lie in the waters around the islands.

Some of them were sunk when the Japanese came.

For on the stroke of noon on December 8, 1941–exactly twenty-three hours after the treacherous blow that, to all intents and purposes, had completely destroyed the U.S. Air Force in the Far East, the Japanese, from Formosa, attacked Cavite naval base.

Twenty-seven four engined bombers, in leisurely unconcern, untroubled by fighter opposition, unthreatened by flak, sent full bomb loads rumbling across the docks and installations of the U.S. Asiatic Squadron.

"Within fifteen minutes"–to quote a survivor–"The base had ceased to be."

Backward and forward ploughed fresh waves of the aircraft; they bombed the docks at Manila, they bombed the fringes of the Pasig river which the city strides. Then the cruisers and destroyers of the Japanese navy concentrated a hail of fire against Lingayen Gulf (north of the Bay), and the landing barges swept ashore with 50,000 men aboard them!

Some of the 366 were sunk during the defence of Corregidor.

Before MacArthur withdrew there from Manila, American demolition parties destroyed every craft that could be of use to the invaders, while later, the stubborn garrison artillery of the island shelled Japanese craft that attempted to make a landing.

But the destruction, both ashore and afloat was later multiplied many times by the subsequent blind necessities arising from modern war, the necessities of bombing and shelling that cause so often the hands of the liberators to be unwittingly dyed in the blood of the people they are endeavouring to liberate!

In that fierce war–the war where the oil reservoirs of Pandacan flamed in December 1941 and the Japanese occupied Government buildings crashed in ruins beneath the fire of liberation, in 1945–crumbled for the Filipinos the restraints and decencies that had until then been imposed by the accommodations of civilisation.

When dawn comes over Manila, and the last gay parties drift from the night clubs home, one feels a haunting despair in the future of "democracy" when democracy can leave so many things unattended, show so little effectiveness in helping the suffering and the sick.

Across the temporary bridges that span the Pasig trudge the grey-faced homeless, the people whose lot it is after five years of "Freedom" to sleep with tarpaulins for their roofs among the cluttered bricks and broken timbers of homes that, once knocked down, nobody has attempted to rebuild.

Here and there the passing police patrols, so necessarily active in the crime infested streets at night, pass, heavily armed to their barracks, and a rest before the darkness falls again.

As the city wakes, fresh detachments of soldiers pass in convoy to one of the many battles that splutter and spark in the villages on its outskirts.

Who are these Huks, these rebels of whom the western world at present hears so little and may, to its surprise, one day hear so much?

Ostensibly, the Hukbalahaps are just one of the many "freedom" movements that spring so prolifically and so confusedly in Asia.

Originally at any rate their party platform was their refusal to acknowledge the Philippine Government's treaty with the United States.

By this treaty, concluded in 1946, the U.S.A. honoured the word she had given many years before and gave the Philippines their independence. To most it seemed a surprisingly generous gesture. To others, sidering how the political and economic structure of the archipelago had been shattered by war, it savoured of a benevolence that was almost incredibly ill-timed!

Among the Philippine people as a whole it generated much genuine goodwill and among the politicians – who had hitherto been comparatively restrained – it provoked an unpleasant scramble for place.

The Huks, among other resistance groups in the war years, had done much to harass the Japanese. It had then enjoyed a most reputable status. Constantly in touch with the American authorities, it was one of the most trusted auxiliaries of the Allies in the Pacific and, thanks to the rather opportunist backing of the U.S. – naturally more interested in the immediate defeat of Japan than in the troubles that might follow that defeat – the Huks acquired status and prestige among the islanders.

On the war's ending, and the commencement of Moscow's attacks upon the west, the name Huk began to acquire a vastly different meaning.

At the head of this private army was Luis Taruc, a lawyer, who decided to make his own bid for power.

He claimed the Treaty had not gone far enough. He stressed the clauses whereby the United States had reserved economic rights for several years to come. And he represented this natural interest of the U.S. in safeguarding her business rights as evidence of America's "Imperialist" aims in the islands!

Taruc did not disband his private army. And the crisis became inevitable. Taruc declared the Government "traitors" and bid for power with violence. The Government declared Taruc an outlaw and a "communist".

At first, it is said, they regarded his threat only as "a nuisance". In fact I heard that certain so-called astute members of the Administration believed in "the Huk menace" only in so far as it might provide further "persuasion" to induce the United States to part with yet more financial aid! Their attitude has changed today. By no stretch of the imagination could certain of the British and Americans I met in the islands—men of experience who had lived in the Philippines for years—be possibly described as "alarmists", yet they warned me it was no longer safe to motor more than ten miles out of Manila!

Taruc has now a price on his head, and it is becoming increasingly obvious that, since Chiang's collapse, he is taking his orders from a headquarters outside the Philippines.

His men have sworn to conquer the capital, and the too lavish generosity of the Americans during the war must certainly have supplied him with arms and equipment sufficient for more than his estimated "front line" force of 20,000 men.

The prospect of increased Chinese aid reaching the wily Taruc brings dismal forebodings to the Filipino administration.

Only recently several G.I.s stationed at the American air base were shot by the Huks, while scarcely a day passes without the report of some village raid where selected victims have been murdered.

Manila itself has been surrounded by a defensive belt of road blocks and check points, and everywhere the grim undertone of war throbs throughout the island.

I became conscious of how these undertones impinge upon the ordinary citizen when, with a number of British friends, I went for a trip to Corregidor. We took a launch out to the island, intending to swim off its shore.

On the way one of them was good enough to expound a little on the history of the place.

He said "When the Japanese attacked their first move was to knock out Clark Field, the American base. They sent over fifty-four two-engined bombers from Formosa. Then more bombers came. Then they attacked with 'Zero' fighters. The American base was a heap of wreckage before their planes had a chance to get airborne.

"The Filipinos have been sensitive about Formosa, and Hainan too, ever since. And their stand has become even more adamant owing to the Huk affair."

At that moment our conversation was rudely interrupted by the roar of Mustang fighter-bombers. There was something tensely urgent about their flight. They passed overhead and disappeared over the Luzon Peninsula beyond.

That evening a statement issued by the Ministry of War said that, for the first time, napalm bombs had been dropped on a Huk concentration.

Rightly or wrongly, the Philippine administration is most concerned about the future of the north Pacific, and most anxious to ensure that the Huks do not find neighbours more amenable than the ones they have at present. The recent treaty with Japan however has presented Manila with a first class diplomatic dilemma.

For MacArthur – the man whom government supporters normally admire so much – has certainly *not* pleased them in his efforts to obtain, in this northerly direction, an anti-communist ally.

And the Filipino disagreement with United States policy in this matter may well be of profound significance in the near future.

During my stay I had the opportunity of meeting Foreign Minister General Carlos Romulo, and on three different occasions he emphasised to me "There can be no excuse at all for ignoring the claims of the Philippines upon Japan".

Genial in appearance, and of jovial humour, General Romulo reputedly possesses one of the best brains in the islands and he is as noted for his eloquence at UNO as he is in his homeland.

Furthermore he is respected for his excellent record during the war, when he served as A.D.C. to MacArthur in the battles around Manila, upon Corregidor and in Bataan.

I met him first in his room at the Foreign Office, after being carefully "vetted" by his *élite* guards, who were equipped with the familiar combination of American uniforms and American "guns" – ranging from pistols to tommy guns and carbines.

Romulo was dressed in the native costume – a delicately embroidered shirt worn outside the trousers.

And, leaning back in his armchair, he put the Philippines' attitude towards the Peace Treaty as simply and concisely this:

"Look around Manila. You have seen the destruction we have suffered through the war. It is a destruction that is comparable only to that suffered by Poland. It is a destruction we suffered as a result of the Japanese – both at their hands and during the process of the Liberation. We cannot hope to assess in terms of money all our sufferings. But if ever a power had a right to be consulted in peace negotiations with another, we have that right. If ever one power had justice on its side in demanding compensation from another we have that justice.

"And we shall continue to press our claims for reparations regardless of what others may think."

Is the Philippine attitude really so inflexible as it sounds? Or would the government of the Republic – anxious for protection against a present "foe" – become a little more tolerant of a past enemy if the United States were to pay in cash its claims against that enemy?

I do not pretend to know the answer. As far as I could see, Romulo, at all events, was in deadly earnest. And yet an estrangement between the U.S.A. and the Philippines over Japan could only serve the interests of Moscow and Peking.

On the subject of Formosa Romulo was no less explicit. But I had the feeling that here the administration as a whole was on more decided ground.

He said: "We remember too well the base that Formosa provided the Japanese. We could never feel secure if it were occupied by another enemy!"

Romulo sighed and then he posed a question. He said "How could we watch with indifference the island of Formosa fall into the hands of those who would put us in peril once again?"

It was, he said, a purely rhetorical question. It was, I thought, one that might yet be of some considerable significance!

The actual technique of the terrorism employed by the Huks may be reasonably compared with that practised by the terrorists in Malaya in their operations against the British.

But the methods originally undertaken for their suppression can scarcely be said to parallel the methods employed by the British.

The reprehensible behaviour of the law enforcing agencies of the Philippines, i.e. the army, constabulary and Special Police, originally made the peasants fear their "protectors" even more than they feared the Huks.

It is to the credit of Minister Ramon Magsaysay – in charge of the armed forces – that he has largely remedied this sorry state of affairs.

He has also adopted an interesting experiment whereby he hopes to find out just how "sincerely Communist" are the rank and file of his opponents.

All bandits captured by his troops are now submitted to a thorough interrogation aimed at ascertaining whether they have in fact been "indoctrinated", or whether they are peasants dissatisfied with their lot, or whether they have joined the Huks through the congenital sense of lawlessness that affects so many of the islanders!

Magsaysay plans to rehabilitate the Huks who surrender and who, he believes, are yet likely to follow more peaceful persuasions.

He envisages organised settlements, such as those that are now being constructed in Mindenao, the largest and perhaps most fertile island in this soil-wealthy region.

Where men have become involved with the Huks for no better reason than "to better themselves" this policy, he believes, will serve the dual purpose of removing the cause of complaint and advertising to other rebels who are not communist at heart that the Government will, for the first time, give them an opportunity of becoming their own masters.

So far the policy is bearing limited fruits. There have been more desertions than usual from the Huk ranks, although on the other hand the threat itself has grown more acute.

But there are other factors apart from economic distress that combine to give Taruc such a powerful faction.

One particularly well-informed Englishman, Peter Richards, Reuter's correspondent in Manila, who has lived in the Philippines for many years gave it as his view that the Huk movement drew its strength from the congenitally rebellious tribes of central Luzon which, for as long as the Irish and Catalonians, had been a constant source of armed insurrection against whatever Government existed. He also attributed the strength of the Huk movement to the refusal of a small proportion of the population in the Luzon area to lead peaceful lives after having enjoyed three years of guerilla banditry during the Japanese occupation. It was this misdirected energy, he said, rather than any extraordinary manifestation of political consciousness, that has made them today the tools of the communists.

It is significant that the Huks–although by far the largest body and given influence and cohesion by the Marxists–are by no means the only illegal armed guerillas in the islands today.

The Americans placed in the hands of the Filipinos for the war against Japan nearly 500,000 weapons and when the war was won they did not ensure their return.

An acquaintance told me–and as he was very close to Government quarters I have no reason to disbelieve him–that over 400,000 permits to carry firearms have been issued, but that for every pistol lawfully carried one could assume two would be unlawfully carried.

Surely there are few places in the world where large placards are displayed outside cinemas, restaurants and night clubs respectfully requesting patrons to deposit their firearms with the attendant.

In one of the banks into which I went a commissionaire responsible for collecting these lethal possessions is equipped with a special office for their temporary deposit, and a tommy gun for their protection.

Violence, murder and sudden death–the toll of robberies, outrages and shooting matches in the streets of this once model capital–far outshine the most sensational of the "cow towns" of Glorious Technicolor.

And as is usual, forced gaity, municipal corruption and an incredible selfishness among the "new rich" contribute their quota to the despair of the poor. Gambling is unlawful–heaven preserve the poor citizen who stakes his miserable pesos in shanty town.

Gambling is unlawful. Yet in the two visits, of necessity short, which I paid to the best known, most publicised casino, I immediately made the acquaintance of two prominent members of the legislature, and while chatting to a newspaper proprietor I discovered that one of the most sought after "guests" was an extremely good looking and notorious lady who was alleged to have shot two of her husbands. She

was now on indefinite bail, pending an appeal against conviction on
the second shooting. Such is life – a very cheap thing in Manila, where
everything else is so dear!

The Manila picture provides to the westerner a very disturbing
aspect of democracy at work. With corruption so evident, the régime
of the much maligned Chiang Kai-shek appears virtuous by comparison, and the bewildered visitor is inclined to wonder just how cor-
ruptly the Filipinos would have run China and how honestly Chiang
could have managed 19,000,000 Filipinos!

It is certainly easy to feel virtuously appalled at the state of the
Philippine Republic today. It is certainly easy to moralise and condemn. Yet it is also, quite surprisingly, impossible not to feel a warm
affection for the wholly improbable, trigger happy, ruinous and immoral place. For the Filipinos have lost so much, and the very corruption of their cities is the corruption that follows the death of
cities.

Not that something should not be done about it. Something *must*
be done. Otherwise, Red Formosa or no, there will one day most
certainly be a Red Luzon.

So far the United States cannot be accused of parsimony in answer-
ing the island's repeated calls for aid. It is not the fault of the Americans
that over two billions of good U.S. dollars, advanced during the past
three or four year, have not yielded more noteworthy results.

But, ironically, it would appear that not until the communists – or
Huks or bandits or patriots – are suppressed can the abuses which
encourage insurrections be corrected.

They say that when MacArthur's bloody jungle-stained soldiers
fought their way back to Bataan the Manila hotels waited for the invaders with lights ablaze and dance music playing.

In evening dress, American and British men and women, as well as
the Filipinos, waltzed, quick stepped and tangoed as the guns thun-
dered around the city's suburbs. Because they did not seem to heed
their doom the cursing, bewildered G.I.s thought they did not know
of it, or knowing of it, cared even less!

Today the guns are rumbling again, and the battle against communism would appear to require more formidable a support than is
provided by the fusillades of champagne corks in the night clubs of
Manila!

Yet, as in the war against the Japs, the war in which because they
could not see just how they could help, they chose (at its commencement only) to ignore, even the petted few are far from oblivious to the
menace.

And that one day they will display against the communists some of
the courage and common sense that they later used against the Japanese

is the belief of all who know the island. Men like Romulo, men like Magsaysay may have their faults, but cowardice or lack of foresight are not among them.

At the moment they are pursuing the policy of the military objective, the physical war to end the Huks. But later, as they realise only too well, they must tackle the moral war as well.

In this particular task the Philippine bosses will find some oddly assorted but very valuable allies.

For Big Business is realising very rapidly the dangers that may be caused by a system that, ostensibly in its interests, imposes intolerable burdens upon the poor. The Church, in a remarkably efficient campaign, is taking a stand on behalf of what the west would call the Rights of Labour and what the Vatican calls Social Justice. Not that the two, except in their opposition to communism, always agree! Far from it.

Two Jesuit priests have organised labour away from the communists and the racketeers. At the same time they are preaching doctrines, that, were it not for their soutanes, would easily earn for them the classification of "Reds"!

As a matter of principle they have led a strike against the most powerful industrial empire in the Philippines, while their "revolutionary" demands for the payment of a living wage to the workers are becoming daily more pressing to the island's industrialists.

Their intervention is noteworthy because the Catholic Church had a deep traditional and general hold on the populace and yet by experience of fifty years of other religions it suffered none of the odium attached to an established Church, while the Spanish régime formed an integral part of the island's culture and tradition. I met one of these Jesuits over dinner which stretched well into the night. Father Hogan, born in Chicago and of Liverpool Irish extraction, is a huge man physically. He impressed me as a man who also thinks big. After the blatant frivolities of the "upper strata" it was refreshing to find someone who had a policy, someone who actually cared about the millions for whom the city of "gaiety" is the city of despair!

I think, unless a Huk bullet removes the Good Father, we will be hearing more of him in the days ahead.

We will also be hearing a lot more of the almost legendary Colonel Andres Soriano.

Soriano ranks among America's reputed "wealthiest ten", with prosperous breweries in the States, Hong Kong and Manila. He showed me a bottle factory which he controls, one of the newest of its kind in the world and probably the largest. Soriano is also the "power behind the throne" of the Philippine Air Lines, now ninth among the world's air fleets in terms of flying miles, and the only air line that flies from London direct to Manila and Formosa. He also owns gold mines which are flourishing.

Soriano, although in a very different manner from Father Hogan, is also doing something to bring back some degree of prosperity to the Philippines.

He brings to his job the enthusiasm and drive of the American—is an ideal employer, works hard himself and insists on others working—plays hard and likes his employees to play hard too. He regards the sweated labour concept as "inefficient", leads off instead with bonuses and initiatives. But he is said, by virtue of the extent of his varied interests, to be too great a power for the Government.

Between the humanitarianism of Father Hogan and the efficiency of this industrial emperor a wide gap yawns. Yet the final objective is similar—a prosperous Philippines that, by its prosperity, will make communism unreceptive.

If it is achieved it will be through the adventurous industrialism of the west, and through the age old spiritual urges of the Church.

In the meantime even the most idealistic Filipinos turn anxious eyes towards the north.

For they believe that what happens to Formosa tomorrow may decide the fate of Manila the day after.

14. *The rôle of Japan*

WHEN Japan signed the articles of surrender in September, 1945, on the deck of an American battleship in Tokyo Bay, her fortunes were at their nadir and no one could possibly have foreseen her return to the comity of nations within six years.

Within seven days of the signing of the surrender, General MacArthur received by special courier, written confirmation of the United States initial post-surrender policy for Japan. It included this paragraph in the section of "Ultimate Objectives".

"The authority of the militarists and the influence of militarism will be totally eliminated from Japan's political, economic and social life. Institutions expressive of the spirit of militarism and aggression will be vigorously suppressed."

In view of present developments comment seems superfluous.

If the Philippines have good cause to apprehend the Hukbalahaps and the extension of Chinese communism through south-east Asia with its big and growing Chinese populations, the young Republic is equally concerned with the inevitable political and military resurgence of Japan. The loyalty of the Chinese communities to their countries of adoption is tenuous, but Japanese economic aims are obvious and practicable; to dominate the Far East.

But politics and war are extensions of economics and it is this cold reasoning that has precipitated the three regional security pacts between the United States and the Philippines, the United States and Australia, and the United States and New Zealand.

The signing of the Security Pact by President Truman and President Quirino and General Romulo in the same hall in Washington as the Atlantic Pact in April, 1945, was described by President Quirino as the "end of the beginning" and he added that they had reached the first milestone on the road towards the enduring security of the Pacific area.

It had been my good fortune whilst in Manila to meet one of the Australian Government representatives. It struck me at the time that the Australian mission might be rather more of a military than a diplomatic or commercial nature and certainly the personnel making up the mission were well qualified to act as military observers.

The U.S. Security Pacts with Australia and New Zealand are evidence that the Dominions are no less concerned with Japan's possible return to power than the Philippine Republic. The southern spread of communism through Malaya and Indo-China is equally feared.

For more than fifty years it has been Australia's plea that what is the "Far East" to London and New York is the "Near North" to Australia.

Australian statesmen have never minced words about their feelings towards what they regard as a permanent threat as old as their history.

Successive Australian Ministers of External Affairs have reiterated the aims of their foreign policy the fundamentals of which are the preservation of the Australian way of life and the preservation of peace. They stress that inseparable from these aims is the closest co-operation within the British Commonwealth and with the United States of America and other friendly nations.

The Australians have warned that since the end of the war there has been a shift of potential aggression from the European to the Asian area and that it is basically necessary in considering Australian viewpoint to remember that the country is situated in the south-west corner of the Pacific with the outlying islands of the Asian continent almost touching their own territories of New Guinea and Papua.

Mr. P. C. Spender, discussed China's present leaders and repeated what is generally felt not only by his countrymen but also by New Zealanders and, indeed, most people who have considered the possible march of events in south-east Asia.

"There are some," said Mr. Spender, and I think he included himself, "who believe that China's present leaders may concern themselves insufficiently with the urgent internal organisation of their own country and may be intent on aggression into other areas across China's present borders, in which event the present pattern which developed in Europe could develop in south-east Asia. But even without actually invading neighbour States or engaging in open intimidation of them, China could either in order to secure markets and raw materials, or as part of communist aims, without much expenditure of resources, foment disaffection and disorder in other countries. The Chinese have a ready-made instrument in the form of the many millions of Chinese scattered throughout all countries of south-east Asia. It has long been Chinese Government policy to retain every possible influence among communities of overseas Chinese, and the communists will undoubtedly try to use for their own purposes these strong ties with the Chinese homeland."

Other Australians have said that above all, any interference with the State of Vietnam by China should be regarded with the deepest concern. They assert that if communism prevails and Vietnam comes under the heel of communist China, Malaya is in danger of being outflanked and it, together with Thailand, Burma and Indonesia will become the next direct object of further communist activities.

Without wishing to labour the Australian attitude, it is certainly desirable to emphasise that the Australians are near to the scene but not too near to lose the sense of proportion. No amount of well meaning tolerance on the part of the British Foreign office towards Chinese intransigence, no lip service about common heritage and stock, will alter Australia's attitude.

Australia regards the integrity of the areas to her north as a matter of primary concern to her own safety and continued existence. In this strategic conception Formosa's rôle is the same to the Australian "bloc" as to the American. If Formosa is threatened, the United States, the Philippine Republic and Australia must be equally concerned and New Zealand only slightly less so.

Here one is unavoidably steered towards ice which is extremely thin. In Sydney and Melbourne the Generalissimo has his Consuls General, Mr. L. M. Wang and Mr. T. W. Liu and in Wellington, Mr. Wang Seng. In Ottawa an Ambassador, Mr. Li Chih, represents the Nationalist Government and Mr. Liu Chih is accredited in Johannesburg as Consul General.

Mr. Nehru whose country turned to Chiang Kai-shek for moral support in its struggle to throw off the British Raj, has dropped the hand of friendship which was so generously and opportunely proffered. India alone of the countries associated in the Commonwealth of Nations has an Ambassador in Peking, the other Dominions, Pakistan,

Ceylon as well as the United Kingdom have gained little or nothing by following the normal course of diplomatic usage.

A very close friend of Chiang Kai-shek's who is also in high office told me that in retrospect not only was the help given to Nehru a mistaken policy but its effect was to make it impossible for Mr. Winston Churchill ever to forgive Chiang Kai-shek.

The significance of this belief may have no bearing on future events unless the British electorate return a party to power which will march in step with the United States and the Dominions as a matter of high policy. In that event, Chiang's forebodings, if correct, could be serious and unhappy.

The British position with regard to Formosa is invidious and fraught with embarrassment. First and foremost there is a split on a matter of major importance in Imperial affairs at a time when unity was never more desirable.

It is only a matter of time before Formosa becomes the subject of acrimonious debate between east and west. When that occasion arises it will require an extraordinary feat of diplomatic contortion to disguise the divergence of British views with those of the older Dominions, whose interest in Formosa is anything but academic.

The political and military alignment in the Pacific with diminished British influence has not gone unnoticed and could become a domestic issue of a nature in which the main point may be lost sight in irrelevant and bitter arguments.

In the fine old Spanish fort of San Domingo at Tamsui built in 1629, Robert Swinhoe established the first British Consulate, in fact the first consulate in Formosa. That was in July, 1861, by which time Jardine, Matheson and other British and American firms were already importing opium for re-export to the mainland and exporting rice, sugar and camphor.

The fort stands on the top of a hill and from its turret the Union Jack flies every day of the year.

Its walls are more than five feet thick at the base and are painted an attractive reddish-brown marred only by the unsightly slogans painted, or rather daubed on, in black paint by exuberant students during anti-British riots in 1950, when the flag was torn down. The Consular staff is somewhat larger than one would expect to find in a small island whose sovereignty is in dispute and whose present rulers must officially be regarded by the Consulate staff as trespassers.

It cannot be a particularly comfortable post specially as most of the consular work involves formal dealings with the local government and not with individual British subjects.

By happy accident the personnel at the Consulate and the vice-

Consulate at Taipeh are the type which an advertisement in *The Times* might describe as "good mixers". By sheer personality they have been able so far literally to keep the flag flying despite the fact that the flag of the Kuomintang was arbitrarily pulled down at the Chinese Embassy at Langham Place in London.

It says a great deal for the tolerance of Chiang Kai-shek's government that this anomalous state of affairs is allowed to continue. It is a pleasant commentary that good sense and good manners continue to overcome a disagreeable position. The difficult situation is aggravated, as has already been mentioned, by the uncompromising attitude of Hong Kong towards Chinese wishing to visit the colony and inelastic interpretation of rules and orders so that even the Consulate is kept ludicrously short of petrol.

A barrister of international repute enjoying the highest honour the English Bar can bestow, told me that it would be technically possible for the Kuomingtang to have a Consulate in Great Britain as distinct from an Embassy. From his researches he was satisfied that whatever instrument accords this privilege had not been rescinded. An enquiry, however, put to the Foreign Office by an interested party on the hypothetical question as to how a Kuomintang approach would be received brought only churlish responses which presumably reflects current official opinion.

As a result of this situation in which Britain recognises Peking while in return Peking merely adds insult to injury, and Taipeh has its seat at the United Nations and Peking has not, something analogous to a legal fiction has grown up between the British Consulate and the Government in Taipeh.

When, for instance, a ship flying the British flag is apprehended, and escorted into Keelung its manifests are checked with the cargo. Unfortunately, on several occasions the manifests have misrepresented the true nature of the cargo and if it is classified as strategic commodities destined for communist China, then the cargo is forfeited and the ship proceeds on its way, without the cargo. The Consulate in the course of its normal duties requests details on behalf of the owner and the insurers, invariably Lloyd's.

But the Consul representing the British cannot make representations, much less protest, to the Foreign Office of a Government which it no longer recognises. At this difficult juncture the compromise is set in motion—the Nationalist Government is side-stepped and the ubiquitous Mr. K. C. Wu is approached in his capacity as Governor of Taiwan which according to the Nationalists, is a province of China. Even the communists regard it as a province. And so, the questions and answers are placed on record almost as if diplomatic relations did exist.

As extraordinary and as humiliating as this may be an even stranger situation exists with regard to liaison with the armed forces of Great Britain and Nationalist China.

The vice-Consulate in Taipeh occupies two rooms in the office of the Government Spokesman. The day after I arrived I called there to register and was amazed to read on a plate outside: "Royal Naval Liaison Officer."

In due course I was the guest of the "Liaison Officer" a Lieutenant-Commander, R.N. His staff included a Leading Writer and a Chinese interpreter; his office was a large room complete with charts on the wall and a safe. But neither the Lieutenant Commander nor the Leading Writer wore uniform and they were, in fact, forbidden to do so. Also, in order to keep up the illusion that they were not in the island at all excepting in the telephone directory and on the name plate outside the office Lt. Commander J. A. Davidson (there is no point in not mentioning his name), had no official access to the naval base or to Admiral Kwei, the Commander in Chief, or to the officers in his navy.

It was quite delightful, therefore, to be one of thirty or forty guests in Davidson's house at a party in which the civilians were heavily outnumbered by Chinese naval officers all of whom spoke excellent English and talked about their days at Greenwich and later on active service with the Royal Navy. Naturally, I never asked Davidson what reason the Lords of the Admiralty had for maintaining an office in such peculiar circumstances, obviously at considerable expense because of the high cost of living. I think the British taxpayer was getting value for his money if only on account of the goodwill which the average Royal Naval officer has a faculty for cultivating.

Now, far away from the enigmatic scene of Formosa I have the greatest regret that I was unable to fly on to Japan which would, after all, only have taken half a day. Too late I learned that the Premier, Mr. Shigeru Yoshida had expressed a willingness to see me for an "off the record" discussion. He was an old friend of my father who knew him whilst he was Consul-General at Tientsin from 1922 to 1925. I met him there and later in London when he was Ambassador from 1936 to 1938.

Mr. Yoshida could have guided me, had he so wished, in my reasoning that the Far East in general will soon be marching to the tune of Tokyo.

The Japanese and Chinese differ greatly in their temperaments and in their history; nevertheless their cultural affinities and geography bring them close to each other.

Basically China can supply the raw materials essential to Japanese industry; cotton, coal, iron, and so on. In return, because of her excessively low production costs, Japan can supply the bottomless

Chinese market on her doorstep with goods at a price which Chinese manufacturers will not be able to lower until China has experienced some decades of political stability.

We do not sufficiently appreciate that events move slowly in the East. The sagacious Oriental boxes cleverly. He prefers to feint, to bargain, to find another way round, to seek a compromise rather than to deliver an impolite ultimatum.

The notorious "Twenty-One Demands" of 1915 by Japan were the aberration of a power drunk military caucus. It was not the typical Japanese way of obtaining an object.

So far as China and Japan are concerned no situation concerning these countries, whether jointly or separately, is ever "hopeless" so long as open hostilities can be averted. Moreover, I believe that Taipeh is in much closer touch with Tokyo than is generally realised and that if a satisfactory formula is worked out, Chiang Kai-shek's sojourn in Japan during his early days will show handsome dividends.

A *rapprochement* has already been made and so long as Japanese eyes look west and south-west, and not south and south-east, Sino-Japanese collaborations will receive the support of the Western allies.

The future of the Far East may well be determined in Taipeh and Tokyo and I venture to say that already the initiative has shifted from Moscow and Peking, from that tremendous land mass that is China and Russia to those little islands of destiny.

FORMOSA

Chronological Outline

(A.D. 605-1951)

Discovery by China

605 A.D. Chinese recorded (unsuccessful) expeditions to force natives of Taiwan, of proto-Malay stock, to acknowledge Chinese

611 A.D. suzerainty.

Late 12th century Natives from Taiwan raided the Fukien (China) coast apparently seeking iron.

1367 Expedition and governor sent to Pescadores, which were to be administered as part of Tung An prefecture. No further mention for two centuries.

1430 Chinese began recording history of Taiwan. Chinese official, eunuch Wan San-ho, driven ashore by storm during voyage homeward from Siam. Chinese explorations for East Coast gold reported to have been unsuccessful.

Japanese and Chinese Settlements

Late 15th century Chinese pirate headquarters on South Formosa; Japanese pirate headquarters on North Formosa (Keelung).

1592 "The trade thus commenced by the pirates was regarded by the (Japanese) nation with hope and finally authorised by the Government. In 1592, merchants of Nagasaki, Kyoto, and Sakai, having obtained special government licences, opened head offices in Formosa, which island was then recognised as the haunt of pirates. These merchants gave the belt of land from Takow to Anping, the name of Takasago, because the scenery was so much like that to be found at Takasago in Harima (Japan). The vast profits of their trade were made use of by the politicians in Hideyoshi's Cabinet." (Takekoshi, p. 52.)

Japanese settlement near Anping a centre for trade to Macao, Annam, Luzon (P.R.), Java. Served as intermediate station for China trade which was prescribed as direct intercourse.

1603 Dutch Admiral Van Warwijk, while attacking Macao (Portuguese) forced to take shelter in Pescadores, realised strategic advantages.

1609 "In 1609, after Iyehisa Shimazu had subjugated Loochoo, the

Shogun Iyeyasu (Tokugawa) sent an envoy to Formosa and invited the inhabitants to become his subjects, but as they had no ruler the mission proved fruitless." (Takekoshi, p. 53.)

1615 Toan Murayama, Governor of Nagasaki, "attempted conquest of the island with his own soldiers, but was defeated. On his return to Japan he was executed by order of the Government." (Takekoshi, p. 53.) Force of 3,000-4,000 men engaged.

Dutch Occupation

1620 Dutch ship wrecked near Tainan. Dutch received permission from Japanese settlement to build a small depot. By subterfuge a large grant of land was secured.

1622 Dutch fleet captured the Pescadores, built fort, using forced labour. Of 1,500 local Chinese employed, 1,300 died; many sent to Batavia as slaves for sale there. Dutch made Pescadores a base for fleet operations against Portuguese at Macao. Six warships, 2,000 soldiers on station.

1623 Chinese officials of Fukien Province opened negotiations, arranged for removal of Dutch from Pescadores to Taiwan, which the Chinese "ceded". A trading station established, Dutch fort in the Pescadores destroyed and guns removed to settlement at Anping.

1623 Chinese population on Formosa estimated to have been about 25,000. Japanese pirate-traders fewer in number; settled further north on coast.

1624 Sugar one of the principal items of export. Dutch attempted to impose export duty on rice and sugar, with consequent serious friction with Chinese and Japanese.

1624 Cheng Ch'eng-kung (Tei Sei Ko; Koxinga) born. Son of Japanese mother by a nominally Christian Chinese migrant father, native of Fukien Province, who had served Portuguese at Macao, then removed to Hirado, Japan, and became vastly rich trader, master of fleet of 3,000 junks.

Small Japanese settlement handled large trade. New Dutch rivals capitalised on opportunity to handle local products locally between seasonal European shipping and to be self-sufficient in foodstuffs.

Spanish Settlement, North Formosa

1626 *May* 10 Spanish landed at Keelung, established fort of Santissimus Trinidad.

1626-1642 Spanish Dominican mission active at North Formosa. Spanish constructed Fort of San Salvador at Keelung. Permanent colonial government set up.

1627 Trouble between Dutch and Japanese settlements flared; Japanese pirate Hamada Yahei, of Nagasaki, attempted violence but was driven off. Vowed to "avenge" insults to Japanese.

DATE	EVENT
	Although Dutch ships were always searched and arms taken off upon entry at any Japanese port, the Japanese refused the same treatment when their ships entered the Dutch port of Anping. In consideration of Dutch interests at Nagasaki, the local governor was forced to be lenient.
1628	Hamada returned and by treacherous ruse seized the person of Governor Van Nuyts. Hostages were seized, carried off to Japan. Dutch forced to pay ransoms etc. Hostages, including Van Nuyts' son, languished, died in Japanese prisons. Japanese forced to quit the island entirely. Fort Providentia, Fort Zelandia constructed at Anping and Tainan (then called Taiwan).
1629	Spanish construct Fort San Domingo at Tamsui (now the British Consulate.
ca. 1630	First Chinese rebellion against Dutch rule. Attack on colony repulsed by Dutch with help of about 2,000 Christian aborigines.
1636	First school on Formosa established by Robert Junius. Seventy boys taught romanised version of local aborigine dialect.
1639	Five schools open; 485 boys enrolled as students.
1640	Dutch attempted to dislodge Spanish from North Formosa. First attack unsuccessful.
1641	Dutch sent ultimatum to Spanish at Keelung.
1642	*August.* Second Dutch expedition against Spanish. Tamsui taken. Crises in China during Manchu invasion from the north drove many people to Formosa, some as Ming loyalists, some merely as refugees in economic distress.
1650	At least 36,000 individual hunting licences alone issued by Dutch to Chinese and few aborignes.
1651	Koxinga, with 25,000 troops, attacked the Dutch settlement via the Pescadores. European settlement of 600, with a garrison of 2,200 men.
1662	Dutch capitulated. Koxinga offered generous terms which were accepted.

Koxinga's Kingdom Established

DATE	EVENT
1662	Koxinga established court as an expatriate Ming loyalist and as independent sovereign at Anping.
1662	Dutch Admiral Bort, with 12 ships, attempted to retake Formosa.
1662	*May* 9. Koxinga died. Succeeded by son Cheng Ching.
1663	Dutch repeated attack, with 16 ships, 1,380 sailors and 1,234 soldiers. Keelung captured and left under Captain de Bitter and 200 men.
1663	Salt manufacturing and land development encouraged by Cheng Ching.
1668	Keelung finally abandoned by the Dutch as an unprofitable station.

DATE	EVENT
1682	Cheng Ching, second ruler of dynasty, dies. Succeeded by 12-year old son Cheng Ko-shung.

Formosa Conquered by Manchu Forces

1683	Manchu fleet occupied Pescadores, conquered Formosa. *July* 19. Formosan court capitulated to Peking Government. Boy king proceeded to Peking to receive investiture as "sea-Quelling Duke." (Hai Ching Kung).
1683	Formosa became a prefecture of Fukien Province. Divided into

     1. Three hsien or districts under civil magistrates
         a. Choolo (?)   (northwest)
         b. Taiwan   (south central)
         c. Fangshan   (southwest)
     2. One *ting* or maritime division
         a. Pangho, in the Pescadores
Schools established in the districts. Triennial exams. A higher school, the graduates of which were to be given preferment in government posts.

1696	First rebellion against Manchu régime, Hozan district suppressed.
1701	Rebellion led by Liu Chow (Ryu Kya-ku) in Kagi area. Rebel leader captured.
1714-15	Entire island mapped by Jesuit missionaries de Mialla, Regis and Hinderer, dispatched by the Court at Peking. Camphor production made a government monopoly; exact date unknown.
1720	More than 200 executed for violating camphor monopoly laws.
1722	Rebellion of Chu Yih-kwei, who declared independence from the Chinese government, had himself enthroned and named his era Yang-ho (Eiwa). Followers cut off their queues to indicate end of submission to Manchu authority. Rebellion based on reaction to camphor trade restrictions. Rebellion put down by 22,000 Imperial troops sent over from mainland. Some suggestion of bribery and betrayal. Chu taken captive to Peking and there crucified.
1722	Revision of administrative districts after Rebellion. New prefecture, Changhwa (Shoka) created from northern part of Chulu. Tamsui made a *ting*.
1723	Great typhoon.
1727	Government Salt Monopoly established. Much contraband production and trade, however.
1730-1770	Constant inter-clan struggles throughout the island.
1731	Aborigine Rebellion, Taikosei and Shoka districts.
1731	Formosan-Chinese Rebellion, led by Wu Fu-sing (Go Fukusei) against the Imperial Chinese government, Hozan area.
1770	Rebellion against the Government led by Hong Chau (Okyo), Hozan area.

DATE	EVENT
1771	Count de Benyowsky attempted to create settlement on the east coast and to attract support of European Governments.
1782	Unparalleled storm devastated west coast settlements.
1784	Lin Shoan-wen (Lin So-bun), a native of Chwangchou, arrived. Founded secret society Tei Ti Fui (Ten Shigai).
1786	Great Rebellion, which grew out of clan feuds, with resentment toward government decisions in favour of one party or the other. Principally rivalry between Chuan-Chou (Senshu) and Changehou (Shoshu) clans.
	(M. de Grammont, in letter of 1789 states "China lost at least 100,000 men in attempting to put down this rebellion cost at 2,000,000 taels.")
1787	Formosa visited by La Perouse.
1787	Lin Shoan-wen raised rebellion, Shoka area, captured northern half of island, set up new government. Named era Shun Tien (Jun Ten).
	Imperial troops sent over from Mainland. Rebellion put down after nine months struggle.
1795	Rebellion raised by Chien Chu-chuan (Chin Shu-zen), native of Huzan who removed his headquatrers to north to rouse old members of secret society in the Shoka area.
1805	Pirate Tsah Ken (Sai Ken) landed at Tamsui, but was driven out by Imperial troops.
	Old clan rivalries flared up. The northern districts in turmoil. *Tsah Ken* sailed south, to stir up rebellion in districts about Hozan and Toko.
	Imperial troops sent from China to restore order.
1808	Pirate Tsu Pun (Shifun), a Cantonese, set up headquarters at Suo. Made attacks across the mountains into the northern settlements. Driven out by Imperial troops sent around the coast.
1809	Civil war generally among the clans.
1811	Rebellion against the government, led by a fortune teller, among others. Quickly suppressed.
1824	A rebellion, leader unnamed, in the Hozan district.

European Contacts Renewed

1824	First efforts by Europeans to reopen trade since the expulsion of the Dutch in 1662. The *Jamesina* and the *Merope*, which surveyed Keelung Harbour in July.
1826	Clan fighting spread around Chuko (Tionkan) until Imperial troops had to suppress it.
1827	The ship *Dhaulle* coasted up the west coast, stopped at Keelung and coasted down the east shores.
1830-33	Uprisings and civil warfare having origins in land disputes; but enlarging into general Hakka vs. Fukienese struggle. The capital city (Tainan) lost to the insurgents, one clan mustering

DATE	EVENT
	30,000 troops. Troops levied in south China province to cross and suppress the rebellion against authority.
	Commissioners and troops dispatched by Emperor from Peking. Attempts to revise administration and lax discipline which had allowed the regular garrison of 20,000 troops to mix in trade, and local affairs.
1832	The ship *Lord Amhurst* visited the West coast.
1833	Canton Register indicate that annually more than twenty junks carried Formosan sugar to Tientsin.
1833	British traders first suggest to their government that Formosa be taken as a British possession.
	From 1833 to 1840 the choice of a new British Far Eastern station lay among Chusan and Ningpo, Formosa and Hong Kong.
1834	Serious outbreak of inter-clan warfare in Hozan area.
1835	Local Tamsui literati petitioned Government to forbid coal mining through fear of "geomantic" consequences, i.e. disturbing dragons.
1841	British ships *Nerbudda* and *Ann* wrecked. Officers with servants, abandoned 240 British Indian subjects to fate on *Nerbudda*. All who reached shore from both vessels and including Europeans, plundered and imprisoned for 11 months. 87 died through ill treatment, 197 executed at Tainan (Aug. 13, 1842), 10 sent to Peking for execution. One European survived.
	"When the news of the outrage reached the British world, excitement was roused to fever heat. . . ." War or further indemnities demanded (Davidson 107).
1842	Clan warfare. Chuan-chou versus Chang-chou.
1847	Third petition and prohibition of coal mining, North Formosa.
1848	Ship *Kelpie* lost. Report that her passengers were sold into slavery on the island; included Thomas Nye (American) and Thomas Smith (British).
1849	Americans visited Keelung, examined coal mines, advocated opening and development as coaling station.
1850	British plenipotentiary asked the Chinese Government to open the Keelung coal deposits, offering British co-operation. Refused by Peking.
1850-60	More than 150 foreign vessels wrecked on west coast. More than 30 plundered by Formosan pirates. More than 1,000 lives lost.
1850	Ship *Larpent* lost (British).
1851	Three survivors of *Larpent* wreck, saved, reveal slavery.
1851	Formosa visited by Sir Harry Parkes, investigating reports of slavery.
1851-52	Americans on the China coast urged the American Minister to China and other American officials in Washington to investigate rumours of slavery of Occidentals on Formosa. No action

DATE	EVENT
	taken. Private inquiries made and some inquiries through local officials.
1852	Clan wars in four areas. Hozan and Kagi seized by insurgents.
1853	Gideon Nye, U.S. Trader on China coast, urged U.S. government to seize and colonise south and east coasts as a measure of security for the rapidly growing U.S. trade in China waters. Peter Parker, U.S. Commissioner to China, agreed with Nye on advisability of seizure of part of Formosa.
1853	Serious warfare among clans at Chureki and Kagi.
1854	Two foreign (?British) ships anchored at Keelung. Coal supplies dug out by ships' crew. Chinese government protested violation of rights. Sir Harry Parkes, then British Consul at Amoy, reported on convenience of such a coal supply for ships from afar, available at a good anchorage.
1854	U.S.S. *Macedonian* sent from Perry's squadron to search for foreign captives rumoured to be on Formosa. Slipshod inquiry conducted by Captain Abbot.
1854	Attempted rebellions against Chinese government at Hozan and Kagi.
1854	Chinese attempted to extend settlement down the east coast but receive no help from the Chinese government.

Era of Foreign Trade

1855	An American, W. M. Robinet of Hong Kong, opened trade with Formosa, first foreigner to do so in modern times (Davidson 400-401).
ca. 1855	Tamsui (Hobe) plundered by populace in rebellions protest against oppressive government. American trader-adventurer named Mooney settled in Takao on a hulk which he used as receiving ship for opium.
1858	British Government dispatched warship *Inflexible* to Formosa to search for shipwrecked foreigners. Swinhoe went along as interpreter.
1858	Further Chinese attempts to push settlements down east coast. Chinese Government indifferent.
1858	Formosa camphor trade engaged in by Jardine, Matheson and Co., and Dent and Company, out of Hong Kong. Mr. Reid, American and Count Putiatine, Russian, persuaded Peking Government to open port of Taiwan (Anping) to foreign trade.
1859	Spanish Dominican Missions re-established on Formosa.
1860	Jardine, Matheson and Co. and Dent and Co. set up first permanent establishments on Formosa.
1860-1870	Jardine, Matheson and Dent engaged in opium import to Formosa, rice, sugar and camphor export.
ca. 1860	France and Germany considered desirability of taking Formosa.

DATE	EVENT
1860	Prussian transport *Elbe* visited South Formosa. Landing party set upon by savages. Commander ordered aborigine's villages destroyed.
	Robert Swinhoe, British, appointed first vice-consul at Taiwan George C. P. Braune, assistant.
	English and French treaties, ratified at end of war, opened Taiwan the French to be at Tamsui 1860, at Keelung 1861.
1861	Robert Swinhoe wrote of Formosan teas; sent samples to various tea inspectors.
1861	*July.* Swinhoe, first British consular representative, took up residence at Tainan, later moved to Hobe (Tamsui).
	Camphor monopoly shared between Jardine, Matheson and Dent and Co.
1861	Rebellions against new taxes imposed by Chinese government General riot in protest of $2\frac{1}{2}\%$ likin tax. Colonists would not submit to a tax measure designed to finance a campaign to suppress rebellions on the mainland.
1862	Natives of Hobe (Tamsui) threaten builders of house for Dent and Co. Agent attacked. British land force of Lascars to enforce punishment of culprits.
1862	Exhibit of Formosan produce at Great International Exhibition, London, 1862.
	Dent and Co. and Jardines settled at Hobe.
1863	American vessel *Lucky Star* wrecked on west coast. Captain, wife and crew harshly treated and released only by payment of ransom by foreigners in charge of the Customs.
1863	Imperial Chinese Maritime Customs opened office at Tamsui. First Commissioner Mr. Howell (British); Second Commissioner Mr. Schenck, (American).
1864	French engineer M. Dupont, employed by Foochow arsenal made survey of Keelung coal districts. Tamsui and Foochow commissioners of customs petitioned that they be developed officially. Petition denied.
1864	*May.* Imperial customs office opened at Takao. Mr. Williams Maxwell in charge.
	British obtain recognition of Takao as an open port.
	John Dodd, trader, established himself on the island.
1864	*December.* S.S. *Elfin* arrived in Formosa from Yokohama with general cargo.
1865	*January.* S.S. *Elfin* returned to Yokohama with cargo of Formosan goods.
1865	Branch office of Takao Customs opened at Anping; W. A. Pickering in charge.
1865	English Presbyterian Mission established by Dr. Maxwell at Tainan.
1865	Rivalry among foreign firms and private wars among

Formosan-Chinese camphor producers complicated relations with local government.

Questions brought before British and American Governments for solution.

Companies engaged in camphor trade included:
    Jardine, Matheson & Co., Dent & Co., MacPhail & Co. at Takao (British), James Milisch & Co. (German), Field, Hastus & Co. (American), Dent & Co. (British) at Tamsui and Keelung.

Swinhoe made a full Consul.

Tamsui and Takao finally opened to foreign residence.

British landed armed forces at Tamsui to enforce clearance of landmark.

John Dodd, trader, investigated tea growing, prepared to purchase tea plants and to set out plantations.

American ship *Rockway* taken by pirates off north shore.

1866   John Dodd secured tea plants from Amoy district to loan out to local planters near Tamsui. Also leased tract of land on savage aboriginal territory borders 20 miles south-east of Koro with intent to exploit the petroleum known to be there. The local mandarins, interfering, forced him to abandon project.

1866   Pirate raids on Anping, from pirate settlement named Koksikong, situated five miles north of Tainan. Three days of rioting and robbery.

December. Naval forces landed at Keelung to rescue the Chinese servant of an officer.

Naval Forces landed to punish natives who had plundered a foreign wreck.

1867   Aborigines refuse to treat with the Chinese or to promise them security such as they agreed to extend to the whites at the south.

June. American ships *Hartford* and *Wyoming* landed 181 officers, sailors and marines in attempt to find captive foreigners, if any, and to reach an agreement with the natives. Unsuccessful.

General Le Gendre, consul at Amoy, visited Tainan where the local officials again disavowed authority over or responsibility for aborigine territory and the East Coast.

1867   Admiral Bell, of the U.S. East Asia fleet, proposed that only assurance of control of aborigines and pirates would be seizure of East Formosa by some powerful ally of the U.S. He urged China to take it. No results.

1867   *March* 9. American ship *Rover* wrecked. Captain, his wife, and crew put ashore in boats. All but one murdered by aborigines. Incident reported to American and British Minister at Peking.

March 26. British naval ship *Cormorant* went to search for survivors.

September. Le Gendre accompanied by a Frenchman M. Joseph

M

| DATE | EVENT |

Bernare and a considerable Chinese force in the Chinese (Amoy) Viceroy's ship, made second visit to Taiwan.

To the discomfiture of local officials, Le Gendre insisted that the Viceroy's orders for a punitive expedition be carried out.

Le Gendre further insisted that General Liu, commander in the south, erect and maintain a fortified observatory. This was a form of compulsion but helped China extend and establish her authority.

Le Gendre visited the territory of the Botan tribe, negotiated with Tokitok, its chief, and secured agreement for co-operation with shipwrecked castaways.

Steam sawmill erected at Suo; timber sent to Foochow. A few foreigners settled at Suo.

Two thousand thirty piculs of tea shipped abroad principally for Tait & Co., and John Dodd. Dodd's sent to Macao.

1867   *December* 18. Great earthquake at north; Keelung harbour emptied of water, followed by tidal wave.

1868   Kindly Englishman named Horn organised group of Pepo-hoans for a settlement to be run on co-operative basis south of Suo. Settlement financed largely by James Milisch, of Hamburg, then resident trader at Tamsui. Other support given by two Scotsmen, one American, one German, one Spanish Mexican, one Goanese Portuguese, together with many Pepohoan.

Area twenty miles south of Suo (Talamo on north to Lamo at south) had never been claimed by nor had jurisdiction exercised over it by the Chinese government. Nevertheless, the Chinese, seeing a lucrative settlement develop, represented to the British Government through Peking that Horn was a pirate who had seized port of the Imperial Domain.

1868   British officials thereupon sent warship, drove Horn out and broke up settlement. Horn and many friends drown while attempting to leave.

Huang-hsing clan becomes troublesome in Banka area. Opposed occupation of hong leased by Messrs. Dodd & Co. Camphor trade interfered with.

Foreign business at a standstill. Settlement at Tamsui endangered. Message sent to mainland asking for foreign gunboat protection.

Crisis mounts. Le Gendre, American Consul, arrives at Tainan aboard American gunboat *Aroostock*, joined Jamieson, British consul with British gunboat *Janus*.

1868   *August*. British agent Pickering set out on foot for Gosei, without a passport, to look after camphor shipment. Threatened with death by Chinese governor, who placed price on his head ($500).

Attacks grew on Protestant and Catholic missions.

Chinese officials refused to honour their pledges.

DATE	EVENT
	British consul threatened to raise rebellion against officialdom. *November* 20. Consul Gibson, with two ships, approached Anping which he threatened to take by force if necessary. Anping forts taken by British marines. Tainan citizens pay over $40,000 guarantee or pledge money which the British held briefly.
1868	Many outstanding difficulties settled through this threat of force.
	Foreigners at Taipeh and Banka attacked. American and British gunboats arrive at the north.
	(Loo Chuo Islanders found to be imprisoned at Taipeh, where they assisted wounded foreigners to the best of their ability.)
	Consular demands on Tamsui officials granted after threat of force. Public admonitions to friendship with foreigners engraved on stone, set up in the streets of Tamsui.
	On representation of Prince Kung and Peking, British Consul Gibson forced to resign.
1868	French engineer M. du Pont surveyed coal resources of island for the Foochow arsenal administration. Report submitted.
1869	Trial shipment of 2,131 piculs of teas direct to New York in two sailing vessels.
1870	Tea trade rapidly expanding; 10,540 piculs exported.
	Large market for sugar in Australia opens suddenly; lasted about five years.
	Last open riots against foreigners as such; sporadic outbreaks in the north by Huang-hsing clan, which attacked hong of Boyd & Co.
	Outbreaks against foreigners hereafter against Missionaries because of their attacks on local religious beliefs, not because of their foreigners.
	Sir Rutherford Alcock, British Minister at Peking recommended to the Earl of Clarendon, Secretary of State for Foreign Affairs, that all foreigners be withdrawn from Formosa, consular representatives withdrawn and the island closed to British trade.
1870-75	Three large junk fleets operated out of Formosa, some going regularly as far north as the Gulf of Liaotung.
1871	Fortnightly steam service between Formosa and mainland, going by way of Hong Kong, Swatow, Tamsui, Tainan and Amoy.
	M. du Pont's coal report taken up for study by Governor-General; dropped.
	August 9. Great typhoon. Four foreign vessels wrecked on North Taiwan.
	December 17. Fishing and trading vessel from the Loo Choos wrecked on the south coast. Few survivors after Botan tribe murdered 54.
	Tea trade rapidly expanding.
1872	Commission sent up to Tokyo from the Loo Choos, asking for assistance in punishing the Botans.

DATE   EVENT

Five British trading firms established at Twatutia (Daitotei) in North Formosa.

   Dodd & Co., Tait & Co.; Elles & Co.; Brown & Co.; Boyd & Co.

Canadian Presbyterian Mission established in North Formosa by George MacKay.

Attacks on MacKay and others thereafter result of intrusive, aggressive and personal actions and local resentment to strange doctrines.

5,200,000 pounds of sugar sent to London.

Peking authorities refused in any way to assume responsibility for east and south coasts of Formosa.

First Japanese Expedition Planned

Japan laid secret plans for a "punitive expedition" to South Formosa. No foreigners in Tokyo given intimation of project.

1873   German schooner wrecked on Miyakohima group. Survivors treated well, given a ship to take them back to native land.

"In 1873 Count Kabayama, then a Captain in the army, and Mr. Mizuno landed in Taiwan-fu from a Japanese ship and travelled overland to Tamsui and thence on to Suao. There were some half dozen different Japanese visitors in the island that year, and being clad in European costume they were looked upon with considerable curiosity by the natives. It was first thought that they were merchants come to take stock of the resources of the island, but the events of the next year proved that they were the advance agents of the expedition which followed."

Japanese organisation of the Formosan Expedition carried forward.

1874   *January.* Okubo Shigenobu presents Emperor with plan for a special "Formosa Department" in the Tokyo government.

April. "Formosa Department" established with Okubo at head.

Chinese Admiral, at Amoy, in consultation with U.S. Consul Henderson asserts that the Chinese Government disclaimed all responsibility for actions of aborigines on Formosa.

Japanese advance plans for "righteous indignation" expedition to effect justice for murder of Loo Chuans in 1871. General Le Gendre invited to become adviser to expedition.

May. Saigo Yorimichi made Commander-in-Chief of expedition.

Lt.-Commander Douglas Cassel, U.S. Navy, made Commodore in Japanese Navy.

Lt. James R. Wasson U.S. Army Engineer, made Colonel in Japanese Army.

Viceroy of Fukien addressed protest to Consul Henderson at Amoy, demanding that Americans cease aiding the Japanese expedition.

DATE	EVENT

Henderson and Williams, U.S. Chargé d'Affaires at Peking noted officially that the Chinese Government did not seem to opppose the Japanese expedition.

Diplomatic corps at Peking urged Chinese to oppose the Japanese, sensing its dangerous precedent.

Bingham, U.S. Minister to Japan, usually pro-Japanese, in this matter counselled against them. European diplomats at Tokyo greatly disturbed.

Chinese officialdom at Peking began to claim authority over all Formosa.

Japanese at home began to prepare for war with China.

Near-rebellion in the Shoka district. Chinese Government feared Japanese would find support among those rebels.

Japanese merchants at Suo made claims against officials, who now feared that they would seize Suo and join with Shoka rebels across the hills.

"Before the arrival of the expedition Japanese visitors had been very numerous and now that troops had followed it was thought that every spot previously visited by the Japanese spies, as they were thought to be, would soon be occupied by Japanese troops" (Davidson, p. 155).

June-July. Japanese troops in small parties explore Central Formosa and the East Coast. While in the Karenko district drew plans, maps, took over 100 samples of soil, to astonishment of local peoples.

August 6. Japanese landings made at Liang-Kiau Bay.

June 21. Two Chinese men-of-war reached Formosa with French "observers" on board.

May 29. U.S.S. *Moncac* tried to put in at Liang-Kiau, for "observation" but storms made anchorage impossible.

British Gunboat followed Japanese ship *Nishin* for "observation". British gunboat *Hornet* landed party of officers to "take observation of Japanese action".

1874

May 22. Battle of Stone Gate, south Formosa, in which the Japanese defeated the Botan savages decisively and indulged in Japanese head-hunting, frowned upon by the Commanders for the adverse impression it might create abroad. Heads taken from aborigines' bodies on battlefield and displayed at camp.

Okubo sent to China to negotiate, with full powers, Le Gendre taken along as adviser. Reached Peking September 10.

Japanese ultimatum presented October 10.

Wade, the British Minister, attempts to become involved in the negotiations, but his services were declined by the Japanese. Japanese mission began to withdraw from Peking, whereupon Chinese came to terms.

Indemnity of 500,000 taels agreed upon, to cover "various expenses of the expedition" and to pay consolation money to families for victimised Loochuans and survivors of the 1871 party.

October 31. Terms signed.

Payments met before December 1st.

General Saigo withdrew with all forces (December 3rd.).

Chinese officials order destruction of every vestige of Japanese occupation, including roads, bridges, buildings.

Chinese Government stimulated to reorganise and develop Formosa.

David Tyzack, mining expert, engaged to make official survey of Formosan resources.

Shen Pao-chen, Imperial Commissioner, reviewed coal reports; decided to recommend installation of modern machinery.

California State Legislature placed high duty on Formosa sugar, effectually closing off that market.

1875   *January*. Special "Formosa Department" in Tokyo Government disbanded.

Emperor of China said to have died without knowledge of the entire Formosa incident.

Measures for reorganisation presented to Throne at Peking.

Military measures taken to establish Chinese control in south Formosa. Aborigines resisted fiercely, many Chinese troops killed.

David Tyzack mining engineer, sent to England for experts and machinery.

William Campbell, missionary, murderously attacked near Kagi. Church property destroyed.

1875   New forts constructed south of Anping, using much material from old Dutch forts at Zealandia. Constructed under supervision of French engineer, M. Berthault.

New Mining machinery from England, purchased by Tyzack, installed at Hattoshi ("Coal Harbour").

1877   Mine at Hattoshi, under Tyzack's direction, produced 200 tons per day. Coal harbour jetty and chutes constructed.

Chinese government decided to declare sulphur a monopoly. Pits worked in desultory fashion by officials; illegally worked by local people.

Government decided to exploit petroleum deposits.

November. First telegraph on Formosa opened. Takao to Taiwan-fu (Tainan) and to Anping. Total about 30 miles.

Because of growing importance of foreign trade, Tamsui was reorganised as a district, with a magistrate and regular government.

First new prefect of Taipeh-fu Hiang Tao.

War with aborigines particularly severe on East Coast.

Hakka community on East Coast in rebellion. Chinese government troops said to have exterminated one community of over 500 persons.

Spain threatens armed expedition after fourteen years of fruit-less negotiation regarding wreck and plunder of ship *Soberana* in 1863. Following Japanese precedent extracted $18,000 from Formosan Government. Evidence clear that it did not get to families of survivors, as represented.

1878   Immigration Bureau founded. Large numbers of Swatow region coolies transferred and settled on sparsely used land. Successful colonisation between Takao and the South Cape.

Two American petroleum engineers arrived with equipment. Sink four wells in Shinchiku district but withdrew (November) because of official obstructionism.

Unscrupulous ships' masters and owners, encouraged by Japanese and Spanish successes, take advantage of Formosa's bad reputation wilfully to destroy ships on the coast followed by charges of plunder and demands for indemnity. American ships blown up in Kwalian Bay, South Formosa, Captains of ship and assisting vessels tried, jailed.

1879   *March.* Prefectural offices removed from Shinchiku to Banka and work on new capital, Taipeh, begun.

Walls and gates completed.

Examination Hall for 10,000 students first buildings entirely completed. Confucian temple and Prefect's yamen under con-struction.

Cost of building new capital fell largely on local "contributors" such as the Lin Family. Lim Pan-ban contributed $500,000.

Examination Hall $34,000. Prefect's Yamen $28,000. Smaller Government Yamen $6,000; Confucian Temple and other Shrines $50,000.

First Civil Examinations given.

1880   MacKaye Hospital established by Canadian Mission.

War Scare. Russia believed to be ready to attack. New forts built (four between Tainan and Taipeh). New fortress at Kee-lung. Takao forts strengthened.

1881   First Military Exams. given.

1882   Lighthouses established at Anping.

1883   Lighthouses at South Cape (Garambi) and at Takao Harbour entrance.

Franco-Chinese War

1884   French ship *Volta* visited Keelung. Chinese slow in providing coal. Captain of ship threatened to fire on forts.

Franco-Chinese undeclared war of reprisals. Formosa block-aded and ports seized as material guarantee for payment of an indemnity which France had demanded of the Chinese govern-ment. French Parliament was not asked to bother with a Declaration of War.

July. British gunboat *Cockchafer* arrived at Tamsui to protect foreign settlement.

Liu Ming-chuan appointed by Peking as Commissioner for Formosa.

July 16. Arrived on Formosa. Arrival acknowledged by salute which caused the French gunboat *Parseval* immediately to clear for action. Captain advised of cause of firing just in time.

July 22. French corvette *Villars* arrived in Keelung. *Parseval* left. French ships prevented German ship *Welle* to discharge cargo of ammunition, torpedoes, telegraph wire, etc., whereupon *Welle* transferred to Tamsui and unloaded.

August 3-4-5. Foreign residents at Twatutia evacuated to Tamsui. Wealthy Formosans evacuated to China mainland. Foreign residents at Keelung evacuated to German schooner *Johann Carl*, thence to British gunboat *Cockchafer*. Removed to Tamsui, leaving only two foreign Customs officials.

1884

Residents during siege: A. Frater and wife, British Consul at Tamsui; P. W. Peterson, British Constable; 10 British members of Imperial Chinese Maritime Customs; 4 representatives of foreign firms; 3 Canadian missionaries; 1 American correspondent (Albert Sutliffe); 1 foreign doctor, a German.

August 4. Three French warships in port of Keelung when ironclad *La Galissoniere* under Admiral Lespes, and gunboat *Lutin* arrived. Admiral Lespes immediately demanded surrender of forts by 8 a.m. the next day.

Governor Liu Ming-chuan ordered Keelung collieries destroyed to prevent use by the French.

August 5. Chinese refuse to surrender Keelung forts. French opened fire, reduced forts to ruins. Marines landed, possession taken of Keelung city.

August 4-10. Tamsui port entrance mined; guns emplaced. Ballast boats and junks loaded with rocks sunk at harbour entrance.

Chinese establish themselves behind earthworks on hills surrounding Keelung. They remained unable to damage the French and French unable to damage them or advance inland.

September 24, 25, 26. French warships arrived to blockade Tamsui, chasing off foreign shipping, boarding and searching the British ship *Waverly*.

October 1. French fleet under Admiral Courbet arrived off Tamsui to give notice of intent to bombard defences.

After the French victory at Keelung, Liu Ming-chuan, Imperial Commissioner, removed headquarters to Banka (now part of Taihoku).

Japanese sloop *Amagi*, under Captain H. Togo, came to watch operations and an occasional British man-of-war made short visits for "observation".

October 7. French forced a landing at Tamsui with some 500-800 men, under cover of heavy bombardment from their ships.

British consul makes formal representation to Chinese general for "barbarous custom" of permitting French soldiers' heads to be cut off and pilloried.

1884   From October coastal lights around the island were extinguished.

October 15. French men-of-war appeared off Anping.

October 17. French men-of-war appeared off Takao.

1885   Despite close French blockade, Chinese managed to land supplies at Pinam (Taito) and carry them overland to Takao.

1885   French forces at Keelung:

Legion Entranger	971
Battalion Afrique	900
Marin Infantry	350
Blue Jackets	800
	3,021

Land force under command of General Duschesnes, "Conqueror of Madagascar".

Rumoured report that China twice offered to cede Formosa to England. Lord Rosebery and Lord Kimberley each refused. France took steps to secure the Pescadores. The British foreign Office feared a final wholesale partition of China.

April. British gunboat *Redbreast*, commanded by Lieut. Stuart, anchored at Tamsui to protect British Consulate and commercial firms.

March. Hills around Kantau, above Tamsui, fortified by Chinese.

Opium captured by French during blockade said to have been sold by them to Chinese buyers at Keelung.

Crews of captured junks set to road-building in and around Keelung.

While blockading west coast the French burned, sunk or destroyed all Chinese and Formosan shipping upon which they could lay their hands.

March 28. Five French ships made rendezvous off Anping and proceeded to capture the Pescadores, which they declared to be French territory on April 1.

April 1. Blockade of Southern Formosa lifted.

April 5. First merchant vessel reached Tamsui after blockade.

April 11. Chinese transport S.S *Pingon* allegedly betrayed by its Chinese master into hands of French.

April 27. Saracen light relit; thereafter at intervals the other lights along coast reappeared.

1855   "An address of thanks for the protection given to foreigners

DATE   EVENT

during the blockade, signed by all the foreigners was, in May, presented to the Taotai, Liu Ao, through the British Consul."

French continued in occupation of Keelung after lifting the blockade elsewhere and life restored to normal at other ports.

Two Frenchman assaulted Chinese girls. One Frenchman killed. French party allegedly took ten hostages and treated them cruelly.

June 9. Treaty between China and France signed. Article IX stipulated that Formosa and the Pescadores should be evacuated. Frenchman on station overjoyed. Over 700 had died at Keelung and were buried there. Of these 150 died of wounds, others of disease.

June 21. French troops, under General Duschesenes, withdrawn from Keelung.

June 11. Admiral Courbet died in the Pescadores. Had urged France to develop Pescadores as a permanent base. Materials had reached Singapore en route. Admiral had won confidence and respect of Chinese residents of Pescadores.

China Adopts Progressive Formosa Policy

1885   Warfare with aborigines continuous; destructive border fires started to drive them back into the hills.

Reconstruction of capital at Taipeh advanced. Streets rearranged, paved; city wall constructed; streets lit with electricity.

1886   New tax system introduced. Subsequent dissatisfaction led to near rebellion. Governor Liu Ming-chuan imprisoned in his own yamen during a trip south to Tainan by the hostile populace.

Campaign against aborigines east of Tokohame and Shoka; Ling Chien-teng led 1,500 troops against tribesmen.

1887   Chinese carry out campaign against aborigines on Giran plain.

General uprisings against government in protest of newly imposed rice-land tax. Yunlin seized, Shoka attacked.

Formosa declared a separate province by Imperial Decree.

Commissioner Liu Ming-chuan declared to be the first Governor, subject ot the Viceroy of Chekiang-Fukien-Formosa.

Province reorganised with four prefectures (Taipeh, Tainan, Taiwan and Taitung) 11 districts and 3 sub-prefectures.

Sulphur Bureau set up in Government.

November. Camphor becomes Government Monopoly after having been abolished in 1869 on foreign protest.

October. Cable steamer, the *Feichau* purchased; cables laid from Dome Bay in the Pescadores to Anping. Increased strategic importance of islands.

1887   *March.* Upon Governor Liu's decision to make Keelung a great harbour, work began on railway to link it with west coast cities.

German engineer named Becker employed. Gauge 3 feet 6

DATE	EVENT

inches; rails of 36 lb. steel; maximum gradient 1:30; curves of 5 chains minimum radius.

December. Customs services placed under Formosan Governor (Liu Ming-chuan).

1888 New capital site projected near centrally located Shoka. Building commenced. Sharp rise in taxes and government expenditures roused antagonism.

March. Telegraph line completed between Tainan and Taipeh, linking Keelung with Takao. Cable laid from Tamsui across straits to Sharp Peak at mouth of the Min River in Fukien. Formosa thus joined the world's telegraph system.

1891 Warfare between Chinese camphor men and aborigines near Tokoham assumes serious proportions.

October. Taipeh-Keelung Railroad completed (about 20 miles). Engines driven by British engineers. Road extending to south beyond city opened for twenty miles.

Government closed its coal mines, thereafter obtaining coal from private miners.

Camphor monopoly once again abolished.

Warfare along aborigine borderland almost uninterrupted. Twelve hundred troops employed in south against them.

Between 1890 and 1895 the campaigns against aborigines brought about sale of human (savage) flesh as meat in the open market of Chinese villages. Especially prevalent on Taiko market. Some salted and sent to Amoy.

1893 Railroad completed from Keelung to Shinchiku (60 miles).

Sino-Japanese War

1894 *August 1.* Sino-Japanese war begins.

First auriferous reefs discovered; gold bearing quartz found in Kyufun hills by a Chinese who had worked in California.

Sulphur exported totalled 5,950 piculs (791,850 lb.).

1895 Armistice and peace negotiations initiated between China and Japan. Rumours spread that Formosa would be ceded as part of indemnity.

Li Hung-chang sent to Japan to negotiate; expected, if possible, to avoid handing over Formosa.

Armistice declared after murderous attack upon Li Hung-chang, China's envoy to Japan.

Formosa Carefully Excluded from Terms of Armistice

"No doubt the higher officials of the island were informed of the signing of the treaty at Shimonoseki soon after it occurred; but to the people in general nothing was known further than the cession of the island to Japan was very probable. To protest against this, a commission consisting of a number of prominent residents backed by all the censors, board secretaries and Hanlins hailing from Formosa and Fukien Province, visited Peking and presented a number of memorials to the Emperor, praying that the island should be not ceded to Japan; and that if China were really unable to hold it, would be far better to present it to England." (Davidson 277).

Plans for "Republic" probably hatched at Peking by this commission.

About March 1 two French warships appeared at Makung; apparently offered to take over the Pescadores "for the duration" with promise to cede them back to China after the war. (Davidson 265)

March 20. Japanese fleet arrived off Pescadores.

March 23. Disembarkation began.

March 23. Japanese under Colonel Hishijima attacked and occupied the Pescadores. Landing made at Reiseikaku. Kompethtai fort taken. Garrison of 500 men made prisoners; 18 guns, 2,663 rifles, million rounds ammunition, 797 kegs, 3,173 bags powder etc. taken.

Few Japanese lost in action, but within few days 1,500 men died of cholera.

Regular Chinese officialdom began leaving Formosa.

Rear Admiral Tanaka became first Governor of the Pescadores.

April. "... The situation became so alarming that the Governor called a meeting of the Consuls, and informed them that he had lost all control over his people, soldiers, and others, and unless Foreign Powers intervened or sufficient foreign aid was provided, as soon as it was officially known that the treaty ceding Formosa to Japan had been ratified Formosa would be thrown into a state of anarchy and rebellion. Furthermore, that he was unable to protect the lives and interests of the foreigners on the island." (Davidson 271).

April. British and German Consuls appeal for protection for their nationals as tension mounted in north Formosa. Germans land 25 sailors from *Irene*, under command of Lieut. Timme to act as guards at Twatutia.

"Among (the forces of Tamsui) were new levies of Hakka hillmen. They were considered by the foreigners to be a dangerous lot to have in the neighbourhood and as they did not speak the same language as the general and other officers, it was feared that misunderstandings might arise with serious results." (Davidson 230.)

1895

April 22. Chinese soldiers rioted in Taipeh; Governor's yamen attacked in belief that he was about to flee with treasury. Troops' pay in arrears.

April 24. Further rioting indicated that soldiers would not admit much interference from superior officers.

April 26. H.M.S. *Spartan* arrived, followed by battleship *Cen-*

turion with an admiral who inspected the situation at Twatutia. Ordered detail of 30 marines, under Captain W. Shubrick, to land for duty at Twatutia. (Davidson 371).

May 1 (?). German gunboat *Wolfe* arrived, bringing a German Admiral to protect (small) German interests.

May 2. U.S.S. *Concord*, despatched from Hagasaki, arrived off Tamsui. Commander Craig, believing situation did not warrant American interference, left again, morning of May 4th.

British contingent ashore included: 6 gunners, marine artillery; 19 privates, marine artillery; 3 non-commissioned officers; 1 bugler, 1 officer (Captain Shubrick).

German contingent ashore included: 3 petty officers and 22 men commanded by Naval Lieutenant Timme.

Bandits and soldiers terrorise countryside and villages throughout May, making the peasants almost hope for the coming of the Japanese troops.

"The militia and volunteer brigades which formed the largest share of the island forces were armed and equipped principally from the mainland but received no pay except when engaged in active service. The organisation of the different native bands was as a rule the work of some rich man or group of rich men, whose motive was the hope of obtaining personal protection. One well-known Chinese was absolutely forced by the mandarins to contribute one million dollars in return for which he was declared commander-in-chief of the Formosan citizen-soldiers...." (Davidson, p. 273)

Republic of Formosa (North)

1895   *May* 23. Republic declared.
Manifesto issued to people. Telegrams sent to European and American powers and to Governors of every district in China. Memorial telegraphed to the Emperor at Peking by the literati:
"The literati and people of Formosa are determined to resist subjection to Japan. Hence they have declared themselves an independent Island Republic, at the same time recognising the suzerainty of the Sacred Tsing Dynasty." (Davidson, p. 278)

"The new authorities believed that the Republic would, if it could hold out for six months of a year, secure due recognition from the powers. The greatest dependence was placed on France, and telegrams passed very frequently between Tcheng Ki-tong and certain Frenchmen. One day a small cruiser, the *Beautemps Beaupre* (appeared), the officers landed and had an interview with the President. This led him fully to believe that the whole French fleet would shortly come to support him. Indeed, it looked as though Tcheng Ki-tong had not been altogether deceiving the people." (Takekoshi, pp. 83-84)

Formosan towns placarded with promises that Russia, France and Germany were sending warships to protect Formosan people.

Upon declaration of independence those not in sympathy were invited to get out. About 150 prominent people left.

May 1-15. Many and increasingly severe riots, especially between Cantonese mercenaries and local villagers whom they pillaged, as at Patlihum, near Tamsui, where a mob of soldiers in a nearby camp drove all male inhabitants from the village and cohabited with the women there for several days.

Northern Formosa in an uproar.

Twenty Camps—10,000 soldiers in all, between Tamsui and Twatutia. Altogether about 75,000 men, conservative estimate. (President claimed 150,000). Hakkas armed by the President, local volunteer troops from mainland, about 50,000 in the North, government arsenal thoroughly equipped. (Davidson, p. 286).

1895   *May* 29. Japanese transports assembled off Agincourt Island, near Keelung. Ordered to land at Samshokaku. First boatload of infantry landed at 2 p.m. Thereafter unloading continued all night.

May 30. Japanese landing complete. About 12,000 men on shore.

May 31. Advance overland begun.

Li Ching-fang, Imperial Chinese Commissioner, fearful for his own safety, refused to land on Formosa to effect formal transfer. Requested the Japanese first to repress rebellion. Finally arranged to meet Governor-General-designate Kabayama on board ship, June 2, off Samtiau Point. Commissioners agreed not to recognise the outbreak of rebellion or to the establishment of the Republic.

Li refused to catalogue Chinese Government property on the island as distinguishable from private property, on the grounds that he had never been on the island. Hence, by permitting the Japanese to draw up their own memorandum, Li completely abandoned the interests of Formosan Chinese private individuals. Transfer of island officially completed at 9 p.m. June 2.

June 5, 2 a.m. "The yellow Republican Tiger gathered in his long tail and laid down and died for lack of nourishment." Attacks on government by unruly soldiery, advance of Japanese from Keelung to Taipeh, caused the president to flee the capital of the ten day Republic. Government buildings looted, by Chinese soldiers. City set afire.

June 8. Tamsui occupied by Japanese. (Davidson, p. 310)

June 17. Ceremony of inauguration of Japanese administration at Taipeh.

DATE   EVENT

First government organised on civil basis soon found unpracticable.

Japanese advance overland, taking Keelung and moving on Taipeh. Rioting and violence threatened the capital. Davidson and two other foreigners volunteered to go to Japanese camp to urge speedy occupation of city and to disclose the lack of organised defence.

Japanese gave little attention to South Formosa until North Formosa was well occupied.

"It was thought that the defeat of the rebels in two of their principal resorts would teach them the futility of battling with the Japanese, and that they would return to their peaceful occupations. But the attacks upon provision trains and scouting parties, within a few miles of Taipeh continued. There was now no other course open but to give up the idea of a peaceful occupation of the island and to prepare for a bitter war against the natives. (Davidson, p. 329)

"Black Flag" pirate chief Liu Yung-fu, formerly commander of Chinese forces in the French war, given charge of organising defences of South Formosa.

British navy landed 50 marines at Anping to protect foreigners as unrest in South grew.

1895   General Liu accused foreigners of aiding the Japanese, after Japanese gunboat came into Anping harbour, anchoring near British men-of-war in a manner which made it difficult for Chinese land forts to direct fire against her.

Foreigners ordered to leave Anping; British sent further troops until 150 marines were ashore. Women and children removed, by Norwegian ship.

British increase forces which included ships *Redbreast, Spartan, Rainbow, Plover*, all of which cleared for action against the Chinese.

Many Chinese fled South Formosa. Governor Liu extorted large amounts of treasure from refugees.

June. Organisation of Southern Republic Chinese Imperial Government ordered its high officials to withdraw from Tainan. About 100 leading citizens and ex-officials called upon General Liu to assume Presidency of Southern Republic.

July 1. British Admiral Buller gave instructions for withdrawal of British forces; advised foreigners to leave. Approach of typhoon season made anchorage of protecting forces unsafe.

Foreign guard withdrew June 30. Customs House closed June 29.

Republic of Formosa (South)

1895   (*June contd.*). When higher officials withdrew from Tainan,

asked General Liu to leave Takao for Tainan in order to protect it (the capital). "He consented and was installed in the Examination Hall, adopting the style of Assistant Commissioner. When Tang fled (from the North) however, the literati and others composing the so-called Parliament elected Liu Yung-fu to the Presidency of the 'Republic" which they determined should continue. (Davidson, p. 352)

Movement continued to have support of Chinese Government. New money issued, guaranteed by wealthy people of Tainan. Postal system, with varied stamp issues, created.

Movement continued to have support of Chinese Government. New money issued, guaranteed by wealthy people of Tainan. Postal system, with varied stamp issues, created.

Strong Japanese forces left Shoka to move southward toward Tainan.

October. Japanese launched campaign to occupy Southern Formosa. Forces moved Southward overland.

October 7. Fifty ships assembled in Pescadores for invasion of South Formosa. Divided; one group south to Boryo, landed 6,330 men and proceeded up coast under protection of warship's guns.

Kagi attacked.

October 12. British ship *Tweed* removed nationals from Takao; Japanese men-of-war opened bombardment.

1895   *October* 13. Japanese men-of-war open bombardment of Takao forts. Entire port fell to Japanese by 4 p.m.

October 10. Nineteen transports, three warships left Pescadores to land at Patechui.

Approach of Japanese from three directions threw Anping and Tainan into panic.

General Liu proposed surrender. Negotiations prolonged. Liu proposed that (1) the Japanese pay up all arrears due to Liu's soldiers; (2) the Japanese to send him and his soldiers to Canton in Japanese transports; (3) The Shimonoseki Treaty be carried out, regarding all people having two years in which to decide ultimate citizenship.

Days spent in stripping escaping refugees of treasure.

October 18. Liu disappeared, escaping to China during night.

October 21. Tainan city occupied, completing operations.

October 28. Imperial Prince Kitashirakawa died at Tainan. Japanese suffered total of 32,315 casualties, of which only 164 were actually killed in battle.

The first wave of Japanese troops were well disciplined Imperial Guards. Later troops which came into garrison and suppress "banditry" were rough, undisciplined, violent and overbearing.

DATE   EVENT

Period of Unorganised but open Resistance to Japanese Control

1895   *Late November.* Hakka uprising near Toko. "Major General Yamaguchi shot five or six hundred. . . ." Two months campaign; 48 Japanese casualties; about 500 rebel casualties. "This was but the beginning of troubles which lasted off and on for several years. These people are called brigands because, though they desired to overthrow the (Japanese) government, the main object of their risings was robbery and plunder. . . ." (Takekoshi, p. 92)

1896   New Year's Day revolt, northern Formosa. There was ruthless suppression; wholesale and indiscriminate slaughter on the Giran plain and Zuiho continued two months. Villages were ruined. In the cities files of prisoners were led to torture daily. Indiscriminate decapitations were followed by burning of rebel heads in public. Reinforcements sent from Japan. Japanese casualties 128 killed; insurgents "more" than 600. (Davidson) "Several thousands of insurgents killed." (Takekoshi)

February 22. Privileges granted to foreigners defined by Proclamation.

1896   *June 30.* Most serious uprising. Japanese driven out of central area. Hori, Shushu, Hokuto, Nanto, Tarimu, Rokko, Inrin, Rato Daihorin all occupied by rebels; Shoka attacked. State of siege proclaimed at Taichu. Army deployed over countryside with orders to kill all Formosans on sight. From 7 to 20 people beheaded publicly every day by Japanese court order.

May 8. Deadline date by which all Formosans not wishing to have Japanese citizenship leave the island or remove to the treaty ports.

Leader of rebellion named Kien-i, of Toroku.

Second Brigade out into field. Thirty Chinese villages destroyed. Japanese casualties 247.

Kien-i reported by Japanese to have accepted an official post. (Davidson, 1898.)

October 30. Uprising at Taihoku led by Lin Ta-peh. Over 360 "brigands" forced to surrender.

November 19. Chung Ki-sung and associated chiefs attacked Hozan.

December 27. Revolt at Taiheicho; the town fortified by Kwa Tia, one of Kien-i's colleagues. Suppressed by Second Brigade.

1897   *January 10.* Hozan again attacked by rebels.

May 8. Taihoku attacked by "more than 600 brigades", under leadership of Cheng Teu-giu. Driven off by local garrison.

June 11. Davidson appointed first U.S. Consul at Taihoku (officially at Tamsui).

1898   *September 21.* Taiping Branch Administrative Office attacked.

September 25. Sankyaksku Court House attacked.

N

DATE	EVENT
1899	Choshuso Court House attacked by 3,000 "brigands" led by Lin Tien-fu and Lin Shao-miao.
	May 15. Japanese establish salt monopoly. Cost of production about quarter cost in Japan proper.
	July 20. Dr. A. Norris Wilkinson appointed U.S. Vice-Consul.
	August 5. Camphor monopoly established by Japanese.
	Old style Chinese schools, about one to each village, attended by 27,568 students under 1,496 instructors.
	Japanese turn official attention to sugar cultivation. Seed cane imported from Hawaii.
1900	Two American sugar cane crushing mills purchased by Government for experimental farms.
	May. Major-General Yamanaka, at head of Second Division, carried out a 25 day campaign against the remnants of Ka Tia's band.
	The North gradually became quieter, although the centre and south of the island remained rebellious, for the Government and was absorbed in effort to pacify immediate neighbourhood of the capital.
	"The proclamations . . . in Tainan and Taichu issued inviting the brigands to surrender were lacking in definiteness, hence the brigands in those districts failed to clearly understand the will of the authorities." (Takekoshi, p. 98).
	By mid-year "the authorities did away with invitations for brigands to surrender."
	In five months, late 1900, more than 5,000 "brigands" were killed. (Takekoshi, p. 99).
	Between 1897 and 1901, the Japanese officially report 8,030 rebels executed and 3,473 killed "in the field". The actual victims were unnumbered.
1901	*February.* Taichu attacked by Chang A-lui and his Toran band.
1902	A general amnesty was offered rebels in central Formosa. Those who returned to village under promise of safety were murdered in a well-planned slaughter May 25, 1902.
	Seven years of bloody war and suppression of "Banditry" (i.e. Formosan-Chinese resistance) are officially acknowledged to have passed before the Japanese could institute civil control.

Beginning of Organised and Ideological Resistance

1907-1928	From 1907 to 1928 there were eight serious conspiracies among Formosan-Chinese. After 1905 the Japanese recognised the ideological element in these rebellions, and the development of organised leadership of one sort or another.
1907	Peipu Rebellion. The immediate cause was an attempt to use Formosans in subjugating the savages.
1909	A village uprising, July 31, 1909, protested police torture

DATE · EVENT

methods. Courts decided that the case against the Japanese policeman, named Shiima, be dismissed.

1910 · An official "Subjugation or Death" programme was launched against the aborigines. An appropriation of 15,000,000 yen was made for the purpose. From May to October, 1910, 4,000 soldiers with all modern arms campaigned against the Gaogan and Atayal tribes in the south.

1911 · The same troops campaigned against Mori-Kouan and the Atayal tribes in central region.

1913 · A similar campaign made against the Kinani and Atayal tribes of the north.

1913 · The Linchi Rebellion of 1913 had as its immediate case the felling of bamboo forests by Mitsui interests, without adequate recompensation to local people.
Rebellion led by Ra Fukusei; 500 Formosans in the Byoritsu area plotted to seize Taihoku, the capital. Nearly all were apprehended and put to death.

1914 · Fourth campaign of the official "Subjugation or Death" programme. Police and 12,000 troops were employed against the 10,000 members (men, women and children) of the Taruk tribe, in mountains back of Karenko.

1915 · Rebellion led by Lo Chun, and Chu Cheung-hong, aided by Chinese in Fukien Province. Many persons prepared to revolt. Upon discovery of the plot, the Japanese began imprisonments. Several thousand conspirators took to the field in the south. Only 51 Japanese were killed, but the Japanese troops beginning August 7, retaliated by exterminating several Chinese villages. After troops restored order by this wholesale slaughter, 1,413 persons were arrested and 866 sentenced to death. An Imperial amnesty saved all but 95 from execution.

1915 · Hsilai-an Rebellion (no details).
Suppression of the *Doka-kai* (Assimilation Society) founded by Itagaki Taisuke, a Japanese liberal, who went to Formosa in November 1914. Not revolutionary in intent; Itagaki merely wished to see a true assimilation of Formosa to the Empire by equality before law, etc. Appeared too dangerous to the Government and was therefore suppressed, with some imprisonments.

1918 · Domeikai organised by Formosan students in Tokyo. Primary purpose was to effect modification of harsh and discriminatory laws. Started monthly publication *Taiwan Youth*. Later changed to a weekly. Failed in attempts to have it removed to Formosa, but during the "liberal" period (1927-30) it was allowed to be published in Taihoku where it became a daily newspaper, the *Taiwan Shinminpo*, suppressed in 1933.

1919 · New subjugation programme. A budget appropriation of 183,000 yen was made for an air corps designed to bomb savage districts and villages, especially of the Niitaka, Ari and Daibu

N*

DATE   EVENT

regions, which were not long thereafter opened up to Japanese timber companies for exploitation.

1921   *Taiwan Bunka Kyokai* (Taiwan Cultural Society) founded by Lin Hsien-t'ang, (Rin Kendo), Ts'ai Pei-ho, Chiang-Wei-sui. This centre of nationalist movement among the moderates was strongly represented in the Taiwan Agricultural Co-operatives.

1921   A petition presented to Tokyo Diet asking for representative Government in Formosa, 1921, was undeeded. Other petitions followed, but Lin Hsien-t'ang, the leader, was severely censured.

1923   Petition for representative government was presented to authorities on February 2, suppressed by police as "rebellious". Three of the petitioners went immediately to Tokyo, and in late February founded (with Tokyo police permission) a "Formosan Magazine" to advocate and defend their ideals. The founders returned to Formosa December 10, 1923.

1924   Forty-nine youths arrested; 14 were prosecuted including the leaders, Lin Hsien-t'ang, Tai Roku and Sho Isu, who were held a year and then sentenced to four months imprisonment. According to Japanese accounts, the Government was forced to arrest "hundreds" of others in order to stop the representative government movement. According to the account of a German in Formosa in 1926, more than 3,000 persons suffered death in the effort to suppress the agitation.

1926   *Taiwan Koyuso Remmi* (Taiwan Workers Union) a Marxist organisation which in 1928 had 6,367 active members. It was suppressed in 1931 and all members have been treated with suspicion and frequently with violence since.

1928   A new era of suppression began in 1928 coinciding with suppressive movements in Japan proper, and by August of 1937 even the most moderate of right-wing organisations officially disbanded. Under these restrictive measures and aggravation of police interference the rightest groups grew more radical, and those who had advocated co-operation with the Japanese began to be silent on that point.

1930   Musha Rebellion of the aborigines on October 26, 1930, was so serious that the Governor-General was forced to resign. Planes and gas bombs were used to subdue the natives. Then the Japanese disarmed and segregated the tribes which had rebelled. Arming the tribe known to be hostile to the rebels, the police encouraged a massacre of these defenceless people. The Japanese press publicly acknowledged this "natural slaughter" as a quick way to solve the problems of the aborigines.

The Minshut Party, Formosa's only modern political party had 800 members in 1930. All walks of life were represented and all degrees of education. The leaders were lawyers, physicians and business men. They made a special issue of the Japanese Government's profiteering exploitation of the opium situation,

DATE   EVENT

which it managed at a handsome profit through the Narcotics Monopoly. The Minshuto had 17 branches.

1931   The leaders suffered imprisonment and the party was dissolved, February 24, after having been allowed no organ for publication of its views.

The Taiwan Youth Party suppressed in Formosa, was reorganised in Shanghai in 1931. It became the Taiwan Anti-Imperialist League. Its members in Formosa were periodically rounded up by the police.

March 23, a large village of aborigines near Heito revolted. The details are obscured by censorship, but the American Consul attributed the revolt to fear of land confiscation and the Japanese policy of removing mountain dwellers to the unhealthy plains, where they do not thrive.

1932   After February 5, there came a wave of arrests and imprisonments for "mongers of false rumours" regarding the progress of the Shanghai Incident.

1934   *Shuyu Kai* plot, engineered by a secret society, the "Friends of the Masses Society" which had branches throughout the island. It was organised in December 1927. Headquarters were in Taiko-gun, Taichu Province. A revolt was planned which miscarried in September 1934. The society had carried on the secret manufacture of rifles and ammunition. The discovery, suppression and drastic punishments were kept secret by the police for two years and one month. Of 425 persons tried for the conspiracy, 31 per cent were farmers, 21.8 per cent were coolies, 15.5 per cent were engaged in manufacturing industries while only 1.2 per cent had had so-called "liberal" education. To give an indication of the representative character of this rebellion and the thoroughness of discontent, it is notable that 198 persons tried were without property, 106 had property valued at less than 1,000 yen and 32 had property in excess of 10,000 yen. The majority were between 30 and 40 years of age.

1936   In November, a poorly contrived plot was discovered among the Formosan-Chinese students of the Second Middle School of Taihoku. They had formed a secret society with an intent to link themselves with a Chinese revolutionary youth movement. The details are unknown; the affair was made public only a year after the apprehension, trial and punishment of the conspirators.

1937   Between 1937 and 1940 police measures designed to cope with the excitement caused by the Sino-Japanese conflict became so severe that it was impossible to get definite facts in confirmation of the many rumours of uprisings and sweeping arrests over the island.

1938   *February* 18. Taihoku airfield (Matsuyama) and Byoritan bombed by Chinese planes. All the public buildings and strategic crossings in Taihoku city were barricaded by sandbags and machine guns, directed not at the invading airplane, but at the Formosan-Chinese population. Not until these barricades were up did the Government sound the air alarm. (The raid came at 11 a.m. the alarm at 2 p.m.)

1940   An American, living in a Japanese quarter, was warned secretly by Formosan friends to get out of that area at the first sign of trouble. A Keelung Formosan-Chinese family is known to be engaged in gun running along the coast. Cautious hints and allusions by Formosans indicated, without supporting facts, that much subversive activity was being carried on, frequently with the Chinese temples as centres.

Two uprisings of non-political origin took place in early 1940. A village set upon and killed two policemen trying to enforce the rice confiscation orders. A village waylaid a rice-rations truck en route to certain mines near Keelung and killed the guards, making off with the week's rice allowance for the miners. Sabotage and internal disturbances fomented by agents of the Formosan Revolutionary League reported by Chinese. Two mysterious explosions, of great violence, occurred in the vicinity of the Taihoku airport during the spring of 1940; no explanation was published.

1940   *The Taiwan Hsienfeng* the official publication of the Formosan Revolutionary League, monthly, appearing in Free China, on April 15, 1940, p. 31, reports the purposes of the Formosan Revolutionary League to be as follows:

1. Disorganisation of Formosa's production and communication facilities.
2. Strengthening of Alishan(?) anti-Japanese guerilla forces in Formosa. ("Alishan" probably refers to Arisan.)
3. Organisation of groups of volunteers for the war against Japan in China.
4. Organisation of strikes among workers, municipal personnel, students.
5. Spread of anti-war and anti-fascist propaganda.
6. Unity of all Formosan revolutionary organisations.

1942   A conference of the Formosan Revolutionary League was held at Chungking on March 20 and 21, 1942. The Chinese Government showed interest in helping the Formosan revolutionaries.

1943   President Chiang Kai-shek, President Franklin D. Roosevelt and Prime Minister Winston Churchill, meeting at Cairo in November, 1943, decided, in the "Cairo Declaration" of December 1, 1943, Taiwan and the Pescadores be restored to China.

1945   Japan surrendered to allies August 15, and Taiwan was returned to China. General Chen Yi, appointed Governor-General of Taiwan, reached Taipeh from Chungking by air October 24 and accepted Japanese surrender the next day.

DATE   EVENT

The Taiwan Director-General's Office was formally inaugurated.

1946   The Taiwan People's Political Council held its first meeting, May 1. President and Madame Chiang Kai-shek arrived in Taipeh November 22 for a five-day visit.

1947   The February 28 incident broke out. The Chinese Government despatched the 21st Division to quell the uprising, On May 16, the Taiwan Director-General's Office was abolished and the Taiwan Provincial Government was set up with Dr. Wei Taoming named Governor.

1948   Elections for legislators in the Chinese Government were held throughout the island on January 21.

1949   General Chen Cheng succeeded Dr. Wei as Governor January 5. On March 1 measures to reduce land rentals to a maximum of 37.5 per cent of harvest were decided on at the Taiwan Administrative conference.
        Dr. K. C. Wu replaced General Chen Cheng as Governor.
        December 23. U.S. State Department issued confidential directive re: Formosa to officials outside U.S. advising them to "play down" any possible importance of Formosa to U.S.

1950   *January* 9. Attempt to haul down Union Jack at Consulate at Tamsui by Nationalist soldiers. Consul, Edward Biggs.
        January 11. The UN Society Council voted down a Russian attempt to oust China from the United Nations.
        February 2. At UN Mr. Warren Austin denied U.S. had aggressive designs, political, military or economic, on Formosa.
        February 6. British recognition of the Chinese People's Government.
        February 13. British chargé d'affaires arrived in Peking.
        March 1. President Chiang Kai-shek announced his resumption of office and assumed his Presidential duties.
        March 15. New cabinet under premiership of General Chen Cheng was formed.
        April 2. General MacArthur in Ryukyu Islands for ceremony of inauguration "Provincial Central Government" at Okinawa.
        April 18. Students hauled down Union Jack at Consulate at Tamsui. Consul, E. H. Jacobs-Larcom.
        April 26. Nationalists completed withdrawal from Hainan Island.
        May 12. President Truman pledged for U.S. support for Free China's retention of a seat in the United Nations.
        May 15. Nationalists completed withdrawal from ChusanIslands.
        May 16. President Chiang issued an announcement to the Chinese people on the withdrawal of troops from Hainan Island and the Chusan Archipelago.
        June 2. Mr. Acheson told Senate Committee U.S. committed to defence of Formosa.

DATE
EVENT

June 27. The United States Seventh Fleet was ordered by President Truman to patrol the Formosan Strait in an effort to localise the Korean war.

July 7. Peking Government sent Note to UN stating "Chinese people will liberate Taiwan without fail".

July 31. General Douglas MacArthur and his top aides arrived at Taiwan for visit.

August 7. Setting up of the United States 13th Airforce Liaison Office in Taiwan.

August 8. S.C.A.P. Liaison Office set up.

August 14. United States Minister Karl L. Rankin, assumed office in Taipeh.

October 15. Popular elections for magistrates were held in Hualien and Taitung.

November 17. William F. Knowland, Republican senator from California, arrived at Taipeh for a week's tour.

December U.S. Government placed complete embargo on exports to Red China, Hong Kong and Macao.

1951   *January* 31. Mr. Gross, U.S. delegate at UN reiterated U.S. attitude re Formosa.

February 7. Soviet draft calling on Security Council to take immediate steps for the cessation of "aggression against China in Formosa and Straits", rejected by 49 votes to 5.

February 13. Similar motion at plenary session of UN rejected by 48 votes to 5.

April 20. U.S. Defence Department announced military mission on way to Formosa.

April 25. Mr. Dean Acheson published text of exchange of Notes between State Department and Nationalist Government on conditions attaching to military aid and mission. i.e., "Logical result of Truman decision of June, 1950."

April 26. German merchant ship *Mai Rickmers* seized with cargo of military materials for Amoy. Reputedly cargo valued at £900,000 confiscated. Released June 1.

May 11. Mr. Herbert Morrison said in House of Commons discussion of Formosa premature so long as war in progress in Korea.

May 14. Major-General Chase, head of military mission announced an additional $50,000,000 for Nationalist army and immediate spending of additional $5,700,000 on navy. Reiterated policy of neutralisation.

June. Mr. Dean Acheson at "MacArthur enquiry" admitted that from October 1948 to June 1950 U.S. policy was based on a recognition of Formosa's strategic importance to U.S. He added that the Truman directive of December 1949 was prepared in expectation of fall of Formosa to reduce damage to U.S. prestige.

DATE   EVENT

1951   *July.* Governor of New York, Thomas Dewey, visited Taipeh.
October. General Cheng Cheng, Premier, tendered resignation.
November. Vice Foreign Minister Shih Chao-ying and Dr. Shen Chang-huan attended UN meeting in Paris representing Nationalists. Second of recent series of earthquakes with heavy loss of life. Major-General Sun Tse-yen executed for treachery on mainland in 1948-49.
November. S.S. *Capella* surrendered to Nationalists, see p. 150.
November. Military Information repeat warning that Chinese communist troops massing on Indo-China and Burma border naming commanding officers.
December. General Pai Chung-hsi pledged that 50,000,000 Moslems in China would rise "as one man" against communists "when counter attack is launched".
December. Official statement that 576 communist underground agents in Formosa had surrendered in response to offer of leniency.
December. Prominent Americans visiting Taipeh included Senators Owen Brewster, John Sparkman and H. Alexander Smith; Congressmen Joseph Martin, Leonard Hall and William Bullitt, author.
December. Nationalist guerillas raided Nanju Island and claimed to have inflicted 400 casualties with light losses including officer commanding raid.
December (31). Maj.-Gen. William C. Chase urged "Ever closer co-operation" between U.S. military advisers and the Nationalist armed forces. He announced increase of military mission from 300 to 700 personnel.

1952   *January.* Cardinal Spellman conferred with Chiang Kai-shek in Taipeh.
January. Communists report Nationalist troops arriving on Burma border via Siam.
January. Letter from Japanese Premier Yoshida dated 1951 published asking for facilities to conclude Treaty with Nationalists.
January. Mr. Churchill, British Prime Minister in speech in U.S. House of Representatives said, *inter alia,* "I am very glad that . . . you will not allow Chinese anti-communists on Formosa to be invaded and massacred from the mainland."
January. Ninety-three members of the Control Yuan passed a resolution impeaching Vice-President Li Tsung-yen domiciled in New York.
January. Brigadier-General Frank A. Allen (U.S. Army) arrived from Korea to confer with Brigadier-General Benjamin Moore, Commanding U.S. 13th Air Force based on the Philippines. They inspected Nationalist military and naval bases and reported they were "pleasantly and deeply impressed".

INDEX

N.B. In many instances further references may be found in the *Chronological Outline*.